THE POTOMAC CHRONICLE

THE POTOMAC CHRONICLE

Public Policy & Civil Rights from Kennedy to Reagan

Harold C. Fleming with Virginia Fleming

THE UNIVERSITY OF GEORGIA PRESS *Athens & London*

© 1996 by the University of Georgia Press
Athens, Georgia 30602
All rights reserved
Designed by Mary Mendell
Set in Minion by Books International
Printed and bound by Thomson-Shore, Inc.
The paper in this book meets the guidelines for
permanence and durability of the Committee on
Production Guidelines for Book Longevity of the
Council on Library Resources.
Printed in the United States of America
00   99   98   97   96   C   5   4   3   2   1
Library of Congress Cataloging in Publication Data
Fleming, Harold C.
The Potomac chronicle : public policy and civil rights
from Kennedy to Reagan / Harold C. Fleming
with Virginia Fleming.
p.   cm.
Includes bibliographical references and index.
ISBN 0-8203-1836-1 (alk. paper)
1. Potomac Institute (Washington, D.C.)—History.
2. Afro-Americans—Civil rights—Societies, etc.—
History—20th century.   3. United States—Race
Relations—Societies, etc.—History—20th century.
I. Fleming, Virginia.   II. Title.
E185.61.F55   1996
323.1'196073'0060753—dc20   95-52513
British Library Cataloging in Publication Data available

CONTENTS

THE CIVIL RIGHTS movement began with protests and court cases. But it also required the hard, day-to-day work of getting laws passed and properly enforced, and of changing institutional behavior. *The Potomac Chronicle* is the story of how one small organization, little known to the general public, gave vital support to the national civil rights movement in the 1960s by serving as a creative broker of talent, ideas, and resources among minorities, activists, and public and private interest groups.

This volume captures in instructive—and sometimes entertaining—detail the evolution of a new, low-key, one-man operation into a power-ful force bringing the principles and requirements of equal opportunity to dozens of new audiences, agencies, and institutional forums. No other organization was so linked both to government offices and the southern civil rights movement, and so trusted by both.

The story of the Potomac Institute weaves through well-known events of contemporary national history: the first almost heady years of the early 1960s, when the civil rights movement was always on the front pages, and ground-breaking national legislation was won; the painful shocks of 1968, when Vietnam protests erupted, and Martin Luther King Jr. and Robert Kennedy were assassinated; the backlash that produced President Nixon; and two decades of struggle to prevent erosion of hard-won gains and to translate promises into reality.

The institute itself was born in 1961 from a unique collaboration be-tween New York philanthropist Stephen Currier and his wife, Audrey Bruce Currier, and a southern white civil rights leader, Harold Fleming. With the coming of the Kennedy administration, they foresaw that the decisive arena for the civil rights struggle would shift from protests and demonstrations to national legislation and enforcement. The Curriers wanted a privately funded presence in Washington that could influence federal initiatives on equal opportunity and urban social problems. They sought out Fleming to head it, and brought him from Atlanta to Washington in 1961.

The initial purpose was deliberately broad: "to create in Washington a center for the cultivation of ideas and associations that will advance public policy affecting race relations." The exact dimensions of its *pro bono publico* role would be determined as it took hold.

The early chapters of this chronicle illustrate how Fleming rapidly put his southern credibility and contacts to work in Washington, becoming an indispensable counselor to the Kennedy administration's civil rights policy debates and assuring southern activists a hearing with federal agencies.

Fleming had a gift for creating opportunities to move the civil rights agenda forward. The new institute quickly gained a reputation for solid technical assistance to federal agencies by launching a series of projects, supervised by Potomac Deputy Director Arthur Levin, to help the Defense Department set new rules for civil rights compliance on the part of their contractors. From these pioneering efforts flowed subsequent public and private affirmative action activities.

In the wake of the Kennedy assassination and President Johnson's growing commitment to a new civil rights act, Potomac helped to calm congressional and bureaucratic doubts by surveys and interchange with southern leaders less visible than the headline-grabbing opponents. Nationally, the institute encouraged public readiness for the new law through a series of reliable, readable publications explaining the numerous requirements in practical terms long before the government documents could appear. In Washington, many government agencies would turn to Potomac for help in integrating new civil rights requirements into their ongoing programs.

Fleming for a time played the classic dollar-a-year man role as the Civil Rights Act of 1964 was implemented in Washington: First, he was borrowed for several months by former Governor Collins of Florida to help design and launch the new Community Relations Service to further the peaceful integration of public accommodations. Later he helped Franklin Delano Roosevelt Jr. organize the new Equal Employment Opportunity Commission. It came as no surprise when President Johnson called on him to help with his 1965 and 1966 Civil Rights Conferences, and wrote afterward to say, "You have had years of experience in the field, and to these you have added good judgment, a saving tolerance and wit, and absolute dedication to justice for the Negro American . . . in a period that was as full of peril as promise."

The ingredients of Potomac's success and credibility had emerged: economy of personnel and resources, independence, flexibility, adaptability, judicious use of humor, and freedom from the need to take credit or compete for funds. The Potomac style was to anticipate useful strategies, to develop reliable applied research, and to collaborate with a wide network of imaginative individuals and organizations. In the words of Vernon Jordan, "We all gathered at the Potomac Institute, interacted with each other and with government officials. We argued, debated, planned and executed."

In early 1967, however, the institute was shaken by the tragic death of the Curriers, both still in their thirties, when their chartered plane disappeared in the Caribbean—a loss that put an untimely end to one of the most extraordinary philanthropic vocations in modern history. But they left behind a charitable foundation, the Taconic Foundation, and its board continued to support Potomac with modest basic operating grants for another twenty years, allowing the institute to maintain the course on which it had been set by the Curriers.

The times, of course, were dramatically changing in 1967. So, too, was the role of Potomac. Presidential leadership on civil rights, no doubt reflecting prevailing public attitudes, soon all but evaporated. As a key player in the Leadership Conference on Civil Rights, that long running coalition of more than a hundred organizations, the institute time and again was called on to protect earlier gains against legislative and administrative efforts to dismantle them. During the Reagan years, perhaps the institute's most critical task was the successful defense of affirmative action guidelines, through well-timed research on the beneficial effects and corporate support already in place, and an influential public information campaign.

Even more important were the strategies that expanded the boundaries of equal opportunity in education and housing. Among them were landmark initiatives on applying Title VI of the Civil Rights Act to a whole new range of government programs, and on applying civil rights requirements to urban growth and zoning. By convening key leaders around the country, Potomac frequently turned isolated legal actions into powerful nationwide initiatives.

Government remedies were not the only sphere of Potomac action, however. Publications and projects also aimed at eliminating historic and often subtle racist practices in mainstream private institutions: corporations, banks and lenders, housing developers, charitable foundations, and professional organizations. A long-running concern with the correlation of race and poverty in America's inner cities led as well to a series of urban technical assistance ventures, often sparked by Program Associate James Gibson.

Among Potomac's most important tools were its timely and practical publications (the special province of Arthur Levin), its strong relations with members of the Washington press corps who appreciated reliable information and analysis, and its formal and informal conferences of "stakeholders" in controversial issues who needed relaxed and off-the-record opportunities to talk.

At Potomac, however, the whole was always greater than the sum of the various activities. Harold Fleming had indeed created a center of good judgment, wise counsel, and selfless sharing of creative ideas and resources that resonated throughout the civil rights movement.

All of us who made up the final board of directors of the institute had served with it for ten or more years, a few of us from the very beginning. When in 1987 we accepted Fleming's retirement and faced with reluctance the decision to close the institute, we asked of him one final task: to spend part of the time of his retirement writing the history of the work of Potomac. We knew that he had always shunned personal publicity and routinely turned credit for ideas and accomplishments to others. Although influential people in government, philanthropy, civil rights advocacy, and the press sought him out and relied on his judgment, the role of Potomac is relatively little known to the public at large. We wanted that rich legacy to be available to future readers.

Fleming agreed to undertake that task, but tragically the work was cut short by his death in 1992, at which time he had finished only about half the story. His notes for the rest, however, along with his speeches and memoranda and the institute's extensive archives, now in the Library of Congress, were all available. We therefore asked his wife and professional colleague, Virginia Fleming, to complete the book. She had for years been closely associated with Potomac, and in her work with the Southern Education Foundation had often collaborated on issues of race and education.

The latter part of this chronicle cannot, under the circumstances, include the personal anecdotes and judgments with which Harold Fleming infused the first sixteen chapters. But his wife has faithfully rounded out the historical record, calling on the recollections of many colleagues so that the complete story can be told.

The Potomac Chronicle is a tale of creative philanthropy, of a pioneering public interest organization, and of less known aspects of the civil rights movement. Above all, it demonstrates the power of optimistic persistence. Harold Fleming and his colleagues knew that the pendulum swing of public attitudes and political style is a recurrent phenomenon. They sustained their agenda of governmental and institutional change through both auspicious and inhospitable times. *The Potomac Chronicle* is the story of that remarkable record.

The Potomac Institute Board of Directors
Philip G. Hammer, President
Lois D. Rice, Vice President
John G. Simon, Secretary
William L. Slayton, Treasurer
Herbert M. Franklin
Vernon E. Jordan Jr.
Melvin A. Mister
Andrew E. Norman

PREFACE

THIS CHRONICLE OF the Potomac Institute was to have been entirely
the work of my husband, Harold Fleming, but his death prevented
him from finishing it. In completing the manuscript, I have used the extensive material that he left, and frequently quoted from his speeches and
memoranda. Following his decision to avoid academic footnotes and references, I have simply listed in Appendix C the references and sources
from which those quotes are drawn; these materials are available in the
Potomac Institute archives at the Library of Congress for those who may
wish to pursue more detail.

Although I have had the primary responsibility for completing the
work, and am of course accountable for errors and omissions, it could
not have been done without many others whose respect and admiration
for Harold and his colleagues at the Potomac Institute prompted help
and support at every turn.

In the beginning, the continuing generosity of the Taconic Foundation
gave me not only the necessary time to house and use the Potomac files
but also the means to call on the talents of Rosa Grillo to turn those files
into proper archives and to research essential points. Throughout this
period Eleanor Ambrose, the first staff member Harold engaged in 1961,
and for thirty-one years his irreplaceable assistant, continued to provide
help with numerous details and the warm presence that was always a
hallmark of Potomac.

The Directors of Potomac kept up sustaining interest and encouragement. John Simon, Philip Hammer, and Herbert Franklin have been
particularly patient readers and careful editors, as has Jane Lee Eddy,
executive director of the Taconic Foundation. The champion editor of
all the Potomac Institute publications, Art Levin, stayed in character

through several drafts and was a tremendous resource. Barbara Wolfson's fresh editorial eye was also valuable.

Some of the most thoughtful insights came from Leslie Dunbar. In fact, everyone I turned to was wonderfully giving of support and memories, including especially Jim Gibson, Bill Taylor, Dick Kleeman, and Helen Hill Miller.

But the indispensable person was John Egerton, author of many marvelous books about southern history and culture and colleague and friend to both Harold and me for many decades. He took on himself the role of literary agent to guide me through the publishing thicket. From his own oral history interviews with Harold and others he wrote the introduction to this volume, recounting Harold's experiences prior to the founding of Potomac. Most important, he nourished this book from start to finish with useful advice and steadfast moral support.

INTRODUCTION   *John Egerton*

LIFE, HAROLD FLEMING was fond of saying, is a chain of accidents, a succession of improbable and unexpected events. He cited his own career to illustrate the point.

When he was a child, the Great Depression jerked him out of the relative comfort of the urban middle class and thrust him into a crowded household of hard-strapped relatives in the rural South. He returned to Atlanta in time to finish high school, and happened to be standing by when a recruiter from Harvard came through looking for white boys to give the Ivy League a little "geographical balance." Coincidence and timing also had a great deal to do with his summons to military services as a private, his nomination to be an officer-candidate, and his eventual assignment as a company commander of black soldiers in the South Pacific. After returning to Harvard and then to Atlanta, Fleming was about to buy a one-way ticket out of the South in 1947 when a chance encounter led him into a fourteen-year stint at the Southern Regional Council, a private organization dedicated to the general uplift of the South and its people. Eventually, his low-key, seek-no-credit approach to solving social problems caught the attention of two young New England philanthropists who were themselves quiet reformers much like him, and the subsequent collaboration of these three gentle progressives gave birth to the Potomac Institute.

In 1967, barely more than six years after Stephen and Audrey Currier first sought out Harold Fleming, a tragic accident took the lives of the couple, still only in their mid-thirties, and left Fleming and the leaders of the Taconic Foundation, the Currier-led sponsoring "parent" of the Potomac Institute, to steer their own course through the murky waters of public policy-making in Washington. And finally, twenty-five years later, the last sudden and unexpected event, a heart attack, took the life of Harold Fleming at the too-young age of seventy.

The element of chance is certainly a factor in the shaping of history. But it is also true that talented and productive people make the most of their luck, whether it is good or bad; they act on their circumstances more often than they allow their circumstances to take control of them. If Harold Fleming's life was a chain of accidents, that was at least in part because he frequently put himself in the path of history, like a good accident waiting to happen.

He had a special talent for disguising his own hand in the shaping of collaborative efforts to change society for the better. His preferred role was as an anonymous pilgrim joined with others in a quest for the holy grail of justice, pausing in the evenings at inns along the way to eat and drink and review the day's events, and then to rest for a while before resuming the journey. Long before he used up his biblical allotment of three score and ten, Harold had been there and back, and he had the experiences, the anecdotes, the insights, the connections, the accomplishments, and the accomplices to prove it. You can look back through decades of the *Washington Post* and the *New York Times* on microfilm and not run across his name very often—but inquire among some of the old hands in government, in social-action and public-interest organizations, and in the press, and they will have numerous ways of telling you that Harold Curtis Fleming was a self-effacing southerner with an irrepressible sense of humor, an instinctive empathy for people in need, and an unclouded vision of the beloved community of humankind, toward which he was unremittingly tending throughout his adult life.

Adulthood came early in the empty bowl of the Great Depression. Hal, age eight, and his older brother Hughes had always spent some of their summer weeks in Elbert County, a rural East Georgia jurisdiction on the South Carolina border, where their mother's family had roots four generations deep in the yeomanry. But when the boys were driven out to Elberton from Atlanta early in the summer of 1930, six months after the Wall Street crash had signaled a deeper and broader plunge into hard times, Hal saw his winter shoes and socks in the baggage and knew intuitively that he and Hughes would not be returning anytime soon.

Their father was a vice president of a large building materials firm in Atlanta, but his tenuous foothold in middle management was not secure enough to withstand the economic tornado that was careening across the South. Gradually, a stream of relatives retreated to the Hulme family farmhouse near Elberton, where there was no electricity or running water and not enough beds—but more than enough food from the fields and streams and woods to sustain one and all. Even an eight-year-old could see the difference between town and country, between making out and making do. He could also see, perhaps for the first time, that when white people had it rough, black people were in the most desperate straits imaginable.

Back in Atlanta three years later, Hal Fleming soon put the country life behind him. He went on to parlay his voracious appetite for reading into a solid academic record at Boys' High School, the city's finest, and it was then that the field representative from Harvard came along and opened the way for him to make a quantum leap from the red clay hills of Georgia to the ivied halls of the nation's oldest and most prestigious university. (It was also then—or perhaps in retrospect—that it first dawned on Harold Fleming that he himself was a minority token, a southerner of limited means among mostly well-to-do Yankees, and that he would not have qualified for inclusion had he been of a different race or gender.)

It was the fall of 1940. From then until March 1943, as war spread across Europe and North Africa and Asia, Fleming lived comfortably on his university scholarship, majoring in English, working on the campus radio station and the student literary magazine, and moving ahead of schedule toward graduation at the end of the 1943 fall semester. But the plan was short-circuited when he was called to active duty in the U.S. Army the previous spring, and by summer he had been invited to trade his lowly private's stripe for a shot at becoming a second lieutenant in the quartermaster corps. Early in 1945 he was promoted to captain, placed in charge of a company of black soldiers (the army, like most other American institutions, was still segregated), and sent to Okinawa in the Pacific, where plans for an invasion of Japan were reaching the final stages.

It was there—not in Atlanta, not at Harvard—that the social education of Harold Fleming really began. In the South, he had seen "colored people"—the polite designation of the time—only in subordinate roles;

they were everywhere, doing the hard work white people shunned. In the Ivy League, they were invisible (in the Ralph Ellison sense of the term), if not absent altogether. But in the army, Fleming's troops were a disciplined, cynical, often enraged and menacing lot, battle-scarred survivors in a racist war of attribution that followed them wherever they went. As time passed, he found himself more and more on their side:

> I was a white straw boss in a very discriminatory segregated army, and I soon felt discriminated against along with the men under my command. I lived where they lived, ate where they ate. We were always together—and we all saw ourselves as second-class soldiers, spat upon by the rest of the army. This was a very impressive lesson in race relations for me. If you had any sense of fairness at all, and if you weren't totally at the mercy of your prejudices, you could really see plainly how mindless and dehumanizing the discrimination was. I had gotten to know these men. I knew some of them were very nice guys, and some were so alienated and coarsened by life that they weren't admirable people at all—but in the eyes of most whites, they were all the same, just worthless. The amazing thing to me was that most of them managed to rise above that crap and be responsible, loyal, productive soldiers.

The lessons lingered when Harold Fleming returned to Atlanta after his discharge in the summer of 1946, and when he went back to Harvard that fall to complete his final year of undergraduate study. Then, in the summer of 1947, he was back in his native city with a *magna cum laude* degree, a Phi Beta Kappa key, a twenty-five-year-old liberal white southerner's impatience with Old South rigidity and reaction—and on top of all that, not the faintest prospect of a job. Reading the *Atlanta Constitution* each morning was an exercise in frustration, a refresher course on just how debilitating and self-destructive the segregationist mindset was. "I've got to get out," Fleming told himself. He was ready to leave the region for good; he had already sent letters to New York, inquiring about jobs in journalism and the book-publishing trade. He resolved to be there come September.

Only one thing gave him pause. There on the *Constitution*'s editorial page was the daily column of executive editor Ralph McGill, a deep-dyed son of the South but a decent fellow, by all appearances, and once every week or so he took up the race question and pleaded for fairness, pleaded with his fellow white southerners to do right by the millions of Negro citizens in their midst. Hal Fleming thought this boss man sounded pretty enlightened. He decided to go down to the paper and ask for an appointment to see him.

As he did with practically all the petitioners who appeared at his office door, Ralph McGill waved Fleming to a chair and listened with an occasional weary sigh to his pitch. The editor's first impression of his visitor is not recorded. What he saw, though, was a thin, bespectacled young man whose blond hair was receding prematurely from his furrowed brow, and what McGill heard from this seemingly mature and earnest young fellow was a curious blend of ideas and perceptions from Harvard and North Georgia and the South Pacific, spun out in a rambling ribbon of free-form conversation. Like many a southerner, this guy was a good talker.

For his part, Fleming had a clear recollection of that first meeting with McGill, and it would still be vivid and detailed years later:

> I was there out of curiosity more than anything else. What kind of guy was this, and why was he writing these things? He said, "I just feel compelled every once in a while to write something about this crazy system. We're in for a terrible time down here. It's going to take years and years to overcome these problems. You're probably making the right decision not to stick around. If I were you, I would just get the hell out." He didn't offer me a job, and I didn't ask him for one. We talked on for a bit, and then I got up to leave. McGill said, "Before you go, let me tell you about an interesting outfit here called the Southern Regional Council, an interracial organization. It's a very balanced, decent, courageous group—Southerners who feel the way you do about the racial thing." He saw that I was listening, so he said, "Hold on a minute." And then he picked up the phone and called George Mitchell.

George S. Mitchell, a former Rhodes scholar with academic expertise in labor economics and a southern liberal's preoccupation with the region's social problems, had recently taken over as executive director of the

Southern Regional Council. The organization was small and struggling, and money was so tight that Mitchell sometimes had to dip into his own meager resources to borrow payroll funds. That would have been more than enough to make him frantic with worry, but Fleming found him to be remarkably calm and easy-going. After they had talked for a few minutes, Mitchell turned their conversation into a job interview.

"He asked me if I was in a big rush to get up to New York," Fleming recalled, "and when I told him I had a month or so to kill, he said, 'I just lost my director of information because I don't have enough money to pay him a decent salary. He left me with a half-finished publication. I can scrape up a little dough to pay you if you'll hang around here for two or three weeks and finish the job for me.' So I replied, just as casually, 'Sure, that sounds okay to me.' The next day I went in to work—and I stayed there for almost fourteen years."

It was to be a memorable time in Harold Fleming's life, a time when his energy and idealism were drawn to a great cause—ending segregation—and he carried with him an ever-growing sense of being in the right place at the right moment in history. The fact that he was a southerner by birth had been impressed upon him as simply another of those circumstantial accidents over which he had no control, but now he was a southerner by choice, and he came to terms with that, the good and the bad of it, and found it to be an identity he could accept with a certain equanimity. He made many new and lasting friendships in those years—binding ties with others, white and black, who wore the same minority tag as he: southern liberal.

The Southern Regional Council (SRC) stalwarts of the late forties were not radicals at all. Politically, they were almost all traditional Democrats in the mainstream of the national party—which meant they favored Harry Truman, not the reactionary Dixiecrat Strom Thurmond or the left-wing Progressive party candidate Henry Wallace (and certainly not the Republican Thomas E. Dewey) in the 1948 presidential election. SRC was also considered more moderate than the reformist Southern Conference for Human Welfare and its spinoff faction, the Southern Conference Educational Fund, both of which had labored under the burden of slanderous criticism from the reactionary right since the day they were founded.

Practically all the critics of the two "conference" groups—including Ralph McGill—accepted without much question the charge that they were infested with Communists, even though only a handful of their members could be shown to have such ties. Even more preposterously, SRC was recklessly smeared with the same red brush. It was Fleming's job as director of information to deflect such explosive and potentially devastating strikes, answering them with fact-filled counterattacks.

From the time of its founding in 1944, the Southern Regional Council had been caught on the horns of a policy dilemma. Its more conservative members were reluctant to attack the segregation laws, fearing the wrath of reactionary whites; it would be better, they argued, to work at a gradual expansion of opportunities for blacks, thus eventually making the "separate but equal" myth a reality. The council's progressive wing, made up of more forthright advocates of social change, maintained that legally enforced segregation could never be made truly equal—and in any case, it was antithetical to both the ideals and the laws of the United States and most of its constituent assemblies outside the South.

The internal debate raged on for eight years without resolution; every time a vote that might break the deadlock seemed imminent, caution took over and the decision was tabled for further study. Harold Fleming's personal convictions were decidedly in favor of the progressives, but he struggled to maintain an attitude of neutrality in order to keep open his channels to all sides. "From the time I got involved in 1947," Fleming said, recalling his earliest days at SRC,

> it was absolutely clear to me that everyone in the organization knew desegregation was inevitable, and the vast majority believed it was the right thing to happen. But they differed greatly on the timetable. Some thought it would take forever, that it wouldn't happen in our lifetime; others saw—correctly, I think—that there would never be a better time to start than right then. To speak out for equality, though, let alone integration, was to more or less automatically cut yourself off from Southern society, Southern traditions; it was to become a pariah.

Finally, in December 1951, the SRC board of directors adopted a new "Statement of Policy and Aims" (drafted by Harold Fleming for an ad hoc committee), making explicit for the first time the council's intention to work for a society free of racial discrimination. "The South of the future," toward which the organization pledged itself to work, must be a place "where segregation . . . will no longer be imposed," the document read, and "every individual will enjoy a full share of dignity and self-respect."

During the ten years he served as SRC's information officer, Fleming earned a solid reputation as a cool-headed, even-handed manager. Within the organization, he was increasingly relied upon for leadership in keeping reluctant members aboard on the South's long-overdue journey toward social reformation; to those on the outside—especially in the press—he came across as a helpful, knowledgeable, and always amiable figure.

With several of the most prominent members of the southern press— Ralph McGill of the *Constitution*, Harry S. Ashmore of the *Arkansas Gazette*, John N. Popham of the *New York Times*, and others—Fleming developed close relationships based on mutual trust. He worked as an editorial associate of Ashmore on a pivotal study of racial inequality in the public schools in the months preceding the Supreme Court's *Brown v. Board of Education* ruling against school segregation. Popham's morning-after analysis of that decision on the front page of the *New York Times* on May 18, 1954, quoted Fleming prominently, and in the years that followed, SRC enjoyed a high profile in the *Times*, thanks in large measure to the very effective keystone combination of Fleming to Popham to Catledge (the last being Popham's managing editor, native Mississippian Turner Catledge).

In the months after *Brown*, Fleming seemed to be everywhere at once, writing articles for such magazines as the *New Republic* and the *Progressive*, being interviewed by non-southern journalists who came with increasing frequency to cover the spreading race relations story, and challenging the claims of such SRC critics as editors Thomas R. Waring of the *Charleston News and Courier* and James J. Kilpatrick of the *Richmond News Leader.*

There is no "solid South" bonded in bitter, die-hard defiance of social change, Fleming kept saying; in every state, there are many ordinary citizens of both races whose basic impulse is to be responsible and cooperative and law-abiding. The court's decision "has set in motion a vast, uneven process of change in the South. The only thing that can be said with absolute certainty is that the process is under way and, whatever setbacks lie ahead, it will not be reversed."

Calm, reasoned, affirming words were what many people came to expect from the Southern Regional Council—and more often than not, Harold Fleming was the spokesman who delivered the reassuring message to them. When George Mitchell announced his retirement from the executive director's post in December 1956, it seemed almost a foregone conclusion that Fleming would be called up to take his place.

The change in staff leadership at the Southern Regional Council coincided with a time when the leadership of the conservative white South, having absorbed the reality of *Brown v. Board of Education,* was organizing a militantly defiant opposition to the U.S. Supreme Court and all other voices of federal authority on the issue of segregation. The fledgling Citizens' Council of America—sometimes called the "country club" or "white collar" Ku Klux Klan—was spreading like wildfire across the Deep South. It was in the spring of 1956 that four out of every five southern members of the U.S. Senate and House of Representatives signed a hostile manifesto of resistance to desegregation, and it was soon thereafter that violent opposition greeted the first attempts of black citizens to enroll their children in all-white public schools in such upper-South communities as Clinton, Tennessee, and Little Rock, Arkansas.

In his four-year tenure as SRC's executive director, Harold Fleming would witness the full emergence of both the civil rights movement and the last-ditch defense of the white supremacist "Southern way of life." Inspired by the constitutional interpretations of the federal courts and the voices of black leaders in religion and the law, millions of southerners of African descent gave themselves to a historic movement that would in time transcend race and region. In angry reaction, millions of southerners of European descent (Fleming's ethnic heritage, obviously) followed their firebrand leaders into a tragic repeat of the defiant estrangement that a century earlier had brought on the Civil War. The relative handful of white southerners who refused to align themselves with the advocates of Old South segregation and white supremacy were hard-pressed to find indigenous institutions that promoted interracial cooperation and equity. SRC was one of the few.

Though its membership remained small—a few thousand, compared to the half a million dues-paying members of the Citizens' Council—the Southern Regional Council was remarkably visible and influential in the turbulent decade (1955–65) when the civil rights movement was in full flower. It established subsidiary councils in most of the southern states. It conducted what amounted to adult education programs aimed at preparing southerners, white and black alike, for the responsibilities of thoroughgoing democracy. And perhaps most importantly, it conducted an ongoing program of research and publication that put vital information in the hands of countless thousands of men and women who aspired to a more perfect union.

It had been one of Harold Fleming's tasks previously to manage and direct the council's public information program, which included dissemination of research. After he became SRC's chief of staff, he brought in Leslie W. Dunbar, a political scientist at Mount Holyoke College in Massachusetts and a native southerner, to be director of research, and the subsequent output of the council enhanced its reputation as the most authoritative source of information on race relations in the South.

SRC researchers and investigative reports studied incidents of racial violence in the region, and minority access to the ballot, and the role of the church in the race issue. They probed into the status of the black minority in schools and colleges, in labor unions and corporations, in housing and health care, in the pages of the press and in the powerful new medium of television. Through the last years of the 1950s and on into the 1960s, SRC kept up a steady drumbeat for social change. Out of all proportion to their numbers, this little band of progressive southerners reached out from their base in Atlanta to play a helpful role in the transformation of the South.

It was in this time—in November 1960, to be exact, right after the election victory of Democratic presidential candidate John F. Kennedy—that twenty-nine-year-old Stephen R. Currier and Audrey Mellon Bruce Currier, his twenty-six-year-old wife, sought out Harold Fleming, then an "early middle-ager" at thirty-eight, and went with him on a fact-finding bus ride through Fleming's natural habitat of rural Georgia.

Fleming sometimes cited his first encounter with the Curriers as another of those chance meetings in the string of accidents that made up his career, but for the Curriers it was hardly coincidental; they and their advisors had been following the work of SRC and its director for a couple of years, and it was with deliberation and firm intent that they sought out Fleming and drew him into conversation.

Two years earlier, the Curriers had made a spectacular entrance on the stage of American philanthropy by concentrating a substantial portion of their vast inherited fortunes into a new charitable enterprise, the Taconic Foundation, through which they hoped to encourage programs of forward-looking social change in the United States. Stephen Currier, descended from a distinguished Jewish family that included the lithographer Nathaniel Currier of Currier and Ives fame, had spent most of his boyhood in Italy and then had gone for a time to Harvard before turning to other interests, among them art and architecture. It was Marshall Field, the Chicago merchandising magnate and a close family friend, who helped to open Stephen Currier's eyes to progressive causes and a vocation of service.

During his brief stay at Harvard, Stephen met Audrey Bruce, a Radcliffe student and daughter of diplomat David E. K. Bruce. Though they were both from upper-class families, Audrey Bruce's inheritance was of a different order of magnitude: far more than a hundred million dollars from the estate of her late grandfather, the industrialist/financier/philanthropist—and Republican—Andrew Mellon. All in all, there were more than enough differences in the two families to generate some consternation on both sides when Stephen Currier and Audrey Bruce eloped in 1954, and then pooled their resources to make a forceful impact in the philanthropic community.

Within four years they had established themselves as sensitive, caring, intelligent, and generous benefactors. With the creation of the Taconic Foundation (the name coming from the mountain range in Vermont where the young couple had chosen their favorite retreat), Stephen and Audrey Currier were ready, in the words of their soon-to-be counselor and friend Jane Lee Eddy, "to look out over the edge of the social horizon and chart a course with real meaning for their generation."

Among foundations leaders of that time, Stephen Currier was decidedly different. There may have been activists like him in earlier generations, men such as Andrew Carnegie, Julius Rosenwald, and one or two others. But by the 1950s and 1960s, most foundations had become professionalized institutions. Currier came among them with a determination, a passion, to be a force for change—for democratizing, liberalizing change. Leslie Dunbar, later Fleming's successor at the Southern Regional Council, not only benefitted from that determination but modeled his later work as executive director of the Field Foundation on what he had seen Currier demonstrate: that a foundation could be a *participant*, not merely a money dispenser.

First among the Curriers' chosen advisors was New York attorney Lloyd K. Garrison, whose interest in social reform might well have come genetically, at least in part, from his abolitionist ancestor, William Lloyd Garrison. In any case, it was the younger Garrison, with his abiding interest in race relations and the South, who first brought Harold Fleming and the Southern Regional Council to the Curriers' attention. Currier increasingly wanted to be an integral part of the civil rights movement, and he wanted to fund an organization to that end.

Perhaps there was some accidental history in this after all—call it destiny, or whatever. Here were two young, quiet, even shy people with a deep sense of empathy for the multitudes who had been excluded from the American dream, and with the resources to address some of the problems, even to make a sizable dent in them. And here was another slightly older young man who had in common with them a Harvard connection—and also shared something else, much more important: a quiet sense of concern, and a willingness, indeed an eagerness, to serve others without a thought for praise or credit. They saw in each other, these three, an opportunity to step in and be useful, to turn their undivided attention on the problems of racial and social inequality in the South and the nation.

And so, after a brief acquaintance, they founded the Potomac Institute in Washington. There was no master plan, no grand agenda for saving the nation—just some common ground where progressive, reform-minded men and women in and out of government could meet, looking for ways to work together for the good of all. Harold Fleming was the low-key director, the amiable host with method in his mirth; Stephen and Audrey Currier were in the background, giving unobtrusive advice, support, resources. Here began what was destined to be a brief but brilliant partnership in the fine art of public service.

And the rest, as they say, is history.

PART ONE

CHAPTER 1 ■ *The Birth of a Notion*

THE POTOMAC INSTITUTE was conceived, appropriately enough, in the back of a bus.

The chartered vehicle was roaring through rural Georgia, an area still in 1960 as loyal as ever to its segregationist tradition. The young man who sat next to me shared my unhappiness about the persistence of racial caste in Georgia and elsewhere in the South. Stephen Currier was a wealthy New Yorker, who at age twenty-nine was emerging as a creative philanthropist quite different from the usual representatives of the breed. Several years earlier, he and his wife, the former Audrey Bruce, a granddaughter of Andrew Mellon, had resolved to invest a major share of their substantial charitable giving in the struggle for racial equality. The Taconic Foundation, which they created in 1958, helped finance many of the organizations working to advance racial justice.

One such organization was the Southern Regional Council, (SRC) an Atlanta-based association of black and white southerners promoting an end to discrimination and segregation in the states of the old Confederacy. Despite its shoe-string budget and constant harassment by professional race-baiters, some in high public office, SRC was routinely identified in the national press as "the South's most respected interracial organization." (Admittedly, competition for this honor was not very keen at the time.) As a newly returned veteran, I joined its staff in 1947 and became its executive director in 1957, about the same time the Curriers began their philanthropic activities.

My first awareness of them came by way of Western Union. The telegram went something like this: "Having heard many fine reports of the Southern Regional Council's work, I am sending today a contribution of $2,500. Best wishes for the New Year. Stephen Richard Currier." It was a small gift by present standards, but a significant windfall in those hard-pressed days—certainly large enough to arouse my curiosity about the donor.

Soon afterward, I met the Curriers and some of their principal advisers, who would help guide the newly formed Taconic Foundation for years to come. Their chief mentor was Lloyd K. Garrison, whose reputation as lawyer, educator, and humanitarian was prodigious. That he was a descendant of the noted abolitionist William Lloyd Garrison was an interesting but incidental sidelight; it was his own experience as a champion of racial equality and other progressive causes that gave significance to his role as adviser to the Curriers.

Others who figured prominently in the affairs of Taconic were a gifted young lawyer named John G. Simon, who would one day be its president; Jane Lee Eddy, who became its resourceful executive director; Dorothy Hirshon, a knowledgeable participant in educational and civic affairs; and Edith Entenman, an innovative child psychologist. It was with this informal "family" that I soon found myself involved, first as a supplicant for the Southern Regional Council, and later as a fellow trustee of the foundation.

By that November day in 1960 when Stephen and I were sharing the bus ride through Georgia, I had come to appreciate him not only as a donor but as a friend and collaborator as well. Nevertheless, I was unprepared for the question he suddenly put to me.

"What would you think of starting something new in Washington? Whether he knows it or not, Kennedy's going to be saddled with enormous racial problems. And he can't just ignore them like Eisenhower."

He went on to recount what a friend had told him about a discreet but influential operation in London that regularly brought together public policy makers and private citizens to brainstorm new approaches to national problems.

"It occurred to me," he said, "that we might set up something like that to help deal with civil rights in the new administration. How would you feel about taking it on?"

But the circumstances that brought Currier to Atlanta gave us no opportunity to explore the idea further. The occasion was an unusual one. At the invitation of Mrs. Ruth Field, Currier had joined trustees of the Field Foundation on a two-day whirlwind excursion to Atlanta and points south. Morris B. Abram, a progressive Atlanta lawyer, was the local host. He was determined to give the group as varied an exposure as possible. The schedule included everything from civil rights activists and black community leaders to "wool hat" politicians and leaders of the business establishment—not easy to arrange in a rigidly segregated state governed by Herman Talmadge and his fellow white supremacists.

Ordinarily, the board of a liberal New York–based foundation would have been about as warmly welcomed in Georgia as General William Tecumseh Sherman on his scorched-earth march from Atlanta to the sea. What made this visit different was the presence of the Field Foundation's president, Adlai E. Stevenson. He was extremely popular in Georgia, and everybody from the governor on down meant to see that he and his companions got VIP treatment. My role was clearly defined. I was supposed to arrange for our foundation guests to meet and talk with blacks and whites who worked together against racial restrictions—the people Talmadge denounced as "those race-mixing radicals."

As part of my assignment, I had arranged a large luncheon meeting in the barebones offices of the Southern Regional Council. The room was jammed, and the seats around our improvised banquet table were filled to capacity. Since I was to introduce Stevenson, I had placed myself next to him. Just as the food was being served, I was called away briefly. When I returned, my seat was occupied by a stocky, curly haired man who was displaying a sheaf of papers to Stevenson with one hand and eating my lunch with the other.

"Who the hell is that," I asked a staff member.

"Some kind of adviser to Governor Stevenson," he replied. "I think his name is Ball."

I learned that George Ball, who would later serve as Kennedy's under secretary of state, had flown to Atlanta to confer on the text of a foreign policy paper he was helping Stevenson prepare for the president-elect. They were no doubt also discussing Stevenson's prospective role in the new administration, which subsequently turned out to be ambassador to the United Nations rather than secretary of state, as Stevenson had hoped.

The bus tour of the Georgia countryside was like nothing so much as a royal procession. At every stop, the local citizenry was gathered in front of the courthouse or at the base of the obligatory Confederate soldier's statue—invincibly facing north, of course. At the sight of Stevenson step-ping from the bus, the local high school band would strike up an ear-splitting Sousa march and the crowd would cheer wildly. As this scene was repeated over and over, I mingled with the spectators—blacks and whites, overalled farmers and white-collar townspeople—and marveled at their enthusiasm for this polished speaker who had recently for the third time missed the chance to become president of the United States.

In one town, a state legislator had gathered his neighbors on the front porch for a conversation over iced tea and lemonade. In another, the ladies of the local chapter of the United Daughters of the Confederacy showed off a succession of antebellum houses, in each of which the dining-room table groaned with home-made confections. In Washing-ton, Georgia, we visited the home of Alexander ("Little Alex") Stephens, that remarkable Georgian who opposed secession, then later reluc-tantly agreed to become vice president of the Confederacy. I have a vivid memory of Lloyd Garrison musing over a yellowed poster that offered a handsome reward for the capture of his great-grandfather, dead or alive.

Philip Hammer, a public-spirited economic planner, a long-time friend, and a veteran of good causes, was one of the Atlantans on the tour. He has reminded me of a stir created by one local Stevenson enthu-siast. As we entered one of the fine old houses, two scrawny legs were seen protruding from the shrubbery. On investigation, they proved to belong to an ancient little man who clutched in his hand a faded ballot bearing the name Adlai Stevenson. This, it turned out, referred not to our guest, but to his grandfather, who had run unsuccessfully for a second stint as vice president on the ticket with William Jennings Bryan in 1900. In his eagerness to show this relic to the extant Stevenson, the unfortu-nate man had lost his balance and fallen head-first from the veranda into an hydrangea bush.

When the excitement died down, the party, surfeited with tea and cookies, was loaded onto the bus for the pellmell ride back to Atlanta. There, we were rushed to the Abrams' home for the first of two large dinner parties, to which an assortment of Atlanta dignitaries had been invited. There were two such affairs—only one of which I was expected to attend—since Morris had prudently invited incompatible guests for different nights. But this well-laid plan went awry; Governor Talmadge came on the wrong night and found himself inadvertently shaking hands with the race-mixing executive director of the Southern Regional Council. A little later, Morris took me aside to tell me that Talmadge had asked indignantly, "What is he doing here?" "Tell him," I said, "that I asked the same about him."

In the midst of this activity, I found an opportunity to tell Lloyd Garrison about Stephen's proposition. He reacted enthusiastically. But once he and Stephen and the other foundation people had decamped, I found myself with sorely mixed feelings. I was a born-and-bred southerner, however heretically reconstructed, and all my working experience had been in the South. Moreover, in my fourteen years with the Southern Regional Council, I had never been more satisfied with the work I was doing or more optimistic about the prospects for major change in our race-plagued society. Why abandon this for an uncertain and arguably presumptuous undertaking in Washington?

The idea was, nevertheless, tempting. It had long since become clear to me and others of like mind that significant change in the South simply would not occur without major federal intervention. The federal courts by themselves were not enough; leadership from the executive and legislative branches as well was essential. Kennedy's election had brought with it an atmosphere of excitement and anticipation, a sense that great things were now possible. The thought of playing some part in bringing about such achievements in civil rights was more than a little appealing. Moreover, my reluctance to leave the Southern Regional Council at so decisive a time was tempered by two fortunate circumstances: SRC was in better shape, financially and otherwise, than ever before; and there was already on staff a person who was superbly equipped to assume the position of executive director. This was Leslie W. Dunbar, who had abandoned a scholarly career to become research director of SRC. (He would later serve with distinction as executive director of the Field Foundation.) If I decided to leave, I could do so with a clear conscience.

When I next saw Currier in New York, he resumed our discussion as though there had been no interruption. I confessed that I had not been able to reach a decision. "That's all right," he said. "We don't have to decide right now. Why don't you put something on paper that will help us look at the possibilities?" With some relief, I agreed. But of course as of that moment I was irrevocably headed for Washington.

Currier's proposition raised a spate of questions to which I had no self-evident answers. Could the would-be operation really make a difference? What form should it take? What kind of board and staff should it have? Should it have members, subscribers, fellows, resident scholars? How would it be funded? Should it seek government contracts? Solicit direct-mail contributions? Have branch offices or chapters? Publish a journal? What kinds of activities would be most productive? And, most troublesome of all, what if we set up shop and were greeted by total indifference?

The memorandum I finally sent to Currier offered only general answers. I suggested that the proposed operation should keep its board, staff, and budget small. Its style should be simple and low-key. It should be helpful to like-minded organizations and should not compete with them for money, recognition, or functions. It should work through relationships of trust with key people inside and outside of government. It should be rigorously independent, which meant steering clear of federal grants and contracts. In time, it should have offices adequate to serve as its headquarters and a meeting place for people involved in its area of activity. But the immediate object should be to get in the swim, to start talking with people and exploring possibilities for useful action.

This formulation appealed to Stephen Currier. Both he and Audrey shunned flamboyant and self-promoting activities. As observers invariably remarked, Audrey was extremely shy and seldom volunteered her views, except among intimates. Stephen could also be reserved in strange company or large gatherings. They insisted that their personal benefactions be given no publicity and that their privacy be respected. So it was to be expected that they would want any new activity with which they were associated to do its best work behind the scenes.

For my part, their predilections were all to the good. Experience had convinced me that attention-getting fanfare was often at odds with effectiveness. The old saying that you can accomplish anything if you are willing to let others take the credit is an overstatement, but it contains a lot of truth.

We also found ourselves in agreement about the kinds of activities such an institute should engage in. It should bring together those persons whose sharing of ideas promised to lead to useful action. Its reports and recommendations should be keyed to immediate and practical civil rights problems that called for action not yet contemplated by government and major private institutions. It should augment its small staff with consultants who were not just theorists but seasoned practitioners in their fields. It should establish itself with the news media as a reliable source of background information and analysis. And, once suitably housed, it should open its library and meeting facilities to others who shared its concerns.

In a sense, Potomac was to represent a new organizational breed. The Brookings Institution had long existed, and there may have been a scattering of others, but the designation "think tank," so familiar now, was a novel name and concept then. What Potomac was to be was different even from that. It was to be a place of thought and research, yes, but a place also of commitment and advocacy. There would be others, but it can fairly be said that Potomac was a first, if not *the* first, of this new breed: an organization with a firm point of view, identifying itself with reforming efforts, and at the same time devoted to accuracy and intellectual rigor.

In addition, few groups at the time were either inclined or equipped to give systematic attention to the complex institutional changes needed to remedy racial inequities. Race relations were most often addressed in either moral, political, or sociological terms. The novelty lay not in what we were proposing to do, but in the fact that we were proposing to do it.

We decided that I should devote the next few months to testing the water in Washington, and so, with some regret, I handed in my resignation at the Southern Regional Council. Since my family would remain in Atlanta until the end of the school term, I rented an apartment in Foggy Bottom to serve as temporary lodgings and makeshift office. The name of the area tallied perfectly with my state of mind as I set out to scavenge advice along the banks of the Potomac.

CHAPTER 2 ■ *Through a Political Lens*

AS JOHN F. KENNEDY settled in the Oval Office, civil rights problems were not uppermost among his concerns. Thanks in large part to his telephone call during the campaign to Mrs. Martin Luther King Jr., expressing concern for her jailed husband, he had won the election by virtue of strong support from black voters.

With respect to racial issues, his predecessor's act was not hard to follow; Eisenhower had made no effort to conceal his distaste for federal intervention on behalf of civil rights. That, coupled with Nixon's campaign courtship of southern conservatives, had brightened Kennedy's image among blacks and liberals and won him—or so he must have thought—a certain amount of indulgence from them. Moreover, the choice of Lyndon B. Johnson as his running mate had mollified southern political leaders and installed as vice president a past master of consensus politics.

Kennedy and his aides were not oblivious to the nation's racial problems, at least as those problems were then perceived. To a degree that in retrospect seems astonishing, racism was viewed as a distinctively southern phenomenon. Racial tensions had exploded from time to time in such northern cities as Detroit and Chicago. But these were viewed as isolated events, overshadowed in the public consciousness by the running drama of racial oppression in the South. And not without reason. Seven years after the *Brown* decision, school segregation in the South was still virtually intact. Blacks for the most part were limited to the lowest paying jobs, often in segregated work places. Housing discrimination, traditionally abetted by federal officialdom, was flagrantly practiced throughout the country. Worst of all, millions of blacks were denied the right to vote by methods ranging from outright violence, intimidation, and economic reprisal to subtler techniques of fraud and evasion. In the face of these persistent discriminations, blacks were increasingly unwilling to pursue their grievances exclusively through court action. Martin Luther King and his followers had set an inspiring example with their nonviolent boycott of segregated bus service in Montgomery, Alabama. In February 1960, black college students had launched the first wave of sit-ins protesting segregated eating facilities, and other planned confrontations were in the making.

The political challenge, as viewed by the new administration, was to steer a circumspect course between the demands of the civil rights movement and the opposition of congressional leaders whose power bases depended on the continued subordination of blacks. Kennedy was painfully conscious that his victory in the election had been razor thin. Furthermore, the loss of Democratic seats in the Congress had left him with a perilously narrow margin of support for his legislative program. How could he hope to quicken the pace of progress in civil rights without alienating essential allies in Congress and jeopardizing his hopes for building a strong national consensus? He gave his answer during the campaign, when asked about his plans for civil rights legislation.

> First, there is a good deal that can be done by the executive branch without legislation. For example, the President could sign an executive order ending discrimination in housing tomorrow. Second, the President could compel all companies which do business with the Government, and after all that is nearly every American company, to practice open, fair hiring of personnel without regard to race, creed, or color. . . . In addition the Department of Justice can pursue the right to vote with far more vigor. . . . So I would say that the greater opportunity is in the Executive branch without Congressional action.[1]

He later had cause to regret his blithe promise to wipe out housing discrimination with "a stroke of the pen"; it was almost two years before he could bring himself to face the supposed political hazards of such an edict. Nevertheless, the general approach described in his campaign statement did become the operating policy of the administration. No new legislation was sought in the first year; in fact, the president coldly repudiated one well-meant effort to identify him with a civil rights bill, drafted at his request by Representative Emanuel Celler and Senator Joseph Clark. Both he and his brother Robert, the new attorney general, repeatedly declared that they regarded the vote as the principal right through which all forms of discrimination could ultimately be eliminated. Executive action focused on those areas that were most obviously in the federal domain, such as government-related employment, rather than areas that involved sensitive national-state relations, such as federal assistance programs. Least of all was there any intent to tie the president's personal prestige to crusading initiatives likely to stir the passions of the multitude.

Kennedy was not long in providing an example of the kind of presidential leadership he had in mind. Surveying the inaugural parade, he asked why the United States Coast Guard contingent included no blacks. Because, he was told, there were no blacks enrolled in the Coast Guard Academy. Kennedy directed his aides to see that the situation was remedied, and soon afterward the academy was engaged in a talent search for black candidates. The same sort of sensitivity prompted the appointment of blacks to high-level positions in the government. Among them were Thurgood Marshall as judge of the Second Circuit Court of Appeals, Robert C. Weaver as head of the Housing and Home Finance Administration, George L.-P. Weaver as assistant secretary of labor, Carl Rowan as deputy assistant secretary of state, and Lisle Carter as deputy assistant secretary of the Department of Health, Education and Welfare.

The first formal use of presidential authority for civil rights came, so long urged by SRC and others, on March 6, 1961, when Kennedy signed Executive Order 10925 requiring employers holding federal contracts, as well as federal departments and agencies, to take "affirmative action" assuring equal employment opportunity irrespective of race, religion, or national origin. It was a forceful decree. It conferred on an invigorated president's Committee on Equal Employment Opportunity broad enforcement powers over private firms employing some twenty million workers. As would soon become evident, mustering the political will to use these sanctions was quite another matter. Yet the bold provisions of the order gave heart to those who hoped to find in Kennedy a strong champion of equal rights.

Late on the afternoon of the signing I joined three former colleagues from the Southern Regional Council for an audience with Vice President Lyndon Johnson. Despite some disagreement within his inner circle of advisers, Kennedy had named Johnson chairman of the president's committee. Johnson was in high spirits when he received us in the cavernous office he had retained in the Capitol. The moment we sat down, he launched into an animated monologue that continued with hardly a pause for the forty-five minutes or so we were with him. He expressed profound satisfaction with the sweeping authority the order had conferred on the committee.

"If any of these contractors think they can get around this order, they're gonna find out we've got 'em right here," he said, forcefully grasping the part of the anatomy in question.

As he talked on, however, his exuberance gave way to a darker mood. He had been deeply offended by the attacks on him by liberal Democrats (including some of those closest to John Kennedy) who had tried to block his nomination as vice president. Imagine, he exclaimed, their trying to smear him as a Dixiecrat opposed to the interests of minorities and working people. He spoke feelingly of his early days in Texas when he taught Mexican-American children in the public schools, and of his lifelong championship of "the little man, the underdog." He referred proudly to his having engineered, in 1957, the first federal civil rights legislation of this century.

Although he left us little opportunity to interject comments or questions, Johnson adroitly associated us with his views by dropping an occasional "I don't have to tell you fellows," accompanied by a conspiratorial wink. Clearly, we as liberal southerners, black and white, could not fail to appreciate the outrageousness of his critics' charges.

"As y'all know," he intoned, "I was one of those radical New Dealers under FDR; I was one of those 'communists' that helped run the National Youth Administration."

Suddenly, the room resonated with a loud buzz. Johnson leaped to his feet, turned off his wrist alarm, clasped the two of us nearest him in a powerful embrace, and declaimed, "I need your help!" And then he was gone. It was a typical—even stereotypical—Johnson performance. Yet such was the force of his personality that it swept away any doubts about his determination to get results. What we did not take into account were the dark strains of suspicion and vindictiveness in his makeup that would often cloud his judgment, make needless enemies, cause him to shut out unwelcome advice and criticism, and finally shackle him to a war that proved disastrous to him and to the country.

In considering what executive actions we should press for, we were not starting from scratch. Before I left the Southern Regional Council, we had submitted to the White House a set of recommendations titled *The Federal Executive and Civil Rights*, put together with the help of the ablest students of government and civil rights we could find. Several other private groups—among them, the Leadership Conference on Civil Rights, the National Urban League, the National Association for the Advancement of Colored People, and the National Association of Intergroup Relations Officials—also put forward their recommendations. And, since its creation in 1957, the U.S. Commission on Civil Rights had developed a number of proposals for presidential action, which were packaged up for consideration by John Kennedy and his advisers.

Although differing in some details, these organizational proposals had much in common. Each group gave high priority to Kennedy's promised executive order on housing discrimination; strong executive action requiring equal employment among firms doing business with the government; various efforts to hasten desegregation of public schools, public accommodations, and interstate transportation; prohibition of discrimination in federally funded activities; and more forceful action by the Department of Justice in support of black citizens' efforts to register and vote. These proposals seemed a logical starting point for the operation we were trying to bring into being.

One of the first persons I sought out in Washington was Harris Wofford, an imaginative activist lawyer whom I had known since the mid-fifties. During travels in India, he had developed a deep admiration for Gandhi's philosophy of nonviolence, an affinity that later led to a close association with Martin Luther King. He was one of the first staff members of the Civil Rights Commission, serving as counsel to Father Theodore Hesburgh, president of Notre Dame University. As John F. Kennedy's campaign adviser on civil rights, he had initiated the proposal that Kennedy call Coretta King, the gesture that was such a decisive factor in the election. He was now dividing his time between the newly formed Peace Corps and the White House, where he served as the president's assistant for civil rights.

One of Wofford's first actions in the White House had been to institute frequent informal meetings of the administration's chief civil rights functionaries. This small group gathered weekly in his office to brainstorm the urgent problems of the moment and to exchange ideas on strategy. To my pleased surprise, Harris invited me to sit in on these meetings, which I did for the eighteen months that the "ad hoc committee" continued to exist. This exposure gave me invaluable insights into the way civil rights problems were perceived in the upper reaches of the administration, as well as the political and bureaucratic roadblocks that had to be surmounted if significant new action was to be taken.

Most of the members of Harris's committee were men I had worked with in one context or another. Berl Bernhard, who had served as counsel to Chairman John Hannah of the U.S. Civil Rights Commission, was the new staff director of the commission. John Feild, who had headed the Michigan Fair Employment Practices Commission and had come to Washington to work for Senator Philip Hart, was now executive director of the president's Committee on Equal Employment Opportunity. Adam Yarmolinsky, a friend since college days, was special assistant to Secretary of Defense Robert McNamara. Louis Martin, deputy director of the Democratic National Committee, was a shrewd adviser on political and racial matters. Frank Reeves was a respected Washington lawyer who had worked in the Kennedy campaign and was now a White House aide. William L. Taylor, a lawyer with the Civil Rights Commission (and later its staff director), buttressed the White House effort with indispensable staff work.

One central figure in the administration's management of civil rights whom I did not know was Burke Marshall, an antitrust lawyer who had been appointed assistant attorney general in charge of the Civil Rights Division. The first reports I had of him had an almost legendary flavor. His judgment and ability had won him recognition in legal circles, but his most celebrated trait was said to be an uncanny ability to reassure and persuade others while uttering hardly a word. In the standard account of his first meeting with Robert F. Kennedy, he is reported to have sat in prolonged silence with the also taciturn attorney general. Yet, muted or not, he was in a position to exert greater influence on the administration's civil rights performance than anyone except the president and the attorney general.

I entered Marshall's office for the first time assuming that it would take a lot of doing to establish a relationship with so reserved a man. I was altogether wrong. From the first moment, I felt an easy rapport with this lanky, mild-mannered man. He was not very talkative, to be sure, but what he said inspired confidence, and any suggestion of undue solemnity was belied by a puckish glint behind his horn-rimmed glasses. He seemed to take it for granted that we would be working closely together.

He spoke of some immediate concerns on which he felt Potomac could be helpful. Most urgent were problems of southern law enforcement. Protests against voting discrimination were beginning in Mississippi, and Burke was worried about the prospect of physical and economic reprisals against the protesters there and in the other Deep South states. (Events would soon demonstrate that his fears were more than justified.) Perhaps we could arrange a confidential meeting with knowledgeable persons from that area? I assured him we would.

Complementing the White House ad hoc committee was a more formal new body that was to play an important part in planning and implementing executive actions. This was the Subcabinet Group on Civil Rights, composed of departmental and agency officials of assistant secretary rank, also chaired by Wofford. It included some of the most talented and effective individuals in the new administration: Jack Conway for the Housing and Home Finance Agency, Hyman Bookbinder for the Department of Commerce, Alfred Fitt for the Department of the Army, Adam Yarmolinsky for the Defense Department, Tom Powers for the Department of Labor, James Quigley and Lisle Carter for the Department of Health, Education and Welfare, and others of like quality. The deliberations—indeed, the very existence—of this group were unpublicized. To the best of my knowledge, none of this committee's discussions or decisions was ever leaked during the three years or so of its active existence.

The new arrangement was well conceived. Harris's ad hoc committee identified problems and opportunities, anticipated political and bureaucratic roadblocks, and brainstormed alternative courses of action. If a presidential mandate seemed necessary, Harris undertook to get it. If a proposed approach called for action by all or a number of agencies, the issue was taken up by the Subcabinet Committee, whose members were in a position to see that the actions decided upon were taken in their respective jurisdictions.

Most of the issues dealt with in this way were of one of two varieties—internal issues affecting practices of the executive branch itself, and external problems that could be dealt with only by suspending standard agency procedures. For example, it was revealed that the Civil War Centennial Commission, chaired by none other than Ulysses S. Grant III, was planning to hold an all-white commemoration of the firing on Fort Sumter in a segregated Charleston hotel. Not until faced with a personal demand by the president, and the threat of defunding, did the commission finally agree to move its observance to the desegregated Charleston Naval Station. Harris felt justified in interpreting the president's action in this case as a mandate for barring the participation of federal officials in all segregated meetings or other events.

Blacks who asserted their right to vote in rural Fayette and Haywood counties, Tennessee, soon found themselves unemployed and denied credit. Many were reduced to living in a "tent city," where food was scarce. The ad hoc committee, backed by a written request from the president, induced the Department of Agriculture to provide surplus food supplies for distribution to the victims of economic reprisals. Some fourteen thousand of them were sustained in this way while the Justice Department sought more permanent relief through the tortuous processes of litigation.

Various government facilities and services that had long accommodated to southern law and custom were directed to conform to the new federal commitment of desegregation and nondiscrimination. Among them were southern offices of the U.S. Employment Service and the Bureau of Apprenticeship and Training, federal employee associations and recreational activities, national parks, language institutes funded under the National Defense Education Act at southern universities, and lunchrooms and other amenities in federal buildings.

Black servicemen and their families stationed in the South were subject to the same indignities as local black residents—segregated off-base housing, schools, and public accommodations of all kinds. Worse yet, the military police used their authority to enforce the local discriminatory practices. When Adam Yarmolinsky brought these abuses to the attention of Secretary McNamara, he ordered the military police to desist, and directed that, where off-base facilities were segregated, every effort should be made to provide racially nondiscriminatory alternatives on military bases. (Such orders were not always brilliantly executed; some military bases contracted with the segregated local school system to run the on-base, integrated school and left to service families the choice of which one to use.)

Welcome as the reforms were, they were not sufficient to root out all the manifestations of officially sanctioned bias in the military. Most conspicuous was continued segregation of southern National Guard units, which were normally under state control. In order to buy time and build public support for action on this hot issue, the president appointed a Committee on Equal Opportunity in the Armed Forces, chaired by a prominent Washington lawyer, later a federal judge, Gerhard Gesell. Another of its members, appointed at my suggestion, was Benjamin Muse, a retired army colonel from Virginia, with whom I had worked closely in the Southern Regional Council. The committee subsequently issued a forceful report that paved the way for elimination of remaining official discrimination in the military.

Potomac's role in the administration's new initiatives was to serve as an informal adviser and a link to a network of private individuals and organizations that monitored compliance with the new policies, forwarded complaints and criticisms, and provided helpful intelligence about criticisms and about developments in their states and localities.

It can justly be said of the Kennedy administration's first year that never, before or since, has a president and his staff involved so many influential and talented appointees in civil rights initiatives. Able as they were, though, their improvisations could not produce the kind of broad, systematic changes that civil rights advocates wanted and the situation required. It is probably true that no amount of presidential commitment could have secured early passage of strong civil rights legislation. Yet, without it, presidential executive action was bound to be too hobbled by political constraints to achieve more than scattered and piecemeal reforms. Early on, Harris Wofford had urged the civil rights community to be mindful of these limitations. In a speech to the National Civil Liberties Clearing House, he said:

I do not mean that the new avenue of executive action will be easy. This course has plenty of contradictions and it will not resolve the built-in political contradictions. The need for enactment of vital measures for the general welfare may still at any given moment have to be weighed against other actions to advance civil rights. Since these social measures have the most direct impact on our racial minorities, so many of whom are at the bottom of our economic ladder, the weighing process is sometimes painful. You may on occasion disagree with the result of the weighing of priorities. But for your disagreement to be effective you will need to look at the process through a political lens that takes into account the major contradictions shaping this problem.[2]

It was a thoroughly reasonable statement. The trouble with this "political lens" approach, however, was that the demands and expectations of civil rights advocates and those for whom they spoke had already gone far beyond the narrow confines of "political feasibility." What could be gained by horse-trading with an Eastland or a Russell was no longer even close to enough.

In a memorandum to Berl Bernhard on the need for more preventive rather than merely responsive action, I characterized the administration's predicament in the following gloomy terms:

The President and the Executive Branch are vulnerable at many points: e.g., whenever a high-ranking Federal official addresses a meeting at a segregated hotel, whenever servicemen are discriminated against in off-base establishments, whenever the I.C.C. rules are flouted, whenever foreign diplomats are denied service because of their color, whenever Federal employees encounter discrimination in the course of official business or travel, whenever leased Federal property or private concessions on Federal property are operated on a discriminatory basis, whenever law and order break down, or the rights of demonstrators are flagrantly violated.[3]

My memorandum concluded: "These problems are not new. What is new is the readiness of the protest movement to create the issue for the Federal Government in the most dramatic and embarrassing terms."

CHAPTER 3 ▪ *The Wild Blue Yonder*

BY THE END OF March, our fledgling operation had been christened the Potomac Institute and legitimized as a nonprofit, tax-exempt corporation under the laws of Delaware. The formative board consisted only of the three of us—Stephen Currier as president, Lloyd Garrison, and myself. Later, we would be joined by John Simon and Phil Hammer; Andrew Norman, publisher and philanthropist; Vivian Henderson, economist, civil rights activist, and president of Clark College in Atlanta; Vernon Jordan, then head of the United Negro College Fund; William Slayton, then executive vice president of Urban America; Melvin Mister, then an official of the U.S. Conference of Mayors; Lois Rice, then Washington representative of the College Entrance Examination Board; and Herbert Franklin, partner in the Washington law firm Lane and Edson. It would be hard to imagine a group better suited to guide an organization like the Potomac Institute. Each of them was accomplished in his or her field, thoughtful, imaginative, and deeply committed to human and civil rights.

Aside from its charter and initial board members, the Potomac Institute had little substance. I had not yet found suitable office space in Washington's tight real estate market, my answering service was a poor substitute for a secretary, and I was still dividing my time among Atlanta, Washington, and New York. Not that this was of great concern, for we had expected it to take at least three months to bring the new organization into being.

Events were moving at such a pace, however, that we were denied the luxury of a leisurely start-up period. For one thing, I felt an obligation to arrange promptly for Burke Marshall and his associates to hear at first-hand about the problems confronting black would-be voters in the Deep South. With the help of my former co-workers at the Southern Regional

Council, I brought representatives of the Justice Department and the Civil Rights Commission together with people from a dozen communities in Georgia, Alabama, and Mississippi. In a two-day off-the-record meeting at the Sheraton-Park Hotel, the southern participants described in detail the formidable obstacle courses that local officials had built between blacks and the ballot box. Their first-hand accounts posed a sobering challenge for the administration's civil rights lawyers.

Problems of a different sort were troubling the staff of the equal employment effort. They felt it was vitally important to collect racial employment data that would enable the president's committee to evaluate the performance of government agencies and private employers covered by the Executive Order. In the absence of such information, there was no way to hold employers accountable for progress, or the lack of it, in the hiring and upgrading of minority workers. On the other hand, talk of a racial census rasped on sensitive nerves in the civil rights community. In the past, the keeping of records by race had been a major device for singling out blacks as targets of discrimination. Civil rights groups had worked hard to get this insidious practice eliminated. Could these groups now be persuaded that there were valid grounds for reversing their strongly held position?

To help find an answer, John Feild proposed a survey of the major civil rights organizations. The objective would be not merely to record their existing positions on racial identification, but to explore the possibility of a consensus that would resolve the dilemma confronting the new federal program. Feild reasoned that this could best be done by a private organization like Potomac, which shared the values of the civil rights groups and had no ax of its own to grind.

The issue was a familiar one to me, and one that would become much more contentious, for different reasons, as time went on. The argument over "color blindness" versus "color consciousness" continues to this day to plague public policy makers and divide traditional allies in the struggle for an equitable society. In 1961, however, the issue was not seen as a major threat to whites, since no one then could reasonably argue that minorities were the beneficiaries of preferential treatment. Rather, recordkeeping was seen as a threat to the minorities they would be intended to help.

I could sympathize with the apprehensions of the mainline civil rights and civil liberties groups. I remembered vividly my first-hand observations of the cruel effects of racial classification in the segregated army of World War II. That racist policy achieved its ultimate absurdity in the classification of Puerto Rican soldiers, who were assigned to "Puerto Rican White" or "Puerto Rican Colored" units depending solely on their complexions. Brothers of differing shades of pigmentation often found themselves separated by this arbitrary color bar. To witness—much less be victimized by—such a system might well make one a lifelong enemy of all forms of racial labeling.

On the other hand, I also remembered the difficulties encountered by the Southern Regional Council when it set out to gather voter registration data in counties of Mississippi and Alabama during the fifties. Incredible as it seems today, neither the Justice Department nor any other official agency collected such data, or showed any interest in doing so. This information was vitally important to lawmakers such as Senator Paul Douglas, who were arguing the need for voting rights legislation. Their efforts were being nullified by pious protestations from southern members that blacks in their home districts were perfectly free to use the ballot but were just not interested. SRC undertook to explode this myth by documenting an absence of blacks on the voting rolls that could only be explained by wholesale discrimination; it was hard for a county with a large majority of black residents to explain away an all-white registration. Our efforts to get hard data were countered by local registrars with bland claims of color blindness. ("Why, we wouldn't think of keeping a record of our registrants by race. That would be unconstitutional!")

The same kind of hypocrisy provided an impenetrable shield for employers intent on evading equal employment requirements. Clearly the issue of racial identification was not a simple one.

Given the circumstances, it seemed to me, as it did to Currier and Garrison, that we should undertake the requested organizational survey, notwithstanding the embryonic state of the institute. Fortunately, a well-qualified consultant was available in the person of Charles H. Slayman Jr., former staff director of the Civil Rights Subcommittee of the Senate Judiciary Committee. Guided by a questionnaire that we developed in consultation with John Feild, he set about interviewing the chief civil rights advocates who rode herd on federal policy. For a time, it looked as though no agreement could be reached. Some interviewees felt it was time for a change, that the benefits of racial data in enforcing the employment order outweighed the dangers of abuse. But others, including the NAACP's influential Washington Representative Clarence Mitchell, disagreed; in their view, the potential harm of identifying workers by race was too great to risk.

After several weeks of stalemate, however, a middle ground gradually emerged. As summarized in Slayman's report, the prevailing view was overwhelmingly against entering racial, religious, or ethnic designations on individual personnel records. It was generally agreed, however, that employers could be required to determine and report the makeup of their work forces by means of periodic "head counts"—that is, simple observation of the number of minority workers in each unit. Although this rough method was subject to some degree of error, it was regarded as accurate enough to indicate whether satisfactory progress was being made, while safeguarding individual employees from discriminatory use of the data. With a few exceptions, the respondents also agreed that it was acceptable to give employees the option of self-identification, so long as this was done voluntarily and anonymously.

Reassured by this consensus among civil rights groups, the president's committee adopted the head-count requirement and optional self-identification for those government agencies and private firms covered by the executive order. Since that time, civil rights organizations have strongly supported racial data collection as an essential part of the compliance process.

Even before the racial data survey was completed, Potomac was asked to take a far larger part in the development of the equal employment program than we could have anticipated. The genesis of this involvement was a telephone call I received from Adam Yarmolinsky soon after he went to the Defense Department. The Pentagon—in fact, the administration generally—had been embarrassed by widely publicized charges against the Lockheed Corporation, one of its biggest contractors. The aircraft company's plant in Marietta, Georgia, had been awarded a lucrative contract to build the giant C-41 (later C-5A) cargo plane. No sooner had the contract been announced than NAACP Labor Secretary Herbert

Hill released an omnibus complaint of discrimination signed by scores of black Lockheed employees. Documented in the complaint was every conceivable form of discrimination—hiring and wage inequities, segregated toilets and cafeterias, even racially separate assembly crews. The Air Force decided it badly needed an adviser in the Atlanta area who was familiar with the local business community, understood labor relations, and was sympathetic to fair employment practices.

I suggested to Adam that he talk with Phil Hammer. Soon afterward, Hammer called to report that he had agreed to serve as a temporary consultant to the Air Force and was finding it a heady, though hardly remunerative, experience. He was being paid a fraction of his standard daily rate for an assignment that was playing havoc with his firm's workload. "Ask not," I reminded him, "what your country can do for you. . . ."

Fortunately, Hammer was not alone in this effort. Some of Kennedy's political friends in Georgia, anxious to spare both the president and Lockheed further embarrassment, also pitched in, and within a short time the Marietta plant had initiated reforms that delivered its huge contract from danger.

So matters stood one day in early May when I received a message from Joseph Imirie, assistant secretary of the Air Force for materiel, asking me to meet with him as soon as possible. Imirie, with whom Hammer had been dealing, was by background a tough, action-minded business executive. I assumed Hammer had suggested that he talk with me in a general way about the Lockheed affair. But I had barely got seated in his Pentagon office before it became clear that he wanted more than casual advice.

"The Lockheed situation is making progress," he said, "but that's not enough. We need a system to see that things like this don't keep happening. The President has signed an executive order and we're going to see that our contractors comply with it. The Secretary of Defense wants the Air Force to serve as a model on this for the entire Department. I've talked with Hammer and others about your Potomac Institute. They say you're the best in the field. I want you to work out a program for us that will do the job. When can you start?"

In the wake of this rapid-fire volley, I stared speechlessly at Imirie.

"Mr. Secretary," I began finally, "I'm afraid Mr. Hammer was too generous . . ."

"No he wasn't," Imirie cut in. "I've checked you out with the President's Committee, the Secretary's Office, and so on. They all say the same thing." That, I reflected, would be John Feild, Adam Yarmolinsky, and, for all I knew, Burke Marshall, Harris Wofford, and Berl Bernhard as well. Small world.

"Mr. Secretary," I began again, "I appreciate these good opinions. The problem is, the Potomac Institute isn't really in operation yet. At the moment, it's just me working out of an apartment."

But Imirie was not to be deflected. "Well, you're going to be operating, aren't you? Why not start now?"

"You should also know," I said, "I'm new to the workings of government programs."

"Then we'll learn together." He stood up and shook my hand briskly. "My people will get in touch about a contract." The meeting had lasted less than ten minutes.

As I taxied back across the Potomac, I considered a problem that I had not raised with Imirie—and that would not have impressed him if I had. That was our resolve that Potomac should abstain from contracts with government agencies. To study Air Force procurement processes and design an appropriate employment compliance program would be a fairly expensive proposition—too expensive to fund out of our small initial budget. Unfortunately, the key person I needed to consult about this was not readily available—Stephen Currier was traveling in Spain. I took the problem to Lloyd Garrison, who advised me to cable Stephen and ask whether he felt the assignment was important enough to warrant an exception to our self-imposed rule.

Currier's reply arrived two days later. He was pleased but also dumbfounded by the suddenness and scope of the Air Force proposition. "APPROVE EVERYTHING DETAILED IN LETTER WITH DELIGHTED APPREHENSION," said his cable; "COMMIT US AT WILL WILL PHONE MONDAY CONGRATULATIONS." In our subsequent telephone conversation, he added one condition: the contract must be rigorously nonprofit. By this, he meant that Potomac should be reimbursed for direct expenses only, accepting nothing for its own overhead or operating expenses. This seemed straightforward enough, but I soon learned that government contracting officers were resistant to any departure from standard procedures. In fact, they seemed suspicious of our self-effacing proposal. The ultimate compromise was that the contract should stipulate an overhead rate but that we would be free not to claim it.

By the time the contract was ready to sign, I had recruited a project team of three professionals who were willing to take leave from their jobs for what we thought would be a brief period. An obvious choice was John Hope II, a highly regarded manpower specialist with the Race Relations Center at Fisk University and a former senior staff member of the wartime Fair Employment Practices Commission created by President Roosevelt. Another was Arthur J. Levin, director of the Anti-Defamation League's Southeastern Regional Office in Atlanta and one of the South's ablest human relations experts. The third team member was Ronald Haughton, a professor at Wayne State University and an expert on labor relations and personnel management. As Air Force liaison, we were assigned two officers whose names Dickens would have relished—Colonel George Boxall and Captain Otto Kattwinkel. Later Major Lorimer Peterson also joined the project. They traveled with the Potomac team and saw to it that we were suitably cloaked in the authority of the Secretary's Office.

This official chaperonage was more than a gesture of courtesy; without it, I doubt that we could have carried out our assignment. There was a prodigious amount of information to be gathered, both in the Pentagon and at Air Force installations around the country. We needed to know the total number of contractors, the dollar volume of their contracts, the geographical range of their operations, the chain of command through which contracts were administered, how and by whom they were monitored, and a host of other details. To extract all this from an intricately entwined military hierarchy and civilian bureaucracy—both of which tended to take a xenophobic view of outsiders—required a lot of high-level support.

Not that the Potomac team ever experienced discourteous treatment; on the contrary, Levin and Hope, who did most of the field work, got VIP treatment at the installations they visited. But when the questioning turned to such sensitive matters as lines of authority, workloads, job descriptions, and salary levels, the atmosphere grew wary. Fortunately, all of us had a healthy appreciation of the therapeutic uses of humor. Our fondness for banter had a relaxing effect on our uneasy hosts; they probably concluded that we were too lighthearted to be much of a threat to their prerogatives. We did, in fact, take an open-minded approach to our assignment. We had started with no fixed opinions about the specifics of the prospective equal employment compliance program and were willing to follow wherever the facts seemed to lead. One preconception, however, we all shared—the fair employment requirement should be, not an appendage, but an integral part of the overall compliance process, subject to the same degree of accountability as other conditions. This grew out of our conviction that if the new requirement was treated as a curiosity, divorced from existing standards that contractors were expected to meet, it was likely to be bypassed and neglected in everyday enforcement activity.

We got no sense that the contract managers we met were necessarily hostile to the principle of equal employment opportunity—or "EEO" as it was soon known in that world of initials. But it was evident that they were not disposed to let EEO concerns interfere with their primary mission, which was to assure timely delivery of military hardware and services, as well as harmonious relations with established contractors. The challenge, as we saw it, was to devise a system that would cause them to give as high a priority to the fair employment requirement as to anything else in a contract.

Of course, our project was subject to certain hazards. If the senior Air Force officers with whom we were dealing became unhappy enough, they could exert great pressure on the Secretary's Office to call the whole thing off. One sorehead with the right political connections would be enough to generate unfriendly congressional attention. And, even if we were allowed to complete our work, the resulting recommendations could easily end up in the "round file"—a common enough fate for consultants' reports in Washington.

One evening in Harrisburg, as we relaxed over a pre-dinner drink with Boxall and Kattwinkel, we fell into a discussion of these gloomy possibilities.

"Why should you worry?" grumbled Boxall. "You can just go on and do something else. My career could be on the line."

"Relax, Colonel," said Art Levin. "We're convinced you're going to come out of this as the first EEO general in the Air Force."

"Or the first EEO casualty," said Boxall as the waiter put our food on the table. Just then he noticed that Kattwinkel was sitting hunched and motionless, his chin resting on his chest and his eyes closed.

"Katt!" he exclaimed. "Is anything wrong?" Kattwinkel remained silent and unmoving.

"Katt! What's the matter? Are you all right?"

When Kattwinkel still did not respond, Boxall reached over and shook him vigorously. Kattwinkel's head snapped up.

"Jesus Christ!" he shouted, "I'm saying grace!"

"Oh," said Boxall, "then put in a good word for me, will you?"

CHAPTER 4 ▪ *Stormy Weather*

MY FORMER CO-WORKERS in the South saw to it that I was kept fully occupied. They produced a steady stream of complaints and suggestions to be pursued with appropriate people in the administration. I also continued to convene working sessions in which people inside and outside government could consider how best to deal with segregation in interstate transportation, public schools, restaurants, retail stores, theaters, golf courses, bowling alleys, and so on.

Fortunately, by midsummer 1961 Potomac had a permanent address—a Victorian townhouse near Dupont Circle that was well suited to our purposes. It was conveniently located both for out-of-town visitors and for government people, who often stopped in to confer over a sandwich at noon or a drink in the evening.

The evening occasions, familiarly known as "fiveses," became something of an institution. Several times a week at the end of the day, some combination of federal officials and people from the private sector with civil rights concerns gathered in my office for convivial shop talk. Although these sessions were utterly informal and spontaneous, the talk often focused on a particular problem or policy issue. How much of consequence grew out of these discussions, it would be hard to say. But they did serve to strengthen many useful relationships and provide a relaxed forum for the testing of ideas. And over many years, there was never any lack of interesting and interested participants.

There was a great deal to talk about. Atlanta and New Orleans were under court order to desegregate public schools in September, in the face of their state officials' rebel yells of defiance. The Student Nonviolent Coordinating Committee's sit-ins at lunch counters, restaurants, and other facilities across the South went on; but hostile, sometimes violent resistance had brought the rate of change to a crawl. Despite repeated federal court rulings prohibiting it, segregation was still enforced in railroad and bus terminals in the lower South. The Justice Department's Civil Rights Division had initiated some sixty investigations of voting rights violations, but even when violations were well documented, a long, slow process of litigation still lay ahead.

Hanging over all these problems like a massive thunder cloud was the danger of large-scale violence and disorder. William Manchester, in *The Glory and the Dream,* has commented on the optimism, bordering on naivete, that he feels animated the new frontiersmen and caused them to reject the notion that there were "dark places in the American mind" inaccessible to reason and civility. In his view, it was these atavistic flaws of human nature that caused the storm clouds to burst into violence, taking the Kennedys and their lieutenants by surprise.[4]

Manchester has a point, but I doubt that it is the main one. As event after event demonstrated, the rampages of bigotry that bloodied the South were less the result of uncontrollable "redneck" sentiment than of the delinquencies of economic and political leadership. Wherever local business leaders and government officials joined in a firm stand for obedience to law and preservation of public order, racial changes usually took place with a minimum of disruption. Where these authority figures traded in fear and demagoguery, or otherwise signaled their unwillingness to deter violence, mob action almost invariably erupted.

I had suggested to Burke Marshall that Robert Kennedy might incorporate this theme in his Law Day address at the University of Georgia in May. Others who were consulted, including Ralph McGill and Morris Abram, made similar suggestions. Kennedy did use the occasion to urge southern leadership to cooperate with the administration in voluntary efforts to achieve peaceful racial change. But to the surprise of many, myself included, he added an unprecedentedly blunt warning: "I say to you today that if the orders of the courts are circumvented, the Department of Justice will act. We will not stand by or be aloof. We will move. . . . We will not make or interpret the laws. We shall enforce them—vigorously, without regional bias or political slant."

This was bold language, and it was put to the test almost immediately. While the attorney general was speaking, a bus was heading south from Washington on the first of the "freedom rides."

Some of the strategy sessions at the White House, and at Potomac as well, had centered on the illegal perpetuation of Jim Crow on many trains and buses and the terminals serving them in southern towns and cities. The question was how to induce a timid and inert Interstate Commerce Commission to promulgate and enforce effective regulations against this flagrant disregard of Supreme Court rulings. We knew that it would take time to get an effective effort mounted, and even more time to bring it to a successful conclusion; but we thought it was high time to start.

James Farmer and his colleagues in the Congress on Racial Equality (CORE) were indeed in no mood to wait for discussion and planning and negotiation. They decided to dramatize the Jim Crow practices by direct confrontation in the heartland of segregation. At one southern bus stop after another, an interracial band of riders defied and ignored the "white only" signs posted over waiting rooms and toilets. Aside from a couple of skirmishes in South Carolina, their journey was uneventful until it crossed the Alabama state line. Then, as they neared Anniston, they were waylaid by a band of Kluxers, who set fire to the bus and savagely beat the riders.

From this point on, the Justice Department became a virtual command post. The attorney general—and finally the president himself—bombarded Governor John Patterson of Alabama with telephone calls that he refused to answer. Robert Kennedy finally sent to Alabama as his personal emissary John Seigenthaler, an able and trusted aide with unimpeachable southern credentials. Seigenthaler extracted from the evasive governor an assurance that a new group of freedom riders, then en route to Montgomery, would have state protection. But Governor Patterson did not keep his word. More mob violence took place in Montgomery, and Seigenthaler himself was beaten senseless when he went to the aid of a young woman who was being attacked. The outraged attorney general sent to the scene a force of six hundred deputy marshals, narrowly averting further violence on a catastrophic scale. The freedom riders who were not too seriously injured, augmented by a contingent of courageous Student Nonviolent Coordinating Committee (SNCC) members, went on to Mississippi. There was no more mob action, but there hardly could have been since the Mississippi state police unceremoniously hustled the riders off to jail.

There were more anxious moments as sympathizers, including a group of nationally prominent clergymen, staged repetitions of the original ride. The tension eventually subsided, and in September the Interstate Commerce Commission yielded to strong pressure from the Justice Department and issued enforceable regulations prohibiting the segregation of bus and train passengers. The administration had emerged creditably from its first federal-state confrontation, although its relations with the civil rights groups were badly battered in the process. Yet the prospects for an improved political climate in the recalcitrant states appeared to be as remote as ever. Despite the heroic labors of Marshall and his overworked lawyers, the Deep South's armor of voting discrimination had scarcely been dented.

The Voter Education Project

It was not surprising, therefore, that in my frequent discussions with Burke Marshall he came back repeatedly to the need for a strong drive by Negro southerners to register and vote. In the absence of such pressure, it was difficult for the Justice Department to mount the investigations and court actions required to bring discriminatory registrars to book. I pointed out to him that the seeming inertia among blacks of voting age in the Deep South was not attributable to lack of interest among the civil rights groups. The NAACP and the Urban League had long maintained registration and voting campaigns in selected parts of the South, as had many local independent black voters' associations. King's Southern Christian Leadership Conference was trying to raise money for similar efforts of its own. The problem was justifiable fear of physical and economic reprisals against both potential black voters and those who sought to organize them.

It was difficult in 1961 to raise funds for any kind of civil rights work, but especially for voting rights activity. Registration campaigns, even nonpartisan ones, were commonly regarded as "political action," and thus believed to be taboo for tax-exempt organizations and for foundations and individuals who wished their contributions to be tax deductible—which meant most large contributors. As a result, efforts to help blacks enroll as voters were sporadic, small-scale, and largely dependent on volunteers.

Marshall was not convinced that registration campaigns were necessarily inconsistent with tax exemption. He thought it likely that a carefully designed project—one that included a significant research component and adequate safeguards against political partisanship—would pass muster with the Internal Revenue Service (IRS) as a "charitable or educational" activity. In order to test this hypothesis, however, it would first be necessary to draft the right kind of charter. If it were approved, of course, it would then be necessary to ensure that philanthropic funds would be forthcoming.

I lost no time in taking up the matter with Stephen Currier, and as I expected, he responded positively. So during the next few weeks we held a series of discussions with Burke Marshall, John Seigenthaler, and Harris Wofford, and subsequently with leaders of the major civil rights groups. It was understood that whatever plan evolved would be an empty proposal unless it was adopted by the civil rights groups, whose participation was essential. There were many knotty problems. Not the least of these were the issues of sponsorship and management, which seemed certain to cause controversy. The national civil rights groups were in competition for public recognition and scarce funds. If any one of them was put in charge of the activity, the others were bound to feel aggrieved. The project would have to be structured so as to enable all the appropriate organizations to participate equitably and with as little competitiveness as possible.

Not surprisingly, the Southern Regional Council came to mind as an acceptable home for the project. SRC was not regarded as a competitor by the other groups, and it had often served as coordinator of multiorganizational southern efforts. When we sounded out Leslie Dunbar, SRC's executive director, we found him receptive to the idea. Wisely, however, he stipulated three conditions: that we help get the tax exemption, that Stephen Currier take charge of the fund-raising, and that the person recruited to direct the activity be the unanimous choice of the participating groups. The latter point was crucial. The project, as we had ten-

tatively conceived it, would require a steady hand on the tiller—someone who could preside over the allocation of funds to the contending
groups, who could say no to strong-minded peers, who could deal effectively with foundations and the Justice Department, who was intimately
acquainted with the South's folkways and contradictions. In short, someone of prodigious talents.

On August 23, at Stephen Currier's invitation, top leaders of the
NAACP, the National Urban League, CORE, SCLC, SNCC, and SRC met
in New York to consider the proposal. In addition to Currier, the Taconic
Foundation was represented by Lloyd Garrison and Jane Lee Eddy. I was
present in a dual Potomac-Taconic role. Currier gave a crisp outline of
the plan. He stressed that, although SRC would provide administrative
and secretariat functions, the project would have considerable autonomy
under its yet-to-be-selected director. He also emphasized the role of
the advisory committee, to be composed of representatives of the five
main civil rights organizations, in the development of overall policy.

Stephen was well acquainted with the major civil rights leaders in attendance, except for Whitney Young, who had only recently been named
chief executive of the National Urban League. Since I knew Whitney well
in Atlanta, where he was dean of the Atlanta University School of Social
Work, Currier had asked my opinion of him.

"He's first-rate," I replied. "You and he will be friends in no time."

When Currier had finished his presentation, Young stood up to respond. Whether it was Currier's patrician manner or the proposal itself
that set him off I never knew, but Young was angrier than I ever saw him
before or afterward.

"Why can't you just give us some funds without all this fol-de-rol?" he
shouted. "I'm tired of white people who don't believe Negroes can be
trusted to handle money responsibly!" He carried on in this vein for several minutes and seemed about to storm out of the room. Everyone else
looked stricken with surprise and embarrassment.

As I recall, it was Roy Wilkins who broke the awkward silence. In his
calm, reasoned style, he gently rebutted Whitney Young's indictment. He
spelled out the logic of having a disinterested, nonparticipating organization as project sponsor. He added that the Southern Regional Council
was a genuinely integrated organization that had the confidence of the

other civil rights groups. As he spoke, the tension leaked out of the room and the discussion turned to the nuts and bolts of the project. Young had little more to say, but in the end he joined with the others in endorsing the proposal. From all appearances, his impassioned outburst was quickly forgotten by everyone, including himself, although as we left the meeting, Stephen dropped me a wry aside: "Friends in no time, eh?" Much to my relief, however, Stephen and Whitney soon developed a warm friendship and a close working relationship that endured for the remainder of their tragically foreshortened lives.

Achieving consensus among the civil rights groups was a relatively simple matter compared to getting certification of tax exemption for the voter registration project, even though we had the assistance of Adrian W. (Bill) De Wind, a law partner of Lloyd Garrison's and a leading specialist in tax law. Notwithstanding his effective services, and my own best efforts to expedite communication among all parties, the IRS was slow to move.

In an interview several years later, Robert Kennedy reportedly said that he intervened with the tax authorities on behalf of the project's application. This does not square with my perception at the time. While I kept Burke Marshall informed of our progress (or lack of it) from time to time—and there was no question of his interest—he repeatedly went out of his way to explain why the attorney general felt it would be improper for him or his aides to try to influence the Internal Revenue Service. I, in turn, assured Marshall that we fully understood and respected that position. Of course, it is possible that Robert Kennedy put pressure on the commissioner or his subordinates without our knowledge. If so, he lacked his usual forcefulness, for it took more than six months of hard negotiation to secure a favorable ruling.

The Voter Education Project (VEP) opened its doors in March of 1962. Providentially, a person had been found who met the demanding requirements for the position of director. He was Wiley Branton, a pioneer Negro graduate of the formerly all-white University of Arkansas Law School who had represented the black plaintiffs in the celebrated Little Rock school desegregation case. He was not only an able lawyer, a skillful negotiator, and a shrewd student of southern character, but he also commanded the respect and trust of the diverse groups within the civil rights movement. It was an extraordinary match of man and mission, made all the more promising by the fact that the Taconic Foundation had been joined by the Field, Stern, and Rockefeller Brothers foundations in pledging substantial financial support. In the two-and-a-half years of the first VEP campaign, their collective contribution was almost eight hundred thousand dollars.

Notwithstanding these favorable developments, all was not serene in the civil rights ranks. Some of the more militant members of SNCC and CORE, foreshadowing the internal divisions that would later shatter these organizations, charged that registration work would divert energy from direct action, which they viewed as the indispensable challenge to racism. Their dissidence was fed by resentment and suspicion of the Kennedy administration, growing out of the handling of the freedom rides crisis. They blamed the Kennedys for not having moved faster and more forcibly to curb the disorders. They were also angered by Robert Kennedy's call for a "cooling off period" when the protest was at its peak. Finally, they were outraged that FBI agents had stood passively by while the riders were beaten. They could not believe that the attorney general of the United States lacked the authority to require J. Edgar Hoover's agents to protect citizens seeking to exercise their constitutional rights. For all these reasons, some of the militants saw Robert Kennedy's emphasis on voter registration as part of a plot to subvert the cause of direct action.

Several usually reliable chroniclers, most writing well after the event, have recorded these suspicions as though they were established fact. Victor Navasky, for example, wrote in *Kennedy Justice:* "the Attorney General and his staff had helped convince the civil-rights oriented Taconic and Field Foundations to subsidize a voter registration drive on condition that civil rights agencies across the board (from the Urban League and NAACP to CORE, SNCC and SCLC) agree to redirect their energies from buses to ballots, from civil disobedience to the Voter Education Project, thereby diverting the energy of civil rights workers from direct confrontation with Southern 'law.'" Milton Viorst, in *Fire in the Streets,* offered a similar version. Godfrey Hodgson, in *America in Our Time,* even suggested that one of the young blacks who urged SNCC to participate in VEP may have been a clandestine agent of the government.

These accounts do an injustice to the individuals, organizations, and foundations—all staunch civil rights supporters before, during, and after the Kennedy years—that participated in the creation of VEP.

The reality as I experienced it was a far cry from the devious plot suggested. As everybody involved, including the civil rights leaders, would surely confirm, no such condition as Navasky describes was—or could conceivably have been—exacted from the civil rights groups. Direct action continued throughout the first cycle of VEP, including the famous confrontations led by King in Albany, Georgia, and Birmingham, Alabama. Moreover, at least three of the five groups—the National Urban League, NAACP, and SCLC—had long been committed to voter registration as a major program activity and had been energetically seeking funds for that purpose. Such SNCC champions of direct action as James Forman, Ella Baker, and John Lewis (who later became director of VEP) favored participation in the voter registration effort. The Southern Regional Council, which had advocated full and free access to the polls by Negro citizens since its inception in the early 1940s, also consistently gave strong public support to the sit-ins and freedom rides.

The only basis for the conspiracy charge, other than pure speculation, was the Kennedys' publicly avowed belief that the exercise of the ballot by blacks was a prime requisite of progress in civil rights. No doubt the bloody confrontations in Alabama strengthened that conviction and intensified their preference for political action over the highly charged encounters of direct action in other areas. But even had there been no freedom rides, there is every reason to believe that the Kennedy administration would have pressed for action to enlarge black political power, and that the foundations and civil rights groups would have moved on that front. The significant new element was not the Kennedys' antipathy to direct action; it was the fact that, for the first time in modern history, there was a declared commitment by a president and his attorney general to back the enfranchisement of southern blacks. No less important, there was also for the first time the likelihood that such an effort could qualify for tax exemption and thus be eligible for foundation funding.

It is true that the apparent agreement reached by the administration and the civil rights groups was flawed by a misunderstanding that had profoundly negative consequences. When the registration workers deployed across the South, they thought they had an implied promise that the Justice Department would protect them and the blacks attempting to register. In many areas, the issue did not arise, as thousands of black citizens were newly registered without incident. But in Mississippi and parts of Alabama, Georgia, and Louisiana, the registration attempts were met by ruthless countermeasures. Most would-be registrants and their VEP mentors were summarily turned away by local registrars. Many found themselves deprived of jobs and credit. Some were threatened, beaten, and arrested on trumped-up charges. When blacks gathered to protest these brutalities, they were herded into jail, where they were denied reasonable bail and access to legal counsel—counsel that was unlikely to have been available, in any case, since local lawyers would not represent them. In the end, three civil rights workers were murdered near Philadelphia, Mississippi.

In some of these instances, the Justice Department brought criminal charges against local officials or sought injunctions from federal district courts. But the prejudices of southern federal judges and jurors, coupled with the defendants' delaying tactics, rendered many of these court actions all but meaningless for practical purposes. Besides, the civil rights workers had little interest in litigation. They wanted effective federal intervention at the time of the offense, not a dubious prospect of vindication long afterward. The Justice Department responded to their calls for such on-the-spot assistance with explanations of the limits of the federal system. In a word, the explanations went, the federal government lacked the authority to preempt the police powers of the states. Writing in early 1964, Burke Marshall described the situation this way:

> There would be vast problems in any attempts at federal control of the administration of justice, through the moderate method of federal court injunctions. Yet vast problems have been created already by police indifference to Negro rights in the South, and they will grow if the trend is not turned. The loss of faith in law—the usefulness of federal law and the fairness of local law—is gaining very rapidly among Negro and white civil rights workers. The consequences in the future cannot be foreseen.[5]

One consequence was that many of the SNCC workers did lose faith, not only in federal and local law, but in the redeemability of the white world generally; the seeds of black separatism and "black power" were taking root. Not until a much stronger voting rights act was passed by Congress, in 1965, would blacks be able to register and vote in significant numbers in the hard-core areas. Elsewhere, however, the first VEP met with much success. Between 1962 and 1964, some seven hundred thirty thousand black voters were added to the rolls in the South—an increase from 26.8 to 40.8 percent of the black voting-age population. Not all of this gain was necessarily attributable to VEP's efforts, but a great deal of it unquestionably was.

In the years to follow hundreds of thousands more blacks would register or be saved from illegal purges of the rolls, in Mississippi as well as less recalcitrant states, thanks to VEP-funded activities. VEP has had its ups and downs over the years, but it blazed a trail for other groups that now concentrate on voting rights of blacks and Hispanics.

The political transformation of the South was won at a heavy cost in anguish and alienation, but without it, American democracy would have faced a doubtful future. If southern blacks had failed to win the ballot, it is inconceivable that the United States could have asserted itself in the international arena as a champion of human rights, or that it could have hoped to serve as a model of freedom and democracy for the people of the Eastern European countries. In all likelihood, the only way to suppress the rising demand of millions of blacks for full political participation would have been by the use of naked force on an unprecedented scale. Under such circumstances, it would not be hard to imagine the emergence of a police state with its corrosive effects on the rights and liberties of citizens of all races.

Thankfully, what we have witnessed instead is the gradual emergence of a political process in which black and other minority Americans can wield real, often decisive power in national, state, and local elections. Nothing symbolizes this change more dramatically than the election in 1989 of the nation's first black governor—this in Virginia, long considered an impenetrable bastion of southern conservatism. Although our society is still afflicted with many intractable racial problems, the gains of the last thirty years give grounds for hope that these problems too will eventually be overcome.

CHAPTER 5 ▪ *The Smallest Gravy Train in Town*

POTOMAC'S ANALYSIS TO apply civil rights compliance to Air Force procurement went forward on schedule and well within budget. In this instance, at least, the taxpayer would be spared a cost overrun. Our project team visited fifteen Air Force installations in different parts of the country, interviewed scores of contracting and procurement officers and contractors themselves, studied tables of organization, and reviewed mountains of data. For some time, we despaired of getting comprehensive figures on the number, size, and distribution of contracts, without which we could make no intelligent estimate of the workload of the EEO program. We inquired in vain of high-ranking military officers, senior bureaucrats, deputy assistant secretaries, and their deputies and assistants. One day Art Levin exultantly reported that he had, at last, found the mother lode of contract data.

"There's this guy who's got it all!" he announced. "He's a GS-9, wears a green eye-shade, and has an office in the basement."

Soon it was time to brief Secretary Eugene Zuckert and the top brass of the Air Force. Our recommendations got a mixed reception. Our plan called for the employment of fifty-one intergroup relations specialists who would be assigned to the principal contracting offices around the country. Their duties would include participation in the pre-award review of major contracts, monitoring the equal employment performance of existing contractors, and helping contractors improve their performance. We urged that these positions be filled by individuals experienced in fair employment and human relations work, that they report directly to the commanding officer or his deputy, and that they be well enough paid to attract people with proven track records. There were many more procedural recommendations, but those pertaining to staffing (or "manning" as it was called in those days) were the most controversial.

The secretary was well disposed toward our proposals, as was the vice chief of staff, but some of the other military officers were openly incredulous. One crusty general, in particular, was consumed by indignation.

"Fifty-one bleeding hearts and bomb throwers!" he snorted. "What in God's name would they do all day? Promote revolution?"

Clearly, no amount of analysis of the huge workload involved in bringing thousands of Air Force contractors into compliance with the Executive Order was going to convince the general that even one "bomb thrower" should be hired. Fortunately, however, his was a minority view. Potomac's basic plan was approved, with the amendment that only nine specialists should be employed immediately, others to be added gradually as the program developed.

Some very tangible political dangers prompted this go-slow policy. Up to this time, federal personnel with full-time responsibility for civil rights enforcement were a nonexistent breed. And the southerners who dominated congressional appropriations committees were fully prepared to use the federal purse strings to keep it that way. Even as artful a dodger as Vice President Lyndon Johnson found it difficult to hire a staff for the new president's Committee on Equal Employment Opportunity without falling afoul of his powerful old colleague, Senator Richard Russell of Georgia. It was understandable, then, that the Department of the Air Force chose to staff up in this field as gradually and inconspicuously as possible. The issue was sensitive enough to require the personal attention of Secretary McNamara. I briefed Adam Yarmolinsky, who then cleared our recommendations with the secretary.

By the end of 1963, the Defense Department had employed fifty-six contract compliance officers, and the number was increasing rapidly as other departments and agencies throughout the federal government followed the example of the Air Force. No doubt many would regard this as one more unfortunate example of bureaucratic proliferation. But the evils of big government are in the eye of the beholder; the same critics might be quite sanguine about much greater increases in the number of air traffic controllers, IRS investigators, or FBI agents. One's priorities make all the difference.

It was agreed from the beginning that if our Air Force study passed muster, we would be expected to adapt the recommendations to the differing structures and contract procedures of the other military service departments; and so we did. This assignment consisted largely of tracking down the Army and Navy equivalents of Mr. Katz, sifting through the data they were hoarding, and tailoring the new recommendations to fit. Art Levin facetiously suggested that by leaving blank the appropriate lines in our original report we could work our way through the entire federal government just by filling in the right numbers and initials. In any case, the follow-on studies were soon completed, and the Army and Navy also began recruiting fair employment specialists for their compliance programs.

Meanwhile, the Defense Department had decided to make a clean sweep of its equal employment obligations. President Kennedy's executive order had directed efforts to end job discrimination not only among contractors but within the federal government itself. The Defense Department, one of the government's largest employers of civilian workers, bore a major share of this responsibility. Department officials asked Potomac to take on, as a final assignment, a study of how the defense agencies might best ensure equal opportunity in "in-house" employment. (Luckily, the term "out-house" employment never caught on.) Encouraged by the favorable response to our contractor employment recommendations, we felt it would be a relatively simple matter to design an acceptable in-house system. So it was that in March 1963—almost two years after we took on our first EEO assignment—we began our third and last Pentagon mission, cheerfully unaware of the mine field we were marching into.

This study differed from the previous ones in that there was a system of a sort already in place. Each of the three services had an office of civilian personnel that was deeply entrenched and had a strongly protective view of its turf. Also existing was a parallel structure established by the Defense Department in response to the Executive Order. This structure consisted of a senior official in each military department designated the Employment Policy Officer (EPO) and a number of deputy EPOs assigned to installations around the country. The problems of overlapping jurisdictions and competition in this dual arrangement had never been resolved. Personnel officers had traditionally exercised full authority over all civilian personnel actions, and they saw no reason why complaints of discrimination and other minority employment issues should be an exception. The Employment Policy line, on the other hand, had been created specifically and solely to see to it that the requirements of the EEO order were fully met. The situation was a stand-off, and the Potomac Institute was called upon, as a disinterested outside arbiter, to examine the problem and recommend a solution.

The Department of the Army, as the Defense Department's largest employer of civilians, was the contract manager and the initial subject of our study. Al Kransdorf, a civilian employee, was assigned as liaison. The Potomac team—somewhat modified by the addition of Furman Templeton of the Baltimore Urban League and educator Jerome Ziegler, since John Hope had taken a senior position with the President's Committee—began another round of site visits to selected installations in different parts of the country. This time, however, our interviewees included a sizable number of employees, particularly minority workers, as well as leaders of minority organizations in the surrounding communities, where most employees were recruited. To no one's surprise, it was immediately obvious that a major overhaul of the system was needed to improve complaint handling and to increase minority hiring, promotion, and participation in training programs.

Midway through the project, I was summoned to the office of Charles Mullelly, the Army's director of civilian personnel. A seasoned veteran of the civil service wars, Mullelly's affable manner was somewhat at odds with the steely glint in his eye. He inquired solicitously about the progress of our study and the cooperativeness of his subordinates in the personnel hierarchy. Following my reassurance on both points and some polite small talk, he came to the point.

"We welcome your study," he said, "but I want to be sure you understand one thing—the Office of Personnel is just what the name implies. We have the responsibility and authority for everything that's done by the Army in the personnel area. I trust your recommendations will recognize that. We don't need anybody outside this office looking over our shoulder."

I explained that we had approached the assignment without prejudgment and wouldn't decide on our recommendations until the study was finished.

"Just so we understand each other," he said. "If your recommendations are acceptable, you'll have my support. If not, there'll be trouble."

"All I can tell you," I replied, "is that our aim is to come up with recommendations that are workable and fair. I hope you'll be able to support them."

I left his office with little conviction that he would approve of anything we could conscientiously propose. If I had read him correctly, he was prepared to oppose any plan that conferred EEO authority on the Employment Policy Officer and his deputies, or to anyone else outside the civilian personnel staff. Should he get his way, the personnel officers throughout the Army would be the sole monitors of their own work, even handling the complaints filed against themselves. Such total lack of accountability would test the character of a saint.

To anyone less passionately turf-conscious than Mr. Mullelly, the recommendations we finally settled on would have seemed quite moderate. They left intact the traditional authority of the Personnel Office, with respect to minorities no less than other employees. They did, however, provide for "outside" review of Personnel's work in two important areas. Specially trained Deputy Employment Policy Officers (DEPOs) would investigate complaints of discriminatory personnel actions and would monitor the effectiveness of affirmative action programs administered by the personnel officers. The DEPOs would exercise no direct authority over Personnel, but their findings would be made available to the commanding officer for any action he might choose to take.

Our recommendations for the Army were not to be formally submitted until we had completed comparable reports for the Navy and Air Force. Nevertheless, I thought it would be prudent to give Mr. Mullelly an advance briefing, on the off-chance that he might accept the logic of our conclusions. Whatever his feelings may have been, he kept them to himself. He gave me a polite but noncommittal hearing and wished me good afternoon.

The trouble he had predicted was not long in coming. A few days later, I was notified that a special hearing on Potomac's work for the Defense Department had been scheduled by the Manpower Utilization Subcommittee of the House Committee on Post Office and Civil Service.

To say that the membership of the subcommittee was conservative would be an understatement. Its chairman was David N. Henderson, a

North Carolina Democrat who later found a more congenial home in the Republican party. Its members included such champions of the status quo as H. R. Gross, the formidable budget cutter from Iowa, August E. Johansen of Michigan, Joe R. Pool of Texas, and Albert Watson of South Carolina. The only member to gladden a liberal heart was Morris K. ("Mo") Udall of Arizona.

The majority philosophy was ominously revealed in the statement of concerns that explained the need for a hearing. In addition to a powerful suspicion that Potomac had been "handpicked to justify preferential treatment for minority groups," subcommittee members were upset by the following perceptions:

(1) that the Department of Defense did not have in-house capabilities, the expertise to develop and/or evaluate equal employment opportunity policies and programs,

(2) that a contract was negotiated exclusively with a contractor, Potomac Institute, Inc., whose financial supporters and principal manpower have had a long-standing and overt policy of sponsoring movements in support of employee programs for minority groups,

(3) that when the contract was executed, the total professional staff of the contractor was limited to two employees,

(4) that the contractor had had no previous research experience as a corporate entity, and

(5) that the Department of Defense was spending approximately $625,000 annually on the direct full-time payroll cost of the equal employment program.[6]

Curiously, the subcommittee did not wish to have any representatives of Potomac testify at its hearings on these charges. Although we were entitled to be present as observers, the witnesses were limited to senior Defense Department officials having manpower responsibilities—namely, Assistant Secretary Norman S. Paul, DOD Director of Equal Opportunity Programs Ralph Horton Jr., and Deputy Under Secretary of the Army for Personnel Management Roy K. Davenport. The reason for this decision we never fathomed. Perhaps it was a tribute to our supposed cleverness, which might thwart the effort to discredit our motives and competence. Or perhaps it was simply a way of emphasizing the subcommittee majority's disdain for Potomac and all its works. In any case, the refusal to entertain our direct testimony contributed to a degree of confusion that often bordered on farce.

> *Mr. Henderson:* Could you tell us who actually in the Potomac Institute performed the work under the first contract?
>
> *Mr. Paul:* Of course, the executive vice president, Mr. Harold Flemming [*sic*], I believe, performed a good deal of the work himself. . . . There was also a John Hope II, Ronald W. Haughton.
>
> *Mr. Pool:* Mr. Chairman, may I ask this? Is that the John Hope that went to Dallas and made the statement that there would be more of the crash promotions [of minority workers]? Is that the same fellow?
>
> *Mr. Paul:* I am not aware of that incident . . .
>
> *Mr. Henderson:* Are you speaking of the gentleman connected with the Potomac Institute?
>
> *Mr. Pool:* This fellow was connected with the equal employment information [*sic*], John Hope III, I believe.
>
> *Mr. Henderson:* What was his assignment immediately prior to his Potomac position?
>
> *Mr. Paul:* He had a number of jobs which appear to have been going on at that time. . . . On October 23, 1961, he joined the President's Committee on Equal Employment Opportunity as a staff member.
>
> *Mr. Pool:* He is at the present time still employed that way?
>
> *Mr. Paul:* He is employed by the President's Committee; yes, sir.
>
> *Mr. Pool:* Also on the Potomac Institute?
>
> *Mr. Paul:* No, sir; he has severed his relations with Potomac. . . .
>
> *Mr. Pool:* When did he serve with Potomac Institute?
>
> *Mr. Paul:* I do not have exact dates, but I can get them. . . . He was brought on as a consultant on this program.
>
> *Mr. Pool:* Was that while he was on the President's Committee?
>
> *Mr. Paul:* No, sir; this was prior to his joining the President's Committee.
>
> *Mr. Henderson:* He was not with Potomac at the time of the execution of the contract? . . .

And so on and so forth. I was reminded of the old Abbott and Costello routine "Who's on first?"

Art Levin and I sat in the spectators' section throughout the two-day hearing, as did John Simon, in case we found ourselves in need of lawyerly advice. (Simon's experience with congressional hearings dated back to Senator Joseph R. McCarthy's investigation of the Army, when Simon was a young officer assigned to the Army General Counsel's staff.) Although we were only a few yards from the congressmen and were key figures in their inquiry, they never acknowledged our presence by a word or glance. I felt as disembodied as the Invisible Man. At one point, a frustrated subcommittee member did ask the chairman if he intended to have anyone from Potomac appear, since "it seems some questions that have been asked could be answered by this group directly." The chairman replied vaguely that the matter could be considered at a later executive session; it was never raised again in open hearing.

Although the questioning was often confused and repetitive, its basic direction was unmistakable. The main questioners were intent on establishing that the Potomac studies were the result of a conspiracy hatched for the dual purpose of defrauding the government and creating a radical-black hegemony in the armed services. The background for such an indictment had been laid a few days earlier by a planted newspaper story about Potomac's president, depicted as a shadowy figure of doubtful motives who was surreptitiously bankrolling the civil rights forces. In the hearing, the hostile members speculated on the sinister possibilities of this connection.

> *Mr. Watson:* Do you know who the president of Potomac Institute is?
> *Mr. Paul:* Mr. Stephen Currier.
> *Mr. Watson:* Since they obviously had no experience as a corporation prior to entering into this contract, what is the background of Mr. Currier? . . . Is he not coordinator for raising funds for civil rights groups such as NAACP, CORE, and others?
> *Mr. Paul:* I believe he is associated with the Taconic Foundation.
> *Mr. Watson:* You do not deny he is coordinator for fundraising activities of these civil rights groups?
> *Mr. Paul:* I do not know of my own personal knowledge. . . .
> *Mr. Johansen:* Am I to understand—possibly Mr. Davenport might be able to answer this—that this contract or these contracts were let

without any investigation of the personnel of this newly formed corporation?

Mr. Davenport: I cannot answer with respect to the earlier contracts. I can answer with respect to the one that has not yet been completed, and I can say that my inquiry did involve an effort to ascertain the extent to which Potomac had the capability to perform a contract in which I had some interest and responsibility. Certainly I was influenced by the fact there had been previous contracts undertaken for the Department of Defense.

Mr. Johansen: Did the work of this institute involve in any way access to classified information?

Mr. Davenport: As far as this contract is concerned, no. . . .

Mr. Johansen: I think we should bring whoever is necessary in here and get answers to these questions. I cannot conceive of a contract being let to a new organization without a security clearance and a check on the background when this Department, policywise, is the most sensitive area in the country today.

On the following morning, Mr. Paul was able to inform the subcommittee that none of Potomac's contracts had involved access to classified material, and accordingly no security clearance was necessary. Evidently the subcommittee had also gained reassurance from some quarter that neither Potomac nor its president posed any present danger to the Republic, since this line of questioning was not resumed. Instead, the members bore in on the supposedly mercenary origins of Potomac's initial contract, with the Air Force, from which the later work had flowed. They apparently reasoned that, if the Potomac contracts were the fruits of an insidious plot, then Philip Hammer must have been a key conspirator; for he it was who first recommended Potomac to the Air Force. Subcommittee members made vigorous and repeated efforts to establish that Potomac's relationship with the Air Force had been born in sin. The fact that Hammer had subsequently joined the board of Potomac struck them as particularly suspicious.

Mr. Watson: . . . What particular expertise did the Potomac Institute have that would qualify them to make such a study as this? They had only been incorporated 3 months prior to your entering into a contract with them. What contracts had they entered into with private or Government agencies prior to that?

Mr. Paul: To the best of my knowledge, none.

Mr. Watson: In other words, you do not know whether Mr. Philip Hammer created this particular institute in order to get a Government contract to pursue this particular study?

Mr. Paul: No, sir; I certainly do not know that he did. . . .

By the end of the first day of the hearing, the congressmen leading the attack were showing signs of acute frustration at their failure to uncover a satisfactory conspiracy. Congressman Udall was critical of the whole process, as for different reasons was Congressman Wilson, who complained: "I have been waiting anxiously for something important to take place here. It may be we do not have the right witnesses here." Oddly, however, the subcommittee chairman continued to show a marked disinclination to hear from the right witnesses. Having already refused to call anyone connected with Potomac, he then rejected the opportunity to question the former Air Force official who started it all. The latter's offer to testify was relayed by Mr. Paul: "When I spoke to Mr. Imirie by telephone—he is now in private industry, having resigned from the Defense Department and the Air Force some weeks ago—but he told me that he knows everything there is to know about this contract and he would be most happy to come back and testify before the subcommittee if it is desired."

The subcommittee showed no such desire, evidently preferring to bombard Paul and his associates with questions that Imirie could have answered from first-hand knowledge. Perhaps they were put off by Paul's sample of what Imirie could be expected to say:

> I have been informed by the Air Force officials that they were the ones who approached the Potomac Institute and not vice versa. They [Potomac] were not engaged in selling themselves on these contracts. As a matter of fact, in the one conversation I have had with Mr. Fleming he indicated to me that this [contracting] was by no means the primary purpose of the incorporation of the Potomac Institute. They are a research organization, and this is the kind of work they hope to do in the future. They were asked to undertake this job and the others followed from that.

An exasperated Congressman Johansen put forward a "tentative hypothesis," which he challenged the witnesses to disprove:

> I am prepared to maintain an open mind until these hearings are completed, but I would like, Mr. Chairman, to see them pursued to the point we get an answer which completely rejects and disproves my hypothesis or otherwise—that is, there was knowledge on the part of Mr. Fleming, possibly on the part of Mr. Currier, possibly on the part of others connected with one or both of these institutions, the [Taconic] foundation which was apparently a going concern, and the Potomac Institute which at the very most was an embryo, I suggest to you that there was knowledge there was going to be a field open for this type of investigation, study, and work, and that the Potomac Institute was a product of planned parenthood. I suggest further that some people knew there would be a gravy train made up, and they were asking for advance reservations on it.

This might have been the final word on the character of Potomac and its principals had not Congressman Udall spoken up:

> I think the moment has arrived for my morning commentary on the proceedings if I may have just a moment. I don't think there's a shred of evidence before us on which we can accept my friend's hypothesis. I certainly shall not accept it until we do have some evidence.
>
> If this were a gravy train, it was one of the least profitable gravy trains that I have seen around here in some time. . . . We have seen here apparently, if the hypothesis is correct, $47,000 given on this first contract which was apparently split among five or six people we have talked about, plus some secretaries and other staff people, amounting to a total take of $6,000 to $8,000 for these people, assuming they didn't do a lick of work.
>
> We have very thick reports here, consisting of some highly professorial language, which would indicate at least some of these people used their dictionaries or their thesaurus to find some big

words to throw into this at the very least. This was a non-profit organization which could not make a profit under the law. Any profits which accrued to anyone came as consulting fees, and on this first contract there was not too much gravy to go around.

It has been suggested that these folks were [not] impartial. I think we lost sight of the important thing . . . The President of the United States ordered this program instituted. There is at least one member of this committee who thinks he did the right thing.

Now, then, if you are going to have an outside analysis of how to put this program into effect . . . I would think that you would want people who are in sympathy with the objectives of the program, who really believed in equal opportunities, and who had had some experience with industrial relations, as these people obviously had, people who had training in fine institutions in Iowa, Michigan, and other places, these were the kinds of people you would want to get.

My final observation would be that I hope we can get our teeth into something here in these hearings. . . . So far as I am concerned up to this point there is no satisfactory evidence to me that these contracts were bad, that the money was wasted, that the Government was cheated, and did not get value received. From the rate at which we are putting things in this record, and from my knowledge of the cost of printing hearing reports, I suspect the hearing record itself will cost $106,000 before we are through.

With these friendly observations I yield.

Friendly or not, Udall's observations had a visibly deflationary effect on the other committee members; thereafter, they seemed to have lost interest in the quest for a "smoking gun" of corruption or radicalism. The Defense Department witnesses were given one last opportunity to give the disgruntled members some comfort. Ralph Horton was asked if he still believed that Potomac's report had been helpful to the department. Horton replied, "Unequivocally. I would say there was a report on this problem that was worth much more [than it cost]. I think that report was of great help; I certainly do."

Norman Paul was also queried, in a more leading fashion:

Mr. Wilson: Mr. Paul, you didn't have anything to do with the original contracts. Do you feel now you might have done it differently had you had jurisdiction at that time or do you feel yourself the report has been worthwhile?

Mr. Paul: I believe it has been extremely worthwhile.

Mr. Wilson: I can't think of a better way to state it.

After a few more desultory questions, and some placatory remarks by the chairman about the "splendid cooperation" of the Defense Department witnesses, the hearing was adjourned.

The subcommittee's published report was a bland document that merely summarized the witnesses' testimony. It charged no wrongdoing or impropriety. By way of salvage, however, Representative Henderson invoked the chairman's prerogative by writing a foreword—not requiring approval by the other members—in which he restated the original allegations.

Afterward, I tried to sort out the lessons that might be learned from this disorderly exercise in congressional oversight. I came up with the following:

Mr. Mullelly had demonstrated that a well connected bureaucrat can make life hard for those who are seen as a threat to his domain.

The hostile Congressmen had demonstrated (once again) how readily a hearing can be used to impugn motives and call reputations into question, with no need at all for supporting evidence.

The Defense Department witnesses had demonstrated that sufficient patience and intelligence can frustrate the most determined inquisitors.

Congressman Udall had demonstrated that one rational voice can stop a posse in its tracks.

Representative Henderson and his friends had demonstrated that a Congressional foray, even one that finds no wrong-doing, can convey a message that prudent administrators will heed. (Not for some time would the Defense Department—or any other federal agency for that matter—enter into another contract in the field of equal opportunity.)

The Potomac team had learned that you can effect needed but controversial innovations in government if you do your homework, keep your head down, and get something in place before your luck runs out.

CHAPTER 6 ▪ *The Art of the Infeasible*

AS THE KENNEDY ADMINISTRATION began its second year, the civil
rights forces continued to press for legislation with mounting impatience,
but to no avail. The Kennedys and their advisers remained convinced that
proposing a strong civil rights bill would result in nothing but alienation
of sorely needed allies on the Hill. Under the circumstances, we saw no
alternative for Potomac but to push the strategy of executive action as
far as it would go. There was little reason to hope it would go far enough,
given the administration's sensitivity to congressional displeasure. Yet,
even if the results were inadequate, we thought the effort in and of itself would help dramatize the need for legislation and lay the groundwork
for the kind of statute that was needed.

Fortunately for the purpose, we had somewhat enlarged Potomac's
staff capacity. Margaret Price, an experienced journalist, served as librarian and research assistant for the next eight years. Eleanor M. Ambrose
became my executive secretary and administrative assistant, a position
that she occupied indispensably for more than thirty years. During the
follow-up of the Defense Department studies, Art Levin's formidable
program and editorial skills were brought to the permanent staff. These
additions, plus the availability of highly qualified project consultants,
enabled us to carry on a variety of concurrent activities.

School Desegregation

High on our agenda was the glacial rate of progress in school desegregation, as well as the racial tension and social disorder generated by
resistance to it. Eight years after the *Brown* decision, most public schools
in the South were still rigidly segregated, and some states had vowed to

close them altogether rather than yield to court desegregation orders. The administration had demonstrated its concern through friend-of-the-court briefs, public appeals by the president, and quiet negotiations in Atlanta, New Orleans, and other localities under court order. The Kennedys were especially disturbed by the situation in Prince Edward County, Virginia, which had thwarted desegregation orders by shutting down the public school system and setting up a segregated private academy for its white children. Robert Kennedy worked with friends in the private sector to create and fund an interim nonpublic school for the black children. These trouble-shooting efforts were a refreshing contrast to the passivity of the Eisenhower years. What was lacking, however, was any kind of continuing, systematic program to enforce, encourage, and facilitate compliance across the board.

Several of the Southern Regional Council's recommendations for executive action had addressed this problem. One of these—partially implemented in 1961—called for requiring desegregation as a condition of federal aid to education, beginning with vocational education and schooling for children of military personnel (those being the areas of greatest federal involvement). Another urged the president to "direct the Secretary of Health, Education and Welfare to assemble and disseminate, for the use of educators and the instruction of the public, educational facts related to the integration process." (The Civil Rights Commission had made a similar recommendation in 1959 and again in 1961.) If this were to be done, the responsibility clearly would rest on the U.S. Office of Education, an agency scarcely known for its boldness in dealing with state and local school officials. The president was unlikely to risk congressional wrath by ordering the secretary of HEW or his commissioner of education to take such a controversial step. The challenge was to find a way short of presidential fiat to get the federal education bureaucracy into the act.

Having pondered this problem, I met with two of the new senior appointees at HEW who could be expected to take a sympathetic view of the matter: Assistant Secretary James Quigley and Deputy Assistant Secretary Lisle Carter. Suppose, I suggested to them, we found that a number of southern school superintendents would welcome helpful information and technical assistance from the Office of Education. Wouldn't this put the office in the tenable position of graciously consenting to meet an expressed need of local officials it was supposed to serve? Quigley and Carter liked the idea, but they were cautious. They stressed that any such strategy would have to be purely private and that there must be no suggestion that HEW was party to it. I assured them that our interests were identical; nothing could serve Potomac's purpose less well than to invite charges that the president's men in the department were plotting an end run to shield the president from political controversy.

A basic question remained: Would an appreciable number of southern superintendents actually endorse the idea? No one could be absolutely certain, but I was strongly inclined to believe they would. Whatever their personal views on segregation, most of them were appalled by the prospect of abandonment of public education. I also knew that many school administrators, in off-the-record discussions, had voiced the hope that their political leaders and the public could be brought to accept the inevitability—and workability—of desegregation. They also expressed frustration at the political constraints that kept them from becoming better informed about the techniques of desegregation and the initial experience with it in other communities.

At the next meeting of the Potomac board, it was agreed that we should carry out an opinion survey of superintendents representing a cross-section of southern school districts. As project director, we engaged Dr. Kenneth B. Morland, a respected social scientist at Randolph-Macon Woman's College in Lynchburg, Virginia. Within a month, Morland, assisted by five colleagues at strategically located southern colleges, had interviewed thirty-four superintendents and school board chairmen in thirty school districts of nine southern states. While no claim was made that this constituted a scientifically valid sample, the school districts' variety of size, location, racial makeup, and historical background lent credibility to the survey results.

The results were surprisingly positive. Thirty of the thirty-four interviewees said they would find it useful to have information on the desegregation experiences of other school systems; three were doubtful that information from elsewhere would be relevant to their special situations; and one replied that there was already more material available than he could use. Nineteen said consultants on desegregation problems would be helpful, and twenty added that conferences would also be useful. A key question dealt with the kind of auspices that the respondents would find acceptable. There was unanimous agreement that the sponsoring agency should be educational in nature and national in scope. A majority said the U.S. Office of Education would be acceptable, although some expressed a preference for a "non-federal" agency—not as far as they themselves were concerned, but because of the anticipated reaction of their boards. Yet, of the six school board chairmen interviewed, none expressed opposition to Office of Education auspices.

Although we gave our friends at HEW a draft report of these and related findings for their use within the department, both we and they felt that the survey results would be most effective if published and distributed under Potomac's own imprint. The report—Potomac's first publication—was issued on April 23, 1962. A mailing including a press release sent to a sizable list of news offices yielded extensive publicity. An Associated Press story ran in many newspapers, and byline articles appeared in the *New York Times,* the *Atlanta Constitution,* and elsewhere. Most welcome of all, however, was the story written by Robert E. Baker of the *Washington Post.* It began as follows:"The United States Office of Education is establishing a clearing house to help public school officials plan desegregation. The new operation is expected to be under way by the start of the fall school term, according to Robert M. Rosenzweig, Assistant to the U.S. Commissioner of Education. He disclosed the plan when asked to comment on a survey conducted by the Potomac Institute which showed that many Southern school officials would welcome help in planning desegregation."

As it turned out, the Office of Education's commitment was probably of more symbolic than operational significance. Under the energetic leadership of newly appointed Commissioner Francis Keppel and his aide David Seeley, who welcomed Potomac's collaboration, much ambitious planning occurred. But putting the plans into action was a slow, laborious process. Most of the agency's permanent professionals were inexperienced in and uncomfortable with a mission involving social change. This, added to the natural inertia of the system, delayed full implementation of the program. The start-up time was by no means wasted, however. The preparatory work paid off when, in 1964, Congress mandated by law the clearing house and technical assistance functions, and provided as well for financial assistance to desegregating districts.

A Federal Role in Public Accommodations

Potomac's search for a federal role focused on public accommodations as well as schools. Two years after five black college students in Greensboro, North Carolina, staged the first nationally televised sit-in, a scattering of lunch counters, restaurants, hotels, and other public facilities, formerly segregated, had opened their doors to blacks. These were mostly establishments in the larger cities of the South, often affiliated with national chains. But for the most part, despite continuing demonstrations, segregated public accommodations were still the rule in the region. Unlike some other forms of discrimination, this one persisted with no visible prospect of federal intervention of any kind. One reason for this inaction was uncertainty, even in some civil rights circles, about the legal justification for federal authority—especially executive authority—to tell private establishments whom they must serve.

It seemed to us that the logical federal agency to initiate serious consideration of the problem was the Civil Rights Commission. Since its creation in 1957, the commission had steadily increased in influence as an advocate of bold new federal civil rights actions. Berl Bernhard, the Kennedy-appointed staff director, had set out to justify his definition of the commission as "the civil rights conscience of the federal government." In this, he was wholeheartedly supported by all but the most conservative of the commissioners, southern segregationists appointed by President Eisenhower to "balance" the membership of the commission. In time, even they became so impressed by the severity and persistence of civil rights violations that they began to join the majority in recommendations that set off political alarms in the White House.

If the commission's relationship with the president and his men was sometimes chilly, with the attorney general and his lawyers it was downright frigid. Robert Kennedy was adamantly opposed to the commission's plans for a public hearing in Mississippi designed to expose the sordid measures used there to deny blacks the vote. He argued that a commission hearing would achieve no practical results, but would undermine the Justice Department's efforts to secure relief through the federal courts. Relations were further strained when the commission publicly recommended that the administration consider withholding federal funds from Mississippi as long as it continued to deprive black citizens of their rights. The president himself publicly expressed his displeasure with so draconian a proposal.

Despite these and other sometimes bitter disputes, both sides had the good sense to stop short of open hostilities. The president rejected suggestions that he use his power to retaliate against the commission by replacing its members or allowing it to expire. Instead, he reaffirmed his respect for the commission's status as an independent body that had a right to make its own decisions. For its part, the commission continued to provide valuable staff services to overworked White House aides and yielded repeatedly, though reluctantly, to the attorney general's insistence that it defer the Mississippi hearing. In the end, the commission's controversial proposals were vindicated; the Mississippi hearing was finally held in 1965 without untoward consequences. And the authority to cut off federal assistance to discriminatory state and local programs was incorporated in the administration's own civil rights bill.

From Potomac's point of view, one of the virtues of the commission was precisely its willingness to air proposals that were somewhat ahead of their time politically. As recent events in this field had demonstrated (and future ones would demonstrate even more dramatically) what seemed totally unrealistic one day could become eminently achievable the next. To limit advocacy and discussion only to those proposals that were currently deemed politically feasible was self-defeating. Indeed, promoting consideration of the "infeasible" was an essential first step toward enlarging the boundaries of the possible.

It was in this spirit that we approached Bernhard and his staff about the need for exploratory thinking on the stalemated issue of public accommodations. After some discussion, it was agreed that Potomac should do a preliminary examination of alternative legal approaches and ways in which the commission might help define a federal role in opening public places to all citizens. Our consultant for this purpose was John Silard, an inventive lawyer who, along with his partner, Joseph L. Rauh Jr., had done pioneering work in the areas of civil rights and civil liberties.

Silard's report consisted in large part of a preliminary but wide-ranging examination of the federal powers that might be invoked against racial discrimination by establishments serving the general public. Chief among these were the Fourteenth Amendment and the Interstate Commerce Clause of the Constitution, the power of federal agencies to prescribe conditions for the use of their grants and subsidies, the authority of the president as national leader and commander-in-chief, and the bases of congressional power to legislate against discrimination by private businesses.

A central question was how far one could go in arguing that such discrimination involved a significant degree of state action. As Silard pointed out, the line between purely governmental and purely private action was not as sharp as commonly supposed. When a policeman evicted or arrested for trespass a black peaceably seeking service in an eating place open to the public, or a court convicted a black citizen for such an alleged violation, was state action involved? When a traveler was refused food service or the use of a rest room because of race in an establishment on or adjacent to a federal highway, state action, again, became a very live issue. When a private firm was granted a license, given a governmental franchise or subsidy, or permitted to operate on state property, was it subject to the same requirements of equal protection as the state itself? If a political party held a private, "jaybird" primary, was it performing an essentially public function in which discrimination was forbidden? (In *Terry v. Adams*, the Supreme Court held that it was.)

Questions of presidential power arose as well. The right of a president of the United States to speak out forcefully for equal treatment and to deplore discrimination could hardly be disputed. But as commander-in-chief of the armed forces was he empowered, perhaps even obligated, to declare "off limits" to all military personnel those private firms that discriminated against black servicemen? Could he enter into reciprocal agreements with other countries providing that diplomatic representatives would not be subjected to racial discrimination? Would such agreements be enforceable by the courts?

Potomac recommended to the Civil Rights Commission that these and a good many other questions be examined in greater depth as background for a commission report to the president and Congress. We rec-

ognized that more was involved than legalistic issues of authority and jurisdiction; there were also practical considerations. What would be the
likely consequences of the various approaches? How could they be effectively carried out? How and by whom would they be enforced? In the
circumstances that existed in 1962, such questions were not susceptible to
easy answers. In fact, the more we considered the limitations and com-
plexities of executive action in the field of public accommodations, the
clearer it became that truly comprehensive and effective remedies could
only be achieved through congressional legislation, remote a prospect as
that seemed at the time.

State Executive Authority on Civil Rights

While the public accommodations study was still in its initial phase,
our examination of possible governmental regulation led us to consider
the potential for executive action at the state and local levels. Several
governors of large industrial states—Harriman and Rockefeller of New
York, Swainson of Michigan, and Lawrence of Pennsylvania—had each
issued a "Governor's Code of Fair Practices" barring discrimination in a
wide array of state and state-supported activities. A few other states had
taken less comprehensive steps in the same direction. But most had done
nothing or had relegated all civil rights concerns to antidiscrimination
commissions of varying power and effectiveness. Given the rising public
awareness of racial issues, we were convinced that this was an area in
which some solid information and encouragement could spark much
needed action.

It did not take long to find a suitable person to take on the necessary fact-finding. The ever-resourceful John Feild put us onto Harold
Galloway, a San Francisco attorney who had helped devise various affirmative civil rights initiatives. Through diligent use of the mails, the
telephone, and personal interviews, Galloway came up with a hefty card
file documenting the diverse types of action taken by progressive governors, attorneys general, and other officials to assure civil rights not
adequately protected by state law. Many of these had to do with the operations of state government itself, such as administrative coordination
and oversight of civil rights responsibilities scattered among departments

and agencies, equal opportunity in state employment and the referral practices of the state employment service, and alleviation of racial isolation in the public schools. Several governors had directed their subordinates not to take part in segregated meetings and not to schedule state meetings or activities at facilities that were known to have discriminatory policies.

A few states went further, using their regulatory and licensing powers to curb discrimination in the private sector. For example, some state contracts for public works, goods, and services forbade discrimination on account of race, creed, color, or national origin. Professionals or firms subject to a state agency's licensing or regulating authority—real estate agents, for instance—were held accountable to the nondiscrimination requirement. In the case of public accommodations, there were examples of reliance on one or more state powers, including licensing, regulation, state assistance, and executive persuasion. The Ohio Turnpike Authority obtained pledges of nondiscrimination from proprietors adjacent to turnpike exits and noted this fact in materials furnished to travelers. New York applied similar pledge requirements to proprietors using the facilities of the state tourist bureau. The California Alcoholic Beverage Control Board had warned taverns that their licenses would be jeopardized if they were found to practice racially discriminatory policies.

A description of these and other actions, and a discussion of the legal foundations on which they rested, were published as a Potomac report, *State Executive Authority to Promote Civil Rights.* John Silard and Art Levin, who put the final version together, took pains to point out that its recommendations were not intended as a substitute for substantive legislation or the establishment of state antidiscrimination bodies. Rather, they were intended to supplement and fill the gaps in existing coverage. The publication was widely distributed, to governors, attorneys general, and other state officials, as well as to state human rights agencies, private civil rights organizations, and the press. The timing was as good as we could have hoped. Requests for additional copies and more information about particular remedies were heartening, as were reports of similar actions effected or under consideration in additional states. Even the later passage of comprehensive federal civil rights legislation did not render the report obsolete; we continued to receive orders and other inquiries for some ten years after the initial publication date. Evidence of the receptive audience that the recommendations continued to receive among state executives was the issuance of an Executive Order in Maryland several years later using the exact language of one of the suggested models.

Fortuitously, about this time Potomac was invited to cooperate with the International City Managers Association (ICMA) and the Southern Regional Council in the preparation of a similar document aimed at local officials. ICMA published the resulting report and distributed copies to its 1,130 subscriber cities, ranging in size from New York and Los Angeles to towns of two or three thousand. Potomac's fruitful cooperative relationship with ICMA, maintained primarily by Art Levin, continued for several years. In 1964 Levin compiled the first comprehensive and descriptive directory of municipal human rights agencies, which was published by the ICMA and incorporated in its yearbook. Later, he helped ICMA develop training sessions and materials on municipal administration of civil rights and equal opportunity responsibilities.

Having carried the message of executive action to all three tiers of government, we christened Potomac's initial series of publications "Son of Federalist Papers."

Fortunately, the prospects for federal civil rights legislation began to appear more politically feasible sooner than we or anyone else anticipated. Well before the Civil Rights Commission, given its contending priorities, could have developed Potomac's recommendations into a full-blown report, a public accommodations title would be incorporated in the first version of a Kennedy-backed civil rights bill.

The next step for Potomac would be our involvement in an ambitious effort to create, in advance of the law, the conditions for peaceful compliance.

CHAPTER 7 ▪ *That Dear Old Slum*

CONSPICUOUS BY ITS ABSENCE in discussions of civil rights legislation was the fair housing issue. This was not surprising. Housing segregation was then, and would be for years to come, the neglected stepchild of civil rights issues. This situation could be explained in part by purely practical considerations that still exist today. The process by which housing was sited, developed, and marketed was complex and hard to regulate. Because blacks made up a disproportionate share of moderate- and low-income Americans, economic barriers frequently served, intentionally or not, to exclude black residents. Some discrimination was practiced less because of raw prejudice than because of fear of neighborhood turnover and declining property values. But whatever motive or mixture of motives might be at work, the resulting denial of housing opportunities to minorities was no less real than that produced by undiluted bigotry. The extent of white resistance to housing integration was revealed by public opinion surveys conducted in 1963. A majority of whites said they were in favor of equality in voting, access to public accommodations, and employment. But only 23 percent felt that blacks should have the right to buy a residence anywhere they chose. This attitude toward race and housing was deeply rooted in the society and powerfully reinforced by government and the housing industry. The all-white suburbs that burgeoned around the nation's cities after World War II were built with the aid of subsidies and loan guarantees by the federal government. Until the late 1940s, the real estate industry's commitment to preserving racially homogeneous neighborhoods had the overt blessing and support of federal housing agencies.

Little wonder, then, that John F. Kennedy was slow to make good on his campaign promise to abolish housing discrimination with "a stroke of the pen." For twenty long months, each time the matter came up for consideration in the White House, some reason was found to defer action. Arthur M. Schlesinger Jr. gives the following account in *Robert Kennedy and His Times:*

> Counter pressure mounted on the civil rights side. An "Ink for Jack" campaign began. Thousands of pens descended on the White House. The President, recalling that the fatal phrase came from Harris Wofford, suggested that they be piled on Wofford's desk. As the issue became a symbolic test of the executive-action strategy, civil rights groups wanted to extend the order beyond housing affected by federal loans and guarantees to cover housing financed by savings and loan associations and even banks. The 1962 elections were drawing near. Democratic congressmen, including northern liberals, were apprehensive about the impact the order might have on the campaign. "There's no question," Robert Kennedy said later, "that we waited until after the election because of the political implications."[7]

In the administration's internal deliberations on the content of the prospective housing executive order, staff members of the Civil Rights Commission had argued vigorously for broad coverage, which it had consistently recommended in its published reports. The Justice Department's Office of Legal Counsel, represented by Assistant Attorney General Nicholas Katzenbach, staunchly defended the limited version. I was present at one or two of these parleys—debates, really. One of the commission staffers' main arguments was that the weak version of the order would be unfair and difficult to enforce, since the small proportion of housing covered would have to compete with the vastly larger market that was left free to discriminate. Katzenbach argued that a stronger order would exceed the constitutional limits of presidential authority.

Although the arguments were couched in legal terms, it seemed clear to me that the central disagreement was not legal, but political. Had it not been for the embarrassment of his much-regretted campaign pledge, Kennedy would probably not have been considering any type of housing order at all. Schlesinger and others have confirmed that even the watered-down order was viewed in the White House as a threat to other important priorities. Winning congressional elections was one of them. Another was the creation of a Department of Housing and Urban Development.

"Executive Order 11063, finally promulgated on Thanksgiving eve, was limited in its reach," wrote Schlesinger. "It proved neither the calamity predicted by opponents nor the blessing anticipated by advocates."

It would be more precise to say that the order did not prove to be the calamity predicted by opponents for the same reason that it did not please the advocates—because its impact was exceedingly mild. It covered no existing housing, not even public housing, and no conventionally financed housing at all. It was limited to new housing built or assisted by the federal government and constructed after November 20, 1962, the date of the executive order. The net effect was to bring under the nondiscrimination requirement less than 20 percent of new housing starts annually. When turnover of existing units was considered, the order covered was a tiny fraction of all housing transactions.

The order did contain a "good offices" provision aimed at existing housing. It directed federal housing agencies to take "appropriate action permitted by law, including the institution of appropriate litigation, if required to promote the abandonment of discriminatory practices with respect to residential property and related facilities heretofore provided with federal financial assistance." But aside from a few efforts at persuasion, largely ineffective, this approach was never used.

There is a phrase from Robert Frost that might well have been carved over the Potomac Institute's door: "what to make of a diminished thing." This was a question we were to put to ourselves many times. It applied perfectly to the new housing order. The civil rights groups, including Potomac, seconded by other more conservative groups, would continue to press for stronger provisions. The immediate challenge, however, was to get as much leverage as possible from the order in its existing form. One way to begin was by developing a working relationship with the president's Committee on Equal Housing Opportunity, a new body mandated by the order to oversee and coordinate implementation of its provisions by the appropriate federal agencies. Another way was to work directly with the agencies themselves. We set out to try both approaches.

In January 1963, the president named as full-time chairman of the committee David Lawrence, former mayor of Pittsburgh and governor of

Pennsylvania, long an influential figure in the Democratic party. Friends and colleagues of ours in Pennsylvania gave us a lukewarm assessment of Lawrence. They conceded that he had a creditable civil rights record; he had issued a Governor's Code of Fair Practices and supported state civil rights legislation. But they attributed this more to political expediency than to gut commitment and predicted that he would be a compliant servant of the administration. I passed this intelligence along to our board, but added a cautionary "let's wait and see."

Lawrence brought with him to Washington a long-time aide, Walter Giesey, to serve as his principal staff assistant at the committee. Shortly after his arrival, he called me at Bob Weaver's suggestion to raise the possibility of Lawrence's addressing the forthcoming annual conference of the National Civil Liberties Clearing House, of which I was the current chairman. Lawrence was invited to speak, and his fine presentation drew enthusiastic applause from the pro–civil rights audience. Giesey and I also set a date for a meeting at Potomac to discuss the role of the new committee.

As a result of that and several other discussions, Art Levin, with some assistance from attorney John Silard on technical matters, prepared an analysis of the order, the responsibilities it conferred on the committee and the federal agencies, and a number of suggested guidelines for carrying them out. Because of the complexity of the housing process, many of these suggestions necessarily dealt with somewhat technical aspects of law and regulation. But our interpretation of the basic mandate was simple enough:

> Meeting this responsibility requires a major reorientation of Federal housing policy and administration. Where once such agencies were neutral on the subject of equal opportunity, they should now be affirmative. Where once the initiative in achieving equal opportunity rested with minority victims of discrimination, these agencies themselves should now act aggressively to root out discrimination and assure that benefits are not color or creed-conditioned. [This] requires that agencies analyze the various ways in which discrimination operates, and eliminate these in detail from Federally-assisted housing programs. It requires that agencies institute policies and practices which will assure Federal aid will promote equal housing

opportunity, and be withheld where benefits are not equally available to all Americans. In essence, this means that provision, rehabilitation, and operation of Federally-assisted housing and related facilities must be based on open occupancy. . . .

The Executive Order establishes this commitment [to an open housing market], and the Committee should publicly declare its strong intention to implement it through broad policy guidance, coordination and review of agency policies and practices, and public education.

Titled *The Federal Role in Equal Housing Opportunity,* this publication was widely used as a guide to compliance with the executive order by the federal housing agencies and the private groups that rode herd on their performance.

Our aim to assist the agencies that had direct responsibility for securing compliance had been given an unexpected assist a few days before the order itself was issued. The occasion was a conference on equal housing opportunity held at Princeton University. The co-sponsoring organizations were the National Housing Center (NHC) and the National Association of Intergroup Relations Officials (NAIRO), the first made up of developers and the second of civil rights workers. I had had a hand in planning the affair, since two old friends and associates of mine were principals—Edward Rutledge of the New York State Commission Against Discrimination, then president of NAIRO, and Fred Routh, an alumnus of the Southern Regional Council and the Michigan Fair Employment Practices Commission, who was NAIRO's new executive director.

In consultation with NHC, they had compiled a list of invitees that included some unlikely bedfellows. Among the forty participants were builders and lenders, government officials and foundation executives, fair housing specialists and civil rights activists, blacks and whites, liberals and conservatives—a mix of people not commonly seen around the same conference table.

The variety of viewpoints made for a spirited discussion. Some conferees ardently advocated the strongest possible executive order. Others no less ardently opposed the use of federal sanctions. Some insisted on the need for "benign" quotas for black occupancy as a precondition of successful integration. Others denounced such arbitrary racial ceilings as blatant violations of civil rights. (The latter issue is still hotly debated more than twenty-five years later.) These views and others, along with their supporting arguments, were subsequently summarized in a report aimed at the White House, government housing officials, the housing industry, and the civil rights community.

Some of those involved were tempted to suppose that the Princeton conference influenced the administration to proceed with the housing order, but, in view of the close timing of the two events, that was hardly likely. The conference did, at least indirectly, have a positive effect on how the order was interpreted by some federal policy-makers. One of the housing officials present was William L. Slayton, head of the federal Urban Renewal Administration (URA), whom I had come to know as a neighbor in Washington's Cleveland Park area. At the conclusion of the conference, we traveled home together on a slow night train, which gave us an opportunity to hash over the discussions of the past two days.

Slayton was smarting from what he considered unfair criticisms heaped on the urban renewal program by civil rights advocates. These were focused mainly on the displacement of low-income residents, particularly blacks, whose deteriorated housing areas were obvious choices for demolition under the large-scale "slum clearance" projects of the day. The land thus cleared was designated for redevelopment, often featuring commercial facilities, public uses, and housing for middle- and upper-income residents. The severest critics condemned the whole process as nothing more than "Negro removal." Others conceded the value of renewing blighted city areas, but faulted the program for failing to rehouse the original residents in acceptable housing in the same or at least comparable areas. Criticism was intensified when, all too often, cleared land remained undeveloped, barren expanses resembling nothing more than bombed-out areas.

Slayton's complaint was that the critics tended to blame urban renewal for deeply rooted social and economic problems that were far beyond the power of the program to resolve. He also felt that the critics failed to acknowledge the Urban Renewal Administration's efforts and achievements in helping displaced citizens to relocate to decent housing from the squalid accommodations they had been renting from exploitative slumlords.

I didn't doubt Slayton's sincerity, but I wondered if his indignation at ill-founded charges might not have made him overly defensive. I asked him if he had made any effort to sit down with URA's detractors, tell them his side of the story and, in turn, give them a fair hearing. No, he replied, but he would like to. We pursued the idea for the rest of the train trip and then at my house until the pre-dawn hours. I woke the next morning with a headache and an uneasy memory of having promised to convene Slayton and his key staff members with the principal fair housing advocates.

Neither Slayton nor I realized at the time that our casual agreement would lead to a long-running series of consultations. Beginning in mid-December of 1962 and extending over nearly two-and-a-half years, Potomac hosted some twenty-nine luncheon meetings, usually involving fifteen to twenty participants from the federal government, local urban renewal agencies, state antidiscrimination commissions, and private civil rights organizations. Slayton might well have felt like the apochryphal lady on the Titanic who reportedly exclaimed, "I ordered ice, but this is ridiculous!" Nevertheless, these sessions at Potomac maintained a remarkable level of interest and participation until the Urban Renewal Administration was terminated by the creation of the Department of Housing and Urban Development and Slayton moved on to work outside the government.

The initial discussions focused, appropriately, on the new housing order and its implications for policy. The Urban Renewal Administration, like other federal agencies with responsibilities in the field of housing, had to decide how broadly (or narrowly) to interpret the new mandate. At our second meeting, in January of 1963, Slayton announced that URA's regulations would go well beyond the minimum requirements of the order. They would apply a nondiscrimination condition not only to residential construction on urban renewal land, but also to "commercial and service establishments, group facilities [schools, parks, etc.], and other publicly owned facilities of all kinds." Moreover, the nondiscrimination covenants would "run with the land"—that is, apply not only to the original contractors, lessees, grantees, or other parties, but to their successors as well.

These were genuine innovations at the time, but, in the view of the activists in our group, they were only a barebones beginning. These participants were eager for the kinds of changes that would make urban renewal a positive force for desegregation and equal opportunity in housing. Many of the proposals advanced and vigorously debated in our discussions centered on the relocation process. URA required the local renewal agencies to assist displaced residents of project areas in finding affordable "decent, safe, and sanitary housing." To facilitate this, the agencies maintained listings of available housing to which the displacees could be referred. The advocates argued that only housing available regardless of race or other minority status should be accepted for listing. This led to a further question: Shouldn't there also be a "clean hands" policy, limiting listings to owners, brokers, and others who practiced nondiscrimination in all their operations (e.g., employment)?

As I observed again and again in discussions of this kind, disagreements were seldom based on opposing ideologies or values; rather, they reflected the differing roles of the participants. The advocates were focused, often single-mindedly, on injustices in the society and the urgent need for remedies. The administrators just as keenly focused on the legal and procedural difficulties inherent in the use of government programs to achieve social change. Accordingly, the proposed policy of nondiscriminatory listings, which seemed self-evidently fair and workable to the proponents, raised pragmatic problems for those who would have to administer it. Might not such a policy, they asked, so shrink the number of listers and listings, at least in heavily segregated cities, that it would be impossible to rehouse all the displaced residents needing referrals? How could the listers be legally required to practice nondiscrimination throughout their operations when they held no contract with the federal government or even the local renewal agency? Wouldn't such a policy have the net effect of forcing many displacees to relocate themselves as best they could, without the assistance of the renewal agency?

Disagreement on this and other issues remained unresolved at the end of many a meeting. Yet it was evident that participants on both (or all) sides of the argument were being forced to reexamine their positions more rigorously. When the same subject came up at a subsequent meeting, the discussion usually was more coherent and the prospect of consensus nearer.

By the time changing circumstances brought the URA discussions to an end, many more issues had been raised than resolved. But some of them had led to significant alterations in URA's policies and procedures. For example, on June 25, 1963, Commissioner Slayton announced "two major steps to increase the effectiveness of urban renewal in providing equal opportunity for housing." One of these dealt with the relocation issues we had wrangled over at such length in the Potomac meetings:

> As part of its concern for the relocation of families displaced by urban renewal, the Urban Renewal Administration also has a responsibility for seeing that these families are assisted in finding housing accommodations that are free from racial or other such restrictions. Consequently as of today we are revising our relocation regulations to prohibit the listing of housing accommodations that are not available to all families regardless of race, color, creed, or national origin.

Another change was based on the recognition that housing discrimination could be effectively attacked only by community-wide planning and action:

> A comprehensive program that examines the needs and requirements of the entire community is essential. The Community Renewal Program of the Urban Renewal Administration offers the means for such an examination. It is a citywide action program for renewal and related activities. Today we are revising our regulations with respect to grants for Community Renewal Programs to make equal opportunity in housing a central factor in the development of communities engaged in these programs. Specifically, we are requiring that CRP's include:
>
> (1) an analysis of the existing pattern of housing occupied by Negroes and other minorities and the extent to which this pattern is a result of discrimination;
> (2) projection of the housing needs of Negro and other minority families;
> (3) development of an affirmative program to increase the quantity, improve the quality, and eliminate barriers to housing for Negro and other minority families.

These policy changes were sufficiently bold at the time to require the personal approval of Slayton's superior, Housing and Home Finance Administration (HHFA) Administrator Robert Weaver. There was a certain irony here. Weaver was not only the highest ranking black appointee in the Kennedy administration; he was also a veteran of many a campaign against racial discrimination, inside and outside government. Yet it was a singularly unpropitious time for him to be perceived as a special pleader for the black cause. That would hardly improve the president's hopes for congressional approval of a Department of Housing or Weaver's prospects for confirmation by the Senate as its first secretary. As real as these concerns must have been, they did not deter Weaver from approving most of Slayton's proposals. On one occasion, however, he did permit himself to refer to the commissioner somewhat wryly as "Abraham Lincoln Slayton."

The president's Committee on Equal Housing Opportunity, under Governor Lawrence's chairmanship, soon recognized the crippling effects of its weak mandate. Its repeated recommendation that the president extend the coverage of the order was seconded by the Mortgage Bankers Association and various spokesmen for lenders, builders, and some realtors, as well as civil rights groups. In an article published in early 1965, I ventured the prediction, "If Constitutional or other doubts [continue to restrain the President from broadening the housing order], it is likely that in time circumstances will force him to ask for Congressional enactment of a fair housing law, however inexpedient that might seem at the moment." In the following year, President Johnson did precisely that, although he was not successful until 1968.

One of my eccentric forms of relaxation was to satirize the developments of the day in irreverent doggerel and songs, rendered to the accompaniment of a venerable ukulele (an instrument fortunately not much seen or heard since the 1920s). At a party given by the Slaytons, I memorialized the urban renewal program with such a rendition, to the tune of "The St. Louis Blues":

I hate to see that dear old slum go down.
I hate to see that dear old slum go down.
There's no place for me in this whole damn town.
I'm movin' tomorrow just like I moved today.

Movin' tomorrow, just like I moved today.
Here comes the bulldozer to push my house away.
I got the blues, got the blues, got the relocation blues.
I'm on the booze, on the booze, 'cause I know I am bound to lose.
I can't choose, can't refuse.
I got the relocation blues.

It says something about Bill Slayton's sense of humor that he insisted on taping this rendition and playing it over the public address system to a large convention of bewildered housing officials.

CHAPTER 8 ▪ *King and the "Cries for Equality"*

AS 1963 BEGAN, ONE could hardly have foreseen the drama, turbulence, and finally horror that would mark that fateful year. President Kennedy's fortunes seemed ascendant. Both he and the American public were enjoying the youthful style and energy of his administration. His attention, as well as the nation's generally, was largely directed toward international developments, which appeared to be going well for him. There were problems aplenty, but they were overlaid by a buoyant spirit of optimism. In short, this was the "brief shining moment" that would come to be sentimentalized in a latter-day legend of Camelot.

For the civil rights movement, however, there was little to cheer about. The long-awaited housing order had proved a disappointment. In February the president finally proposed a civil rights bill, but it was too narrow in scope and timid in approach to stir any real enthusiasm. To make matters worse, the civil rights organizations and their leaders were at odds among themselves, a disunity that threatened to obliterate all possibility of concerted action.

By this time, Martin Luther King was incontestably the most prominent figure in the civil rights movement—and also the most controversial. So widely revered has he become since his martyrdom that few Americans recall, if indeed they ever realized, how tenuous his reputation was before his death. During the brief twelve-year span of his activist career, he was periodically assailed as an upstart, a publicity hound, a hypocrite, an Uncle Tom, a self-anointed messiah, a communist subversive, and near the end, an irrelevant has-been. Denunciation from white racists and right-wingers was only to be expected. But King's detractors also included a number of young black militants and established civil rights leaders.

Relations between King and Roy Wilkins, in particular, were chronically strained. This was probably inevitable under the circumstances. Wilkins was a jealous guardian of the NAACP's reputation as the preeminent champion of the Negro cause. He could only view as a threat King's emergence as the charismatic spokesman of the new nonviolent movement, the focus of overwhelming media attention, and the leader of the Southern Christian Leadership Conference (SCLC), a competitor for both public recognition and scarce funds. King was anxious to avert a public feud, but short of abdicating his leadership role there was little he could do to eradicate the basic causes of friction.

Wilkins made no effort to conceal his irritation. In one nationally publicized speech he inveighed against "the other organizations" that "furnish the noise and get the publicity while the NAACP furnishes the manpower and pays the bills. . . . They are here today and gone tomorrow. There is only one organization that can handle a long, sustained fight—the NAACP." Although this indictment was meant to include SNCC and CORE, the primary target was clearly SCLC.

SNCC had its own bones to pick with King. One area of contention dated back to SNCC's origins, when King was charged with trying to maneuver the new organization into a relationship of dependence, as a sort of youth auxiliary of SCLC. Later, King's refusal to take part in the hazardous freedom ride from Alabama to Mississippi bred resentment tinged with contempt among some SNCC leaders. In their view, "de Lawd," as they derisively styled him, was at once too stodgy, too irresolute, and too concerned with his public image to be trusted. These animosities more than once threatened to precipitate an open break between the young militants and the man who was widely assumed to be their mentor. Yet whenever a final rupture threatened, it was averted by a grudging recognition of mutual self-interest. King needed the vigor and boldness of the youthful activists, and they, in turn, needed King's magnetic presence to attract public attention to their efforts.

Criticisms of King within the movement were exacerbated by the failure of his crusade to score the kind of victories the Montgomery bus boycott had seemed to promise. The most protracted and widely publicized campaign with which he had been associated since Montgomery was waged in Albany, Georgia.

Months of fitful protests there led only to bitter factionalism among the local black leadership, rancorous exchanges among SCLC, SNCC, and the NAACP, and finally a humiliating defeat and withdrawal by King and his associates. Ironically, the individual who emerged from this affair with the most acclaim was Laurie Pritchett, Albany's police chief, whose restrained and wily tactics of containment won him not only favorable media attention but commendation (for keeping the peace) from none other than Attorney General Robert F. Kennedy.

Although only a handful of people knew it at the time, King was the object of an unrelenting campaign of surveillance and vilification waged from within the Justice Department itself. J. Edgar Hoover, the arrogant, seemingly indestructible chief of the Federal Bureau of Investigation, had developed an obsessive loathing for King. He was driven by a fierce compulsion to prove that King was "the most dangerous Negro in America," a tool of hard-core communist advisers, and a lecherous "tom cat" to boot. When Hoover's sycophants reported that they could find no evidence of communist influence on King, he sent back the furious message that such findings were unacceptable. Partly by deceit, partly by intimidation, he persuaded Robert Kennedy to authorize bugs and wiretaps on telephones, residences, and hotel accommodations of King and his associates. One of the tapes, purportedly a recording of a sex orgy involving King, was sent anonymously to Coretta King along with a note implying that her husband would be well advised to commit suicide.

Word of this covert campaign to destroy King came to me by way of a friend who was a reporter for the *Washington Post*. He and his newspaper had been invited (presumably by an agent of the FBI) to publish the allegedly incriminating products of the bugs and taps—an offer, I later learned, that was made to other major newspapers as well. My friend was in a quandary. On one hand, he was aching to expose Hoover's scurrilous campaign. On the other hand, he was appalled by the possible damage such an exposé might inflict on King's reputation and effectiveness. While I shared both of these conflicting reactions, it seemed to me unthinkable that any self-respecting publication should publicize such defamatory (and unverified) material, even if its motive was to discredit the source. As it turned out, neither the *Post* nor any other major newspaper made use of the tapes.

Thanks to diligent use of the Freedom of Information Act and extensive interviews by David Garrow, Taylor Branch, and others, we now know a great deal more about both Hoover's vendetta and King's private life (which was, in fact, no model of marital fidelity). Yet enough remains under seal to enable President Reagan to suggest—even as he proclaimed King's birthday a national holiday—that only after all the files are declassified, decades from now, will we know for sure whether King was a "loyal American." Few, if any, responsible researchers who have examined the facts share the skepticism evinced by Reagan. But such a statement by a president of the United States should stand as a dismal example of the ignoble uses to which the claims of national security may be put.

Quite apart from such heady issues as patriotism and sexual probity, King's personality was one to invite speculation. For all the fervor of his writings and speeches, his public manner was usually formal and reserved, bordering on impassivity. I was struck by this quality in my occasional encounters with him, beginning in the mid-fifties when I was still with the Southern Regional Council. He was invariably cordial, attentive, and responsive to any comment or request, but there was always that sense of inwardness, an air of private preoccupation. Notwithstanding that and his deliberate, somewhat orotund manner of speech, I never detected the slightest trace of the pomposity and arrogance one associates with a "messianic complex." On the contrary, he impressed me as an essentially modest and unassuming person.

This impression was borne out in the rare instances when I dealt with him on sensitive issues. One such occasion arose late one night when, by sheer coincidence, I had just attended a reception hosted by King for the young Kenyan leader Tom Mboya. Returning home, I found an urgent message to call John Perry, an aide to Leroy Collins, the enlightened governor of Florida. When I reached him, Perry was apologetic about the lateness of the hour, but explained that Governor Collins had just learned that King was to speak in Tallahassee the following night to a mass meeting of the Florida affiliate of SCLC. The racial atmosphere there was tense. In an unprecedented action, the state had brought to trial several white men charged with raping a black coed at Florida A&M University. The white supremacists were hoping that King's speech would create a backlash in the white community that would assure acquittal of the accused men.

"What does the governor want me to do?" I asked Perry. "Surely he doesn't expect me to urge King to cancel his Tallahassee speech?"

"Not in the least," said Perry. "He only wants your help in making sure that King understands the local situation. We're not trying to tell him how to handle it." I promised to see what I could do.

It was almost eleven o'clock, but, having left King only a short time before, I decided to take a chance on his still being awake. He answered the telephone himself, as imperturbably as though it were high noon. I told him about Governor Collins's concern and described the situation as Perry had presented it. After a brief silence, he asked me what I would suggest.

"Well, Martin," I replied uncomfortably, "I'm just a messenger in this situation, not an advocate."

"I understand," he said, "but I'd still welcome your advice."

Rape, at least at that time, was a capital offense in Florida. Without any forethought at all, I found myself saying, "I'm a great admirer of your forthright stand against capital punishment. Maybe if you reaffirmed that in this context it would add to the moral force of your position."

There was another silence on the line. Then King said slowly, "That's a very thoughtful suggestion. Of course, I'd have to discuss it with the host group in Tallahassee. It's their occasion, and I wouldn't want to surprise or embarrass them." I murmured agreement, and we wished each other good night.

The next day, I called my friend John Popham, the peripatetic southern correspondent for the *New York Times*, to ask him to alert his city desk to the speech. By the time I reached him, the deadline for regional news had expired, but we thought it was worth a try. If King should act on my suggestion, it seemed only fair that he get some favorable notice along with the brickbats that would surely come his way. The following morning's *Times* did carry a brief news item on the Tallahassee speech. As I recall, it said simply that King had commented on the rape trial, reminding his audience that the death penalty was a moral wrong whether inflicted on a white or a black, one guilty of a heinous crime or one falsely accused. The Tallahassee defendants were convicted and sentenced to prison terms.

That was not the only time I found myself in the role of intercessor with King. In 1960, I became involved as one of several go-betweens in an effort to resolve the stalemate in Atlanta between the black student protestors, with whom King had made common cause, and the white merchants who maintained segregated eating facilities. The chief obstacle to a settlement was the wounded ego of the city's biggest department store magnate, Dick Rich, who felt his store had been unfairly singled out as the main target of the demonstrations. As a result, he adamantly refused to negotiate with the protestors, emphatically including King.

In response to prodding by Ivan Allen Jr., president of the Atlanta Chamber of Commerce, Rich finally conceded that there was one black leader—and only one—who would be acceptable to him as chief negotiator. This was Austin T. Walden, an elderly lawyer who had long spearheaded the black community's efforts to win change through conventional means—by resort to the courts and the voting booths. Walden was highly esteemed by his contemporaries and peers in the adult black community, but was viewed by the student activists—unfairly, in my opinion—as an old fogey, if not an Uncle Tom.

It fell to me to get King's reaction to Rich's grudging concession. Once again, I found myself telephoning him at home, this time on a Saturday afternoon. As we began our conversation, a racket broke out at his end of the line; the din of children laughing and shrieking all but drowned us out. King asked me to excuse him for a moment, turned away from the telephone, and bawled at the top of his voice, "If you chillun don't stop all this fuss, I'm gonna whop your behinds!" Then, in his usual stately tones, he resumed, "Now, Harold, where were we?"

I couldn't resist twitting him a bit. "Martin, that didn't sound very nonviolent to me!"

"We-e-ell," he replied, "in the bosom of your own family it's hard to practice what you preach."

When I finished describing Ivan Allen's initiative and Dick Rich's stubborn position, he promptly brushed aside my misgivings.

"Don't worry about it for a moment," he said. "It's not at all important for me to be involved in the negotiation. I have the greatest respect for Colonel Walden, and he'll have my wholehearted support."

In the end, however, King *was* involved, and in a crucially important way. When the agreement between the business leaders and Walden's negotiating team was made public, many of the students greeted it with anger and derision. In essence, the merchants promised to desegregate the eating facilities simultaneously with the court-ordered desegregation of the city's public schools the following September. In return, the black negotiators promised an immediate end to the "boycotts, reprisals, picketing, and sit-ins, and to bring back a condition of complete normalcy as soon as possible." This was seen by the dissident students as an abject surrender to the white power structure.

In an effort to resolve the controversy in the black community, a mass meeting was held in one of the large black churches. The debate was loud and rancorous. The older, "establishment" leaders who rose to defend the agreement were all but shouted down. King arrived late, just in time to see his father, the Reverend M. L. King Sr. (later popularly known as "Daddy" King) silenced by boos and catcalls. In a rare display of anger, Martin chastised the crowd for succumbing to the "cancer of disunity."

"If this contract is broken, it will be a disaster and a disgrace," he thundered. "If anyone breaks this contract, let it be the white man!"

His passionate statement left the assemblage awed and chastened. The settlement was approved without further challenge, and the "contract" was subsequently honored by the parties on both sides.

Three years after these events, in 1963, the sympathy and admiration I had come to feel for King made it all the more painful to witness what appeared to be the declining fortunes of his crusade. In retrospect, it is possible to discern a pattern in which even the setbacks and defeats of that period were building toward a great surge in the advancement of civil rights. At the time, however, the inevitability of such an advance was anything but self-evident.

In the several preceding years a succession of racial brush fires could at any time have exploded into a raging, uncontrolled conflagration, beginning with the freedom rides of 1961. The enrollment of James Meredith at the University of Mississippi in September of 1962 led to a fearful night of rioting that came to a sullen end only after the belated arrival of federal troops. In 1963, the fiery rhetoric of black militant H. Rap Brown at a Cambridge, Maryland, rally turned that sleepy town into a mob scene. Medgar Evers, the dedicated young leader of the Mississippi NAACP, was killed by an assassin's bullet in front of his home in Jackson; at his funeral, a massive race riot was barely averted. These were only some of the most notable and well-publicized incidents. In scores of

other communities, black protests and the prospect of school desegregation were met with threats and violence.

None of the centers of die-hard resistance surpassed Birmingham in
the ruthlessness with which it punished any show of black discontent.
The Alabama steel town was the spiritual capital of the Ku Klux Klan
and other hate groups. Within a six-year period, fifty cross-burnings
and eighteen bombings in the black community went unpunished. The
official local guardian of the racist status quo was the flamboyant police commissioner Eugene Theophilus "Bull" Connor—the same public
official who had withheld police protection from the freedom riders,
reportedly expressing the hope that they would be beaten "until it looks
like a bulldog got ahold of them."

On April 2, 1963, declaring Birmingham the "symbol of segregation,"
King launched a campaign of demonstrations and boycotts designed to
force the hand of the city's business leadership. Bull Connor responded
with mass arrests of the demonstrators, ultimately including King himself. As King languished in jail and Connor continued his wholesale arrests, the number of marchers dwindled away; the protest appeared to
be hopelessly bogged down.

In near desperation, King and his lieutenants felt it was imperative to
force Connor to show his true barbaric colors. They adopted a course of
action that they had previously rejected as dangerous and unwise, fully
aware that it would provoke harsh criticism, even from some blacks and
white sympathizers—they decided to include school-age youngsters in
their demonstrations. And so it was that television brought into living
rooms across the country the spectacle of black children being fire-hosed,
shocked with cattle prods, and savaged by Bull Connor's police dogs.

My reactions to this atrocity were summed up in a memorandum to
the Potomac board dated May 15, 1963. Since those views were shared by
a good many others of similar persuasion, they may bear quoting at
some length:

> The Birmingham demonstrations were a new departure in sev-
> eral ways. The deliberate involvement of children of high school age
> and younger was the key factor, almost without precedent; this
> sparked the adult community and added mass and excitement to the

theretofore desultory protests. It also led to some breakdown in the non-violent discipline of the effort, which was almost inevitable. In earlier community situations, whenever younger-than-college-age children have spontaneously joined the demonstrations, rock-throwing and other minor forms of violence have broken out. It is for this reason that the protest leadership has consciously excluded the younger group from demonstrations.

The turnabout in Birmingham may alter the character of the movement, since it seems to signify a decision on the part of King et al. that whatever risk is involved is more than offset by the invigoration of the demonstrations through more youthful participation. For the first time, the protesters succeeded in literally filling the jails to overflowing. The violent reaction of the Negro community to the bombings of last Saturday night was a measure of how much tension and excitement were generated. The related events in other cities represented an expectable contagion, and probably presage much more of the same. The Administration was slow to respond to the growing explosiveness of the situation. At least in part, this was because of disapproval of King's timing, which Bobby Kennedy openly criticized, to no evident effect except to anger the Negroes who were by that time solidly committed. Once involved, Justice was determined to put all its chips on negotiation and conciliation. The President in his news conference of May 8 disclaimed all authority for more direct intervention and was hypercareful to say nothing derogatory of Birmingham segregationists; his bland comments further exasperated the civil rights group. Meanwhile, Burke Marshall was working diligently at negotiation in Birmingham—with surprisingly effective results, under the circumstances. Buttressing his efforts was a lot of quiet effort by Bobby Kennedy and other cabinet officers and their staffs to bring positive influence to bear on white Birmingham leadership, through everything from U.S. Steel to the Yale law school alumni.

This earnest effort to activate the economic "power structure" was all to the good. But it was the grossest over-optimism to rely exclusively on this approach, or to suppose that the shaky agreement finally reached could resolve the problem. The President, by denying all authority to intervene, put his aides in the position of negotiating from weakness. Moreover, they were trying to achieve a settlement among private parties (of whom most of the whites were afraid even to reveal their identity) in the face of openly defiant official-dom at both state and local levels. This has never worked anywhere, and anyone who knows Birmingham could hardly expect it to work there. Here, for what they are worth, are some of the conclusions that I think can be drawn from the Birmingham experience:

1. The Administration should accept the fact that troops trained in mob control must be present on a stand-by basis in Mississippi and Alabama for the foreseeable future. If the President had alerted the troops a week earlier than he did—at the point when Wallace's state troopers first entered Birmingham—some of the violence might have been averted. It would have served notice on Governor Wallace, "Bull" Connor, and the public at large that the Federal Government meant business. It would have had a calming and reas-suring effect on the Negro community, which under the circum-stances felt it must take matters into its own hands.

2. The President should either acknowledge that he has the au-thority to intervene effectively in such situations as Birmingham or he should vigorously seek such authority from Congress. This should include not only authority to use troops but also the power to initiate legal actions to protect civil rights—the old Title III that Eisenhower once tried to get, but Kennedy has up to now indicated he doesn't want. He is in an untenable position saying on the one hand that he is helpless, and on the other that he neither needs nor wants more authority.

3. The conciliation function is too important to be done on an ad hoc, trouble-shooting basis by Burke Marshall and his associates, who are already grievously overburdened by their proper duties. There are many techniques to be used, on a preventive rather than merely reactive basis. A top-level conciliator is needed on the White House staff. He should have all the backing and prestige that the Presidency commands, and might rely on the Civil Rights Com-

mission for detailed staff work. Obviously he would have to work in close coordination with Burke Marshall and the Justice Department.

For the good of the Administration itself as well as that of the country, these steps or others like them should be taken soon. Otherwise, we can only look forward to a chaotic series of national crises. The direction and nature of race relations will be in the hands of whoever can and will make the issue in the most explosive way.

Bull Connor's display of police brutality and the national outburst of revulsion it provoked did not cause the administration to take the kind of steps that I and others had urged. But the Birmingham atrocity had a much more profound effect—it moved the president to reexamine his position on civil rights legislation. Against all his political instincts and against the advice of some of his closest advisers, he concluded that he must champion a strong civil rights bill, and do so on moral grounds, whatever the consequences.

On June 11, 1963, he took the case to the American public in a television speech as forceful and eloquent as any he had delivered. I recall vividly the satisfaction I felt as I listened to his concluding words:

> One hundred years of delay have passed since President Lincoln freed the slaves, yet their heirs, their grandsons, are not fully free. They are not yet freed from the bonds of injustice. They are not yet freed from social and economic oppression. And this Nation, for all its hopes and all its boasts, will not be fully free until all its citizens are free.
>
> Now the time has come for this nation to fulfill its promise. The events in Birmingham and elsewhere have so increased the cries for equality that no city or state or legislative body can prudently choose to ignore them.
>
> We face, therefore, a moral crisis as a country and as a people. It cannot be met by repressive police action. It cannot be left to increased demonstrations in the streets. It cannot be quieted by token moves or talk. It is a time to act in Congress, in your state and local legislative bodies and, above all, in all of our daily lives.

> Next week I shall ask the Congress of the United States to act, to make a commitment it has not fully made in this century to the proposition that race has no place in American life or law.

The package President Kennedy submitted to Congress would (1) prohibit exclusion based on race from restaurants, hotels, stores, places of amusement, and other public accommodations; (2) authorize the attorney general to file suits to require desegregation of schools and colleges; (3) empower the federal government to withhold funds from discriminatory programs and institutions; (4) give the president's Committee on Equal Employment Opportunity statutory authority to require government contractors to practice fair employment; (5) create a federal Community Relations Service to help resolve racial disputes through mediation and negotiation.

The bill was a vast improvement over any legislative proposals the administration would have considered even a few months earlier. But in the view of civil rights advocates, it still had some glaring deficiencies. They wanted a more comprehensive fair employment provision ("FEPC" was then the operative term) that would ban discrimination not just by government contractors but by all employers of significant size. Another conspicuous omission was a title prohibiting discrimination in housing. There were also many points of contention as to whether the various enforcement provisions were too strong or too weak. These and other features of the bill would be the subjects of continuing debate, negotiation, revision, and bipartisan consensus building for a full year before a law was finally enacted.

CHAPTER 9 ▪ *Marching and Mourning*

THE BEGINNING OF A do-or-die struggle for passage of civil rights legislation made it more urgent than ever that the major civil rights leaders resolve their differences and forge a more cooperative relationship. Stephen Currier had grown increasingly concerned about this problem. He saw more clearly than most the extent to which tension and divisiveness in the movement grew out of the organizations' competition for funds. Characteristically, he decided to step in where other philanthropic angels feared to tread.

On the morning that brought the news of Medgar Evers's murder, Currier invited Whitney Young and Roy Wilkins to his office to see whether there might be useful steps to take. As a result of that discussion he sent telegrams to scores of key corporate and foundation leaders, inviting them to breakfast with civil rights leaders on one of two dates in June. Young, Wilkins, James Farmer, Martin Luther King, Jack Greenberg, and Dorothy Height made presentations. At the second breakfast King's "Letter from a Birmingham Jail" was read.

The response was positive and required vehicles to receive the funds. Two were organized: one, the Committee for Welfare, Education, and Legal Defense (WELD) was for tax-exempt purposes. A second, named the Council for United Civil Rights Leadership (CUCRL), was to raise money for necessary, but non-tax-exempt, purposes. Currier then hosted an ongoing series of luncheon meetings at which the leadership decided how the money should be divided and spent. Currier and Whitney Young were named co-chairs of the new coalition, and Wiley Branton of the Voter Education Project was later drafted to serve as its staff director.

Currier lost no time in following through on his fund-raising commitment. Within a matter of weeks, CUCRL was able to announce an initial distribution of more than $500,000 out of some $1.5 million pledged. And though the new mechanism did not produce perfect harmony in the civil rights ranks, it did contribute to a greatly improved public display of unity.

This newly achieved accommodation was soon tested as the idea of a march on Washington gained currency. The proposal was put forward by A. Philip Randolph, the venerable head of the Brotherhood of Sleeping Car Porters, and his brilliant disciple Bayard Rustin. It was, in fact, the revival of a strategy conceived by Randolph twenty-two years earlier, which resulted in what might be called the most effective nonmarch of all time.

Shortly after America's entry into World War II, Randolph had urged President Roosevelt to set up a Fair Employment Practices Committee to assure that black workers would be equitably included in the wartime industrial expansion. When Roosevelt demurred, Randolph threatened to organize a massive march on the nation's capital. Appalled by the potential for disruption and embarrassment of such a demonstration, the president capitulated and the march was aborted.

Randolph and Rustin felt that the time was ripe to resurrect the wartime strategy, thereby forcing President Kennedy to put the full power of his office behind civil rights and job opportunities for blacks, and disadvantaged whites as well. Getting a consensus among the civil rights leaders was not an easy task. King was attracted to the idea but conceived of a march in the nonviolent but confrontational spirit of Birmingham, a view that was shared by Jim Farmer of CORE and John Lewis of SNCC. Whitney Young of the Urban League was concerned that a huge demonstration might degenerate into disorder and violence that would discredit the civil rights cause. Roy Wilkins of the NAACP was outspokenly cool to the proposal; his first priority was passage of the president's civil rights package, and he was unpersuaded that a turnout of blacks and white liberals, however huge, would improve its chances in Congress.

Labor and religious groups also had their doubts. The American Federation of Labor–Congress of Industrial Organizations (AFL-CIO) flatly refused to endorse the march, but the United Auto Workers pledged its support and was represented on the steering committee by its president, Walter Reuther. The committee was further expanded to include three prominent religious leaders: Eugene Carson Blake of the National Council of Churches, Rabbi Joachim Prinz, and Matthew Ahmann, an activist Catholic layman.

The negotiations that followed from mid-June to mid-July were a classic exercise in the art of compromise, designed to win the endorsement of the doubters and allay the fears of the faint-hearted. Among the resulting reassurances were these:

(1) The route of the march would be confined to the Mall, between the Washington Monument and the Lincoln Memorial (safely removed from the precincts of Congress on the Hill).

(2) The guiding principle of the march would be nonviolence, but not civil disobedience. There would be no disruption of transportation or other such provocative behavior.

(3) The sponsors of the march explicitly rejected "the aid or participation of totalitarian or subversive groups of all persuasions." Organizational participation was invited only from "the established civil rights organizations, from major religious and fraternal groups, and from labor unions."

(4) Extraordinary measures would be taken to maintain order and discipline. Specially trained marshals and black police volunteers from New York would help the local police keep the peace.

(5) The only placards permitted would be those prepared or approved by march personnel.

(6) The out-of-town marchers—then predicted at some 100,000—would be funneled into the city on the morning of the march and decanted toward home by nightfall.

(7) The committee of co-chairmen would seek a friendly audience with the president at the conclusion of the ceremonies.

One highly charged issue that posed a special threat to unity was resolved with Solomonic ingenuity. This was the question of who would serve as director of the march. The logical choice, by almost any standard, was Bayard Rustin, whose skill and experience as an organizer were formidable and who had the insistent backing of the elder statesman of the movement, A. Philip Randolph. Roy Wilkins, however, declared himself unalterably opposed to that choice. He argued that Rustin's background would be exploited by the enemies of the movement, probably with consequences fatal to the success of the march. (Rustin had served a prison term for refusing to perform military service, had been accused in earlier years of communist affiliations, and was once arrested on a charge of committing a homosexual act.) Even King and Farmer conceded that public attacks on Rustin's character might be extremely damaging. The impasse was broken by Whitney Young, who proposed that Randolph be named director, with the right to choose whomever he wished as his deputy. Of course, Randolph was unanimously elected. And, of course, he promptly named Rustin as his deputy.

Among those strenuously opposed to the march were the Kennedy brothers and their advisers. When the plan was first publicly announced, the president quickly convened a meeting at the White House with the civil rights leaders. He opened the discussion with a strong statement on the precarious status of the civil rights bill and the danger of offending senators and congressmen whose votes were crucial.

"We want success in Congress, not just a big show at the Capitol," he reportedly said. "Some of these people are looking for an excuse to be against us. I don't want to give any of them a chance to say, 'Yes, I'm for the bill but I'm damned if I will vote for it at the point of a gun.'" Vice President Johnson, who was also in attendance, vigorously seconded the president's warning.

Randolph, Farmer, and King strongly defended the march. King concluded with the observation, "It may seem ill-timed. Frankly, I have never engaged in any direct action movement which did not seem ill-timed. Some people thought Birmingham ill-timed."

"Including the Attorney General," the president added good-humoredly.

The meeting ended inconclusively, but shortly afterward Kennedy's pragmatic bent led him to do an about-face. Perceiving that the march, with or without his approval, was inevitable, he wisely concluded that the administration should put itself in position to protect its stake in a positive and harmonious outcome. Accordingly, he gave the march his public blessing and assigned Assistant Attorney General John Douglas as the administration's liaison to the planning process.

As the participants and millions of television viewers could testify, the march was a triumph of meticulous planning and flawless execution. The number of marchers—variously estimated at two hundred fifty thousand upward—exceeded all expectations. For those of us lucky enough to be there, it was an unforgettable experience. The singing and some of the oratory—notably, of course, King's "I have a dream" speech—were inspiring. Equally moving was the spirit of good fellowship and common cause that animated the throng of marchers, black and white, women and men, old and young. All apprehension about untoward incidents soon melted away in the warm August air.

The march was not hailed by everyone as a victory for the civil rights cause. Some critics charged that it was a mere puppet show, with the Kennedys and their wealthy white friends pulling the strings. The fiery Black Muslim leader Malcolm X referred to it scornfully as "the farce on Washington," whose organizers had been brought to heel by "the white man's money." Some SNCC members spurned the carefully ordered events of the march, choosing instead to picket the Justice Department.

These and other critics of the affair found added justification for their views in the dispute that arose over the advance text of John Lewis's speech. As the spokesman for SNCC, Lewis probably reflected the views of most of his comrades when he wrote that the administration's civil rights bill was "too little, too late" and posed the angry question, "Which side is the federal government on?" But the older leaders found such rhetoric unacceptably harsh and out of keeping with the purpose of the march. Lewis resisted their efforts to "censor" his remarks, yielding only at the last minute to their insistence that he moderate his language.

Retrospective analyses have kept criticisms of the march alive. Godfrey Hodgson concluded his comparatively mild critique this way: "But essentially Malcolm [X] was not wrong. The march was manipulated by the federal government and by white liberals for their own purposes, generous as these may have been . . . [T]he Kennedy administration did manipulate the march to its own purposes. It is not surprising, therefore, that even that shining symbol of unity, upon closer inspection, hints at the instability of the liberal coalition."[8]

Murray Kempton, the liberal New York columnist, also smelled cooptation. "If the march was important," he wrote, "it was because it represented an acceptance of the Negro revolt as part of the American myth, and so an acceptance of the revolutionaries into the American establishment. That acceptance, of course, carries with it the hope that the

Negro revolt will stop where it is. Yet that acceptance is also the most powerful incentive and assurance that the revolt will continue."

The detractors may be right in arguing that the march changed no minds in Congress and did not significantly enhance prospects for passage of the civil rights act. It is true that in the immediate aftermath of the march the political arithmetic showed no signs of improving. What might have happened in the longer run we will never know, for three months later an assassin's bullet in Dallas drastically changed the political equation.

Yet to dismiss the march—as some have done—as merely a slick piece of stage management calculated to tranquilize the civil rights movement seems to me unduly cynical. The march was a living demonstration of some possibilities that badly needed affirmation. It showed that large numbers of Americans of diverse ancestry could be rallied under the banner of human rights. It showed that racial harmony, even on a monumental scale, was not just a visionary dream, but could be a realistic goal. And it showed that even the harshest grievances could be forcefully protested with civility and good humor. It is for these reasons that the march is still commemorated more than twenty-five years later as a high point of the peaceful civil rights revolution. It is hard to believe that so memorable a happening had no lasting effect on the nation's conscience.

As a rule, Americans who are old enough to recall Friday, November 22, 1963, can tell you exactly where they were and what they were doing when they heard that the president had been shot. Most of them got the word in the company of others, which, I imagine, made it easier to accept the reality of the macabre news. By chance, I was alone and only yards from the White House, which lent the assassination report an eerie, hallucinatory quality. Returning from a NAIRO conference in Cleveland, I had boarded an airplane at midday, flown to National Airport, reclaimed my car, and was driving to my office. Wrapped in the meditative cocoon of the traveler, I only dimly registered that the streets were strangely empty, almost devoid of cars and people. As I skirted the White House, the grounds were deserted. Then I noticed that the flag was at half mast.

Wondering idly what aged dignitary had died, I flipped on the car radio and heard, ". . . has confirmed that the President is dead." The announcer's voice, inappropriately matter-of-fact, went on to recount the fateful sequence of events in Dallas. My first confused thought was that there must be some mistake. Surely so dreadful an occurrence could not have gone unnoticed or unmentioned in the teeming world of travel I had just left. Did the pilot of the plane and the flight attendants know? Did any of the other passengers? The airport personnel? Why were people not out on the streets commiserating with each other? With some effort, I brought the car to a halt at the curb. For some time I sat there, gazing at the seemingly deserted White House and wondering if and when it would come to life again.

The sense of disorientation continued for me and millions of others through the weekend, intensified by Jack Ruby's murder of Lee Harvey Oswald on live television. Only much later, after endless hours of television images and commentary had turned tragedy into tedium, did the grisly drama in Dallas begin to lose its aura of unreality.

David Brinkley summed it up this way: "The events of those days don't fit, you can't place them anywhere, they don't go in the intellectual luggage of our time. It was too big, too sudden, too overwhelming, and it meant too much. It has to be separate and apart." Yet, all too soon, this awful singularity would fade; similar horrors would be played back on the small screen, like a recurring national nightmare.

In the days that followed, the man whom fate had so rudely thrust into the presidency was the object of much uneasy speculation. Lyndon Johnson was not a widely admired public figure. Many of John F. Kennedy's associates had never been reconciled to him as vice president. In the wake of the assassination they made little effort to conceal their resentment of the crude Texas political manipulator who had supplanted their fallen leader. Foreign policy experts and heads of state shuddered over Johnson's inexperience and lack of sophistication in the international arena. Pundits assessed the danger of a major crisis of public confidence. As Johnson himself would later bitterly remark, "For millions of Americans, I was still illegitimate, a naked man with no presidential covering, a pretender to the throne, an illegal usurper."

Among those beset by doubts and fears were the leaders of the civil rights movement. Their quarrels with John Kennedy had revolved about issues of timing and strategy rather than essential values. They had no doubt that he was personally sympathetic to their goals, and they had lately been heartened by his endorsement of the march on Washington and his new-found willingness to do battle for meaningful civil rights legislation.

Lyndon Johnson, by contrast, was an ambiguous figure. During his long tenure in Congress, he had been identified in the public mind with the powerful southern bloc. Although as Senate majority leader he had departed from tradition by engineering the passage of the first civil rights legislation of this century, that did little to establish him as a principled champion of civil rights. The 1957 law was a product of artful compromise and, as such, was necessarily much watered-down. Six years after enactment, it was more often cited for its limitations than its boldness. Moreover, in Kennedy's shadow as vice president, Johnson had added little luster to his civil rights image. His one major activity in that field (as chairman of the president's Committee on Equal Opportunity) had been clouded by controversy between those who favored strong enforcement and those who preferred to rely on the good will and promises of employers. Johnson's affinity with the latter faction brought him into sharp conflict with Robert Kennedy and other liberal members of the committee.

For all these reasons, civil rights advocates regarded the new president with misgivings. Johnson, obviously anticipating their lack of confidence, moved swiftly to dispel it. Despite the awesome pressures upon him during his first hectic weeks in the White House, he made a point of meeting with the major civil rights leaders, first singly, then as a group.

The members of the Council for United Civil Rights Leadership gathered at the Potomac Institute shortly before their group meeting with Johnson at the White House. Chatting with them as they arrived, I was struck by their air of tension and uneasiness. Although they had been at pains in their public statements to express confidence in the new president, their private views were not so sanguine. Whitney Young, in particular, was volubly pessimistic, and the others were only slightly less so. When they returned later, however, their mood had vastly improved. They reported that the meeting was a great success. Johnson had committed himself to a no-holds-barred drive for passage of the civil rights bill and had assured them that no issue would have higher priority in his administration.

Johnson was true to his pledge. In his first presidential address to Congress, he declared that "no memorial or eulogy could more eloquently honor President Kennedy's memory than the earliest possible passage of the civil-rights bill, for which he fought so long."

From that moment on, the question generally posed was not whether, but when, the civil rights act would become the law of the land.

CHAPTER 10 ▪ *The Compliance Underground*

THE OLD SOUTHERN war horses in Congress found themselves in an unaccustomed position. Their power to block unwelcome legislation, long taken for granted, was suddenly in doubt. Arrayed against them in the civil rights battle was not just the usual coterie of liberals, but also their shrewd former colleague Lyndon B. Johnson, now cloaked in the majesty of the presidency and strongly supported by those Americans who were eager to see John F. Kennedy memorialized by passage of the bill he had initiated.

The civil rights coalition had also acquired a formidable new look. Its Washington lobby was still the Leadership Conference on Civil Rights, an association of more than seventy civil rights, labor, civic, and religious organizations. Among its leading figures were NAACP executive director Roy Wilkins; Clarence Mitchell, the NAACP's influential Washington representative; Joseph L. Rauh Jr., that indomitable champion of liberal causes; Arnold Aronson of the Jewish National Community Relations Advisory Council; Marvin Caplan, of the CIO's Industrial Union Department; and Andrew Biemiller, chief lobbyist of the AFL-CIO.

The new dimension was a freshly mobilized army of constituents—many of them recruited by Protestant, Catholic, and Jewish groups to augment newly activated black voters, students and civil rights workers—in states and communities throughout the country. Never before or since has the national civil rights lobby commanded such political potency at the grassroots. Even the congressmen from conservative districts with few or no minority residents had to take heed.

One measure of this new order was the extent of bipartisan backing for the civil rights bill. The managers of the legislation recognized that without strong support on both sides of the aisle there was no hope of success; there were simply not enough favorable Democratic votes to pass the bill. In the end, two Republican leaders—William McCulloch of Ohio in the House and Everett Dirksen of Illinois in the Senate—would marshal a healthy majority of their party members behind the bill.

The segregationists on the Hill were pessimistic but determined to wage their customary war of attrition. Their main reliance in the House was "Judge" Howard W. Smith, the Virginia octogenarian who wielded despotic power as chairman of the mighty Rules Committee. For years, his decision to bury a bill had consigned it to a lingering death; his committee had thus become known as the graveyard of civil rights legislation. This time, however, he could do no more than delay for a few weeks. Faced with the president's determination to bypass him and his committee if necessary, he grudgingly allowed the civil rights bill to be reported out.

The House moved at record speed to pass the measure. In only eleven days, 122 amendments, most of them aimed at weakening the bill, were voted down. Of 28 amendments accepted, none materially diluted the bill and several actually strengthened it.

Judge Smith still had one last trump card to play—one he hoped might even lead to the bill's defeat. As the debate neared its close, he exultantly introduced his prize amendment. It added to the prohibition on employment discrimination because of "race, religion or national origin" the single word "sex." Immediately and enthusiastically endorsed by the women members, the amendment was adopted. Some of the more sexist representatives doubtless swallowed hard, but in one of the memorable ironies of legislative history, the House proceeded to pass the bill, including Judge Smith's cunning amendment, by a vote of 290 to 130. Much to his surprise, the old Virginia conservative found that he had given women's liberation a big boost.

A more arduous and extended struggle still lay ahead in the Senate, where the southerners had readied their ultimate weapon, the filibuster. This rule of the upper chamber permitting unlimited debate was originally intended to ensure that a strongly held minority view would get a full and fair hearing. It had long been used by the southerners to talk to death any bill that threatened the racial traditions of their region. Although their prospects for victory in this instance were less bright than usual, a filibuster still served their purpose. Even if they could not kill the measure, they stood a good chance of forcing a weary majority to accept amendments that would nullify its strongest provisions. Most objectionable to the opponents were Title II on desegregation of public accommodations and Title VII on equal employment opportunity, or "FEPC" as they preferred to call it. If these could be stripped from the bill, passage of the remainder would be a Pyrrhic victory for the civil rights forces.

The Potomac Institute could do little to influence this protracted battle of verbosity. We had no grassroots battalions with which to impress the Congress, and in any case, we were precluded by our tax-exempt status from engaging in legislative lobbying. There was another, related role, however, for which our kind of operation was well suited. That role was to lay the groundwork for peaceful compliance before and after the bill became law, which was especially critical with respect to the public accommodations title. Unlike other provisions, this one would take full effect as soon as the bill was signed. At that moment, thousands of white-only establishments, many of them in the most recalcitrant areas of the South, would be legally required to begin serving individuals of all races. Widespread defiance could mean black-white confrontations and turmoil on an unprecedented scale.

Despite Lyndon Johnson's speedy emergence as "the civil rights President," the Justice Department continued to be the command center for federal action in that area. And despite the bitter personal relationship between Johnson and Robert Kennedy, Kennedy and his team were still in charge of the department. Thus it fell to them to manage the federal initiative to avert massive noncompliance with the prospective law. In doing so, they built on a precedent set in mid-1963, shortly after President Kennedy issued his call for stronger legislation. This was a series of White House meetings called by the president and attended by influential representatives of the private sector and state and local government—business executives, heads of women's groups, prominent lawyers, labor leaders, governors, mayors, and others. Spurred by the president's exhortations, the participants organized several new national efforts, including a Mayor's Community Relations Service (headed by John Feild), a

Lawyers' Committee for Civil Rights Under Law (co-chaired by Bernard Siegel and Harrison Tweed), and an ad hoc group of business leaders.

Potomac had figured in a modest way in this process; some of our "how-to" publications (*State Executive Authority to Promote Civil Rights,* for one) were handed out to the White House invitees. A friend who attended one of the sessions commented wistfully, "I wish I could get the President to be my distributor."

Operation Compliance

Now, in early 1964, a similar but more sharply focused public/private effort was needed. We took part in several planning sessions with Burke Marshall and his colleagues at Justice and Leslie Dunbar of the Southern Regional Council about how such an effort might be put together. Since the bill was expected to pass within three or four months, there was no time to create elaborate structures or procedures. Fortunately, there were already a good many organizations that could be expected to join in a concerted effort to promote voluntary compliance. Our plan was to work out an appropriate division of labor among our three agencies, select thirty to forty pilot southern cities for concentrated effort and mobilize for that purpose as many existing national and local groups as possible.

Within a few weeks, the project, which we labeled "Operation Compliance," was making headway. The Justice Department's guiding hand in the operation was Assistant Attorney General Louis Oberdorfer, a native of Birmingham, a shrewd strategist, and an efficient manager. Under his direction, Justice assembled a mass of city-by-city detail on the status of desegregation, the location and racial policies of major retail chains and their southern outlets, and the posture of local officials and private citizens whose influence in their communities was crucial.

Oberdorfer had also established a close working relationship with a group of national business executives whose southern affiliates and franchises were squarely in the battle zone. These men did not limit their efforts to their own corporate operations; they also made themselves available for meetings with economic and political leaders in the pilot cities. One of the most active and effective of the business "missionaries" was the president of the Manger hotel chain, Julius Manger, whose combination of charm, good will, and pragmatism won over many a wavering local business leader.

The Southern Regional Council coordinated the activities of some twenty-five organizations with southwide constituencies, as well as dozens of state and local human relations committees. For each pilot city, a representative of one of these groups acted as local coordinator of community activities. The council's headquarters in Atlanta served this organizational network as a clearinghouse for information and materials, a convener of frequent strategy meetings, and a link to the press.

The Justice Department was the logical choice to coordinate the activities of federal departments and agencies. The informal strategy committee for the project that met periodically at Justice included, in addition to the business and other nongovernmental participants, senior officials of the Commerce, Labor, Defense, and other departments, as well as the White House and the Civil Rights Commission. Their job was to relate the policies, programs, and community relations of their agencies to the goals of the compliance effort. Since most of them had important operations in the South, their collective local influence there was considerable.

Potomac provided a kind of overall secretariat for the project. We met regularly with the Justice Department team and key people from the other federal agencies, as well as the ad hoc business group. In addition, Potomac convened officials of national organizations that had constituencies or influence in the South, including their representatives in a regional caucus called the Southern Interagency Conference. It was our responsibility to assure that these various groups received each other's reports and intelligence on the pilot cities. We were also expected to see to the preparation and distribution of useful background material and publications, such as an explanatory summary of the civil rights bill and a statement of the case for voluntary compliance.

The basic and most widely distributed piece was an eight-page flyer titled *Service for All Citizens*. Into it we squeezed a description of the terms and probable effects of the public accommodations title, its moral and economic significance, and suggested steps to orderly and effective community desegregation. This topical breakdown faithfully reflected the strategy we were pursuing in "Operation Compliance," aimed at appealing simultaneously to respect for the law, moral convictions, the spirit of fair play, successful precedents, economic self-interest, and concern for the well-being of the community.

Invoking this combination of values came naturally to long-time southern proponents of racial change, black and white, such as those who made up the Southern Regional Council. For decades they had had to carry on their efforts in an overwhelmingly hostile climate. All the instruments of power and authority in the region were pitted against them. For many years even the national government openly sanctioned discrimination and segregation. A few courageous and uncompromising white southerners denounced racism in all its manifestations as the evil it was; but those who could not be silenced were soon ostracized and ignored.

Less confrontational dissenters, despite their paucity of numbers and power, had one significant point of leverage—the inconsistencies and contradictions inherent in the doctrine of white supremacy itself. It was this phenomenon that inspired the title of Gunnar Myrdal's monumental study of race relations in this country, *An American Dilemma,* published in 1944. Myrdal laid heavy emphasis on the clash of moral values posed by oppression of the black minority on the one hand, and the American ideal of "liberty and justice for all" on the other.

This inner conflict was real enough for many white southerners, but it was not enough by itself to induce them to accept basic reforms. Not until the mid-fifties did they have to grapple seriously with a dilemma that could not be evaded or wished away. Beginning with the U.S. Supreme Court's school desegregation order of 1954, it became increasingly plain that blacks would settle for nothing less than full equality and that whites would have to pay dearly for a last-ditch defense of the racial status quo.

In this new era of painful options, southern communities found themselves faced with a choice of desegregated public schools or no public schools at all, racially open public accommodations or jails overflowing with protesters, black balloting or something akin to federal occupation, economic progress or the stagnation produced by picketing, boycotts, and social disorder. The main struggle was no longer between subjugated blacks and all-powerful whites, or between a handful of idealists and a huge complacent majority. As the hard practical choices proliferated, the conflict was increasingly *within* the white majority, between those who urged defiance at any price and those who were unwilling to dismantle the society rather than accommodate to inevitable change.

In short, the old moral dilemma of the South had taken on a new dimension of self-interest. As James McBride Dabbs, a great southern humanitarian, put it: "The time is ripe for change when justice and expediency meet." My favorite example of this truism occurred when the town fathers of Hoxie, Arkansas, resolved in 1954 to proceed voluntarily to desegregate their public school system. The mayor gave the following reasons for this unorthodox decision: "It's the law of the land, it's inevitable, it's God's will, and it's cheaper."

Our aim in Operation Compliance was to supply the kinds of practical as well as ethical arguments that would strengthen the hands—and the spines—of the so-called "moderates" of the region. Fortunately, we could point to some highly successful precedents for citizen action and forthright public leadership. In Atlanta, a sizable number of women joined together as "Partners for Progress" to get local restaurants, hotels, and theaters to open their doors to black patrons. They not only called on the owners of these establishments to desegregate, but pledged that they would patronize those who did and urge their friends and associates to do likewise.

In Charlotte, North Carolina, the board of directors of the Chamber of Commerce passed a resolution recommending that "all businesses in this community catering to the general public be opened immediately to all customers without regard to race, creed, or color." The Chamber directors also agreed to participate personally in desegregation. When a restaurant owner agreed to begin serving blacks if other members of the group brought blacks as guests, the mayor, a councilman, an editor, a minister, and a banker agreed to do so. Within two months, one hundred restaurants had opened their doors to patrons of all races. One of the participants told the *Charlotte Observer:* "These were Southern men. These were hard choices. But this was too good a town to have it ruined, and they just weren't going to have it."

Among the southern public officials who spoke out for voluntary desegregation were two whom I had dealt with in earlier racial crises—Ivan Allen Jr., by then mayor of Atlanta, and LeRoy Collins, governor of Florida. Allen braved the wrath of many of his constituents by testifying in Congress in favor of the public accommodations title.

> Are we going to say that it is all right for the Negro citizen to go into the bank on Main Street and to deposit her earnings or borrow money, then go to department stores to buy what he needs, to go to the supermarket to purchase food for his family, and so on along Main Street until he comes to a restaurant or hotel . . . [Then] are we going to say that it is right and legal for the operators of these businesses, merely as a matter of convenience, to insist that the Negro's citizenship be changed and that, as a second-class citizen he is to be refused service? I submit that it is not right to allow an American's citizenship to be changed merely as a matter of convenience.[9]

Allen further pointed out to the congressmen that voluntarism was not enough, that without the force of law one businessman could be unfairly penalized for doing the right thing while another could reap an economic benefit by continuing to discriminate.

Governor Collins had also confounded his fellow politicians when, in a Florida-wide broadcast, he branded segregated public facilities as unfair and immoral.

For several months, our compliance efforts had been carried on quietly. Still, considering the involvement of high-ranking government and corporate officials, it was remarkable that it remained unpublicized for as long as it did. As the civil rights bill moved closer to passage, however, our informal steering committee decided we should pull out all the stops, publicly as well as privately. We agreed to ask the president to lend his prestige to our business group by appointing them to a Temporary Business Advisory Committee on Community Relations. The new committee would then be announced by a mass mailing to public and private leaders in southern cities, urging them to prepare their communities for full compliance. While we were putting this plan into effect, an assiduous pair of Washington journalists got wind of our activities and broke the story in somewhat melodramatic terms. On May 27, Rowland Evans and Robert Novak reported in their syndicated column:

> Backed by the full prestige of President Johnson, a civil rights underground secretly is preparing the way to reduce disorder when the civil rights law takes effect this summer.
>
> Probably never in history has so much been attempted behind the scenes to encourage acceptance of a law before its passage. But never was the need greater. At issue here is violent change in culture and custom.
>
> Hotel, restaurant and theater chain executives have been traveling throughout the South, shrouded from public and press, to take soundings from Chambers of Commerce and bi-racial committees in more than 40 cities on the bill's explosive public accommodations section. . . .
>
> In direct contrast to the way massive resistance snowballed 10 years ago, the Administration hopes this year to set in motion a snowball of quick compliance.

A short time later, with President Johnson's official blessing, the "underground" dropped its shroud of secrecy and went public with a letter, signed by Julius Manger as chairman of the Temporary Advisory Committee and widely distributed to southern community leaders. The letter laid heavy stress on the president's endorsement.

> In appointing the Committee, the President expressed the desire that we do everything possible to enlist the aid of business leaders and public officials in securing prompt and widespread compliance with the civil rights act—most particularly the Public Accommodations title—which is expected to be enacted shortly. . . .
>
> We realize that this type of leadership has already been effectively demonstrated in many towns and cities, even in the absence of a law. . . . As a result of such leadership, as of June 10, some privately owned facilities had been opened to everyone, regardless of race, in 397 Southern cities of over 10,000 population.
>
> Yet, even in the most advanced cities, a part of the job remains to be done, and in some it is the major part of the job. If the leader-

ship of your city has not already laid careful plans for achieving community-wide compliance, I urge you to direct your efforts to this end.

The letter closed with a reference to the "how-to" materials enclosed and the business committee's promise to respond to requests for further information or assistance.

Little time remained, however, for more advance efforts. On June 19, the Senate passed the final version of the civil rights bill by a vote of 73 to 27. On July 2, the House followed suit by a vote of 289 to 126, notwithstanding Rules Chairman Smith's dire warning that the result would be "hordes of beatniks, misfits and agitators from the North, with the admitted aid of the Communists, streaming into the Southland mischief-bent, backed and defended by other hordes of federal marshals, federal agents and federal power."

President Johnson signed the bill that same evening, urging all Americans "to join in this effort to bring justice and hope to all our people— and peace to our land."

CHAPTER 11 ∎ *The Way of the Peacemakers*

AT THE SIGNING ceremony for the Civil Rights Act, President Johnson announced that LeRoy Collins, who had completed his term as
governor of Florida, would head the federal Community Relations Service created by the act. His assignment, as the government's chief racial trouble-shooter, was to bring into being an agency for which there
was no blueprint. For guidance, he had only the very general language of
Title X, which mandated the service "to provide assistance to communities and persons therein in resolving disputes, disagreements, or difficulties relating to discriminatory practices based on race, color, or national
origin which impair the rights of persons in such communities under
the Constitution or laws of the United States or which affect or may affect
interstate commerce."

I soon discovered that Collins was not the only one who was about to
venture into this unmapped territory. A few days after the act was signed,
Stephen Currier attended a White House meeting at which the president
put in an appearance. Afterward, Currier and I met for lunch. He told me
that the president had taken him aside, flung an arm around his shoul-
ders, and murmured, "I need your man Fleming."

Johnson had gone on to explain that Governor Collins—along with
two other former southern governors, Buford Ellington of Tennessee
and Luther Hodges of North Carolina (by this time Secretary of Commerce)—would spend some weeks on a crash tour of the South making
speeches and conferring with governors and others on the need for peaceful compliance with the new law. Therefore, Collins would need a knowledgeable deputy who could mind the store and begin setting up the
Community Relations Service while he was on the road. The president
had been advised that I was right for the job.

Neither Currier nor I was enthusiastic about this proposition. We had committed ourselves to a nongovernmental operation, which we had no wish to abandon. On the other hand, we were reluctant, as were most people in those days, to refuse a presidential call to duty. The compromise we finally settled on was that I should accept the assignment on temporary loan from Potomac, for a period of not more than six months. Thus I would become the contemporary equivalent of a New Deal "dollar-a-year" executive.

The personnel office of the Department of Commerce, where the new agency would be lodged, was predictably unhappy about this unorthodox arrangement. They argued, among other things, that, not being a paid employee, I might expose the government to a liability risk by falling down a stairwell. The White House imperative prevailed, however, and I was shortly immured in the huge stone mausoleum that houses the Commerce Department.

As in the early days of Potomac, I found myself involved in a would-be agency that was little more than an idea, and a rather hazy idea at that. There was no table of organization, no permanent staff, no budget, and no funds; just a hastily assembled handful of federal workers, mostly from within Commerce, who had volunteered for temporary assignment to the amorphous new entity. Since Collins was away barnstorming much of the time, as expected, I was charged with the day-to-day responsibilities of putting the the new agency together.

As a rule, a newborn federal agency is allowed an initial period of grace in which to get organized before it is expected to become operational. The Community Relations Service (CRS) was an exception. Since the public accommodations title was effective immediately, CRS was supposed to be ready at once for any fire-fighting that might be required. Yet as complaints began to come in, we found ourselves in an awkward dilemma. Our statutory mandate would not permit us to turn away serious complainants with the excuse that we were not ready for business. Yet not only was our makeshift staff short on experienced investigators and mediators; there were no travel funds to send trouble-shooters into the field.

For a time, we made do with long-distance telephone calls billed to the Commerce Department. One of the few seasoned human relations practitioners then on the staff—Seymour Samet, a long-time professional with the American Jewish Committee—has reminded me of one of those early episodes.

Black residents of a town in Florida complained that a local drive-in theater segregated its patrons by means of a fence separating the "white" and "black" viewing areas. Samet talked by telephone with the proprietor, who heatedly denied that this arrangement was discriminatory. He maintained that it not only preserved harmonious relations between the races, but actually favored blacks, since they were charged a lower price of admission than whites. Samet patiently explained that the law did not recognize discounts as a justification for segregation. He warned the proprietor that if the illicit fence was not removed in short order, CRS would be obliged to take stern measures. He could only hope the man would not call his bluff.

The result was a standoff, which persisted for several days. Then one morning Samet received a call from the recalcitrant movie operator, who informed him that he didn't need to worry about that damn fence any more; a violent storm had erupted the previous night and blown it to smithereens.

"I didn't realize we had that kind of influence," Samet remarked.

Long-distance admonitions, even when abetted by acts of God, did not suffice for long. CRS faced its first major challenge when it was requested to intervene in a school desegregation case in St. Helena Parish, Louisiana. The case had dragged on in the courts for years. Repeatedly, the trial judge had refused to heed the charge of the Fifth Circuit Court of Appeals to order the local school board to proceed with desegregation. Finally, in this summer of 1964, the appeals court had informed the trial judge in the baldest of terms that further delay would not be countenanced. In response, the judge had ordered the board to desegregate its schools in September, ready or not, adding in effect that the blood of the school children would be on the hands of the appeals court. This abrupt and ill-tempered about-face raised the specter of racial chaos in the rural county, which had made no plans for orderly transition and had done nothing to prepare the community for the momentous changes that were now imminent.

It was not only die-hard segregationists who were dismayed by this turn of events. The White House and Democratic party leaders had their own cause for concern. Louisiana Congressman Hale Boggs, a party loyalist and highly respected House Democratic leader, was waging a pitched battle for reelection against a white-supremacist opponent. A racial explosion in the state at this critical stage of the campaign might well demolish his chances for victory. It was hardly a surprise, then, when a message arrived from the White House urgently requesting that Governor Collins talk with Congressman Boggs. After I filled in Collins by telephone, he instructed me to meet with the congressman and report back to him as soon as possible.

Boggs received me with typical southern geniality, putting me at ease (and presumably off my guard) with small talk laced with down-home humor. But once he got down to business, there was nothing casual about him. He made no bones about his political stake in the situation. Yet he wanted Governor Collins to understand that he was concerned about more than his own political fortunes. His position in the House could be vital to the success or failure of the administration's legislative program, including its social agenda, which was even more vital for blacks than for whites. He wanted the law of the land to prevail, but not at the needless price of his defeat and all that would entail. Besides, he concluded, it was a fact that St. Helena Parish was woefully unprepared for a sudden dismantling of its dual school system. The safety and well-being of the black children, as well as the general community, would be served by delaying the effect of the ruling for at least a semester, thus allowing time to prepare the ground for a peaceful transition.

Boggs's argument struck me as an eloquent variation on the familiar refrain "the time isn't ripe." Still, I was impressed by the evident sincerity and effectiveness with which he made his case. I responded mildly that blacks might find it difficult to believe that the parish authorities, after all those years of delay and inaction, would put more time to constructive use.

"What," I asked him, "would you like the Community Relations Service to do?"

"Intervene in the court case," he replied, "and make the appropriate arguments for a delay. I'm sure the court of appeals will seriously consider a recommendation from a national agency of this kind, headed by a man of Governor Collins's reputation."

I promised to convey his views to Collins, who would undoubtedly be in touch with him shortly. To my surprise, he shook his head.

"That won't be necessary," he said. "I just want him to know how I see the situation. You people have your job to do. I'll respect whatever decision he makes."

When I reported this conversation to Collins, he was not inclined to make a snap judgment. Instead, he engaged an expert consultant to investigate the state of affairs in St. Helena Parish and advise him on the best course to take. The expert in question was John Ivey, a highly regarded educator whom both Collins and I had come to know when he was director of the Southern Regional Education Board. I felt reassured, since I respected Ivey's ability and integrity and was convinced that neither he nor Collins would be influenced in a matter of this sort by political considerations.

Ivey returned from Louisiana with a bleak account of social and educational conditions in St. Helena Parish. The economy was depressed, the disparity between white and black schools was enormous, and feelings of racial hostility ran high. The success of their delaying tactics over many years had left the local whites and their leaders smugly confident that they could stave off desegregation indefinitely. Now that their friendly judge had been forced to yield to higher authority, they were dangerously aroused. In Ivey's opinion, to impose immediate desegregation under such circumstances would make sacrificial victims of the black school children. He favored a delay of one year and proposed an ambitious agenda of community preparation that the local leadership should be persuaded to undertake during the interim.

Collins found Ivey's report and recommendations persuasive and was prepared to move on them at once. At the risk of appearing doctrinaire, perhaps even inhumane, I argued against this course of action. I was as concerned as anyone about the safety of the chidren, but I was also sensitive to the fact that they and their parents had fought long and hard, and suffered endless frustrations and abuse, to win the court order. How would they feel if that victory were snatched away by another delay, engineered this time by a federal civil rights agency? I recalled the Little Rock students, the sitters-in, the freedom riders, the young Birmingham demonstrators—all of whom chose to brave great danger to assert their rights. And I remembered Martin Luther King's rueful comment to President Kennedy that he had never participated in any direct action movement that was not criticized as being "ill-timed."

One further objection seemed to me indisputable: If the Community Relations Service as its first public action sought to stay a court desegregation order, it would be discredited in its infancy in the eyes of the civil rights movement and minorities in general. Those who already suspected that it was created to appease civil rights violators rather than to defend their victims would consider their suspicions fully confirmed.

These arguments did not sway Governor Collins. He maintained that the overriding consideration was the safety of the children—and that, he believed, clearly dictated delay. He did concede, however, that CRS could not intervene in a legal action without the approval of the attorney general, then still Robert Kennedy. Since Collins's heavy commitments in the South made it impossible for him to return to Washington, he once again asked me to represent him. I could hardly suppress my dismay when he instructed me to present his case to Kennedy in the strongest terms.

John Perry, Collins's long-time special assistant, went with me to the meeting at the Justice Department. We found Kennedy in the huge attorney general's office, dressed in his well-known casual style—shirtsleeves rolled up, collar open, stockinged feet propped up, hair tousled. I presented the background of the St. Helena school suit, Hale Boggs's views, John Ivey's findings and recommendations, and, finally, Collins's position. I gave no hint, of course, of my own reservations. He heard me out without interruption, except for an occasional half-smile that might have reflected kindly condescension.

When I had finished, Kennedy expressed his respect for Collins as a man of great courage and conviction. He also declared his sympathy with our concern for the well-being of the school children. Then he proceeded in avuncular fashion to demolish the case I had so conscientiously presented. He explained that he had learned from hard experience that blacks were determined to decide for themselves what risks they should take in asserting their rights. This was as it should be. They would deeply resent it, he said, if the government, however well intentioned, should step in at this point and try to undo what they had fought so hard to achieve. All the Justice Department could do, he concluded, was to make every effort to prevent violence and intimidation.

Listening to this rebuttal, I hoped my expression was suitably grave. I also reflected on the contrast between the present Robert Kennedy and that of earlier days. He now seemed a far cry from the man who had called on the freedom riders to suspend their protest, who had commended the Albany, Georgia, police chief for his gentility in rounding up and jailing black marchers, and who had complained that King's Birmingham demonstrations were ill-timed and ill-advised.

Without the Justice Department's participation, no federal intervention was possible. And so it was that St. Helena Parish in September took its first steps toward school desegregation, grudgingly to be sure, but without bloodshed or violence. Hale Boggs was reelected to his congressional seat, which he continued to occupy until 1972, when he died in a plane crash.

The St. Helena episode had a welcome side effect; it shook loose sufficient temporary funding to enable the Community Relations Service to respond to serious crises. In response to an urgent plea by Governor Collins, Secretary Hodges agreed to divert from the Commerce Department's general budget enough money to tide over CRS until it could secure its own appropriation.

Despite Secretary Hodges' wholehearted support, however, the stop-gap funds did not come easily. The obstacle turned out to be an underling in the administrative ranks of the department. It seemed that the funds in question could not flow to CRS without his authorization, which he adamantly refused to give. An exasperated Hodges gathered several aides, including me, in his office and summoned the recalcitrant clerk to explain himself. Hodges brusquely informed the man of the urgency of the situation and of his own determination to have the exchange of funds authorized forthwith.

The lowly bureaucrat (a GS-11) was completely unfazed. While we all gaped in astonishment, he told Secretary Hodges that he had no intention of signing off on the funds. He explained his refusal approximately as follows: "What you have to understand, Mr. Secretary, is that the department has no authority to do what you want. I was here long before you came, and I will be here long after you are gone. If I sign this authorization, I will be personally accountable for the use of these funds. I don't intend to put myself in that position. If you want this authorization signed, you will have to sign it yourself and personally assume any liability that may result."

After a few moments of ominously charged silence, Hodges got his temper under control.

"All right! All right!" he exclaimed. "If that's how it has to be done, I'll do it. Get the thing on my desk and I'll sign it. Now!"

So far as I know, the GS-11 was still there when Secretary Hodges left office and no doubt remained there until he took his well-deserved retirement. For me, the episode served as a useful introduction to bureaucratic obstructions—and to the fact that they are not always as irrational as they seem.

During my six months with CRS, I spent a great deal of time coping with administrative roadblocks, crashing through them when possible (rarely), crawling over or under them (occasionally), or circumventing them (fairly often). In this maneuvering, I had several advantages over career executives who struggled with similar problems. First and foremost, I did not have to worry about protecting my long-term prospects in government; given my temporary, on-loan status, I could if necessary risk the displeasure of the permanent hierarchy. Second, having in effect been drafted by the president, I felt comparatively free to call for support from White House aides when the stakes were high. Finally, Governor Collins's popularity and prestige ensured that other senior officials would go out of their way to help our mission succeed.

Even a "loaner," however, was well advised not to take unnecessary liberties unless he positively enjoyed doing battle. Those who lived by the system were especially quick to take offense at anyone who went over their heads in an effort to bend the rules. This was impressed upon me early on as we considered the issue of staff size and grade levels.

Collins had been strongly advised by well-wishers in the administration (presumably aides at Justice and the White House) to settle for a very small cadre of high-quality personnel—he recalled seventeen as the recommended number. This was fine in principle, but unrealistic in practice. A staff of that size would be swamped by the clerical, administrative, and professional demands that even a small agency could anticipate. Many of these duties might be regarded as extraneous to the basic mission—for example, responding to congressional inquiries and demands, preparing budgets and testimony, maintaining personnel records, processing complaints, and the like—but they were nonetheless inescapable.

Based on preliminary discussions with specialists at the Civil Service Commission, I estimated that the agency would need an initial staff of at least forty and should plan for substantial increases as its operations grew. But Collins was uneasy about proposing a staff of this size lest he be regarded as "empire building." I suggested to him that he seek the advice of John Macy, the creative public administrator then serving as chairman of the Civil Service Commission. With Collins's enthusiastic agreement, I called Macy, explained the situation to him, and asked when we could come to see him.

"I'll come over there," Macy replied. "How about right now?"

Macy emphatically assured Collins that the larger number we were considering was not only justifiable but modest—probably excessively modest under the circumstances. Moreover, he added, an agency with as sensitive and demanding a mission as CRS should have a larger-than-normal allocation of supergrades, the coveted high-paying positions GS-16 to GS-18.

"I'll put it in the works myself," he added, "as soon as I get back to the Commission."

He was as good as his word. Not more than half-an-hour later, I received an irate telephone call from our chief contact on the Civil Service Commission staff.

"Who do you think you are?" he thundered. "Going over my head to the chairman to wangle all those supergrades! You don't deal with the chairman, you deal with me!"

"I accept that," I replied. "But are you saying that Governor Collins, who has cabinet rank, can't call on Chairman Macy for advice?"

"I didn't say that!"

"Well, that's what happened. And, just to keep the record straight, the additional supergrades were Macy's idea." Whereupon, he hung up.

The proposed staffing, supergrades included, was approved in short order. I considered it fortunate, however, that I never had to have further dealings with the outraged Civil Service official.

Bureaucratic red tape and delayed funding were not the only barriers to the organization of the new agency. We were also severely hampered by White House insistence on the immediate creation of a large and prestigious National Citizens Advisory Council that was meant to enlist opinion leaders from all walks of life in a crusade for peaceful implementation of the Civil Rights Act. This overriding priority reflected President Johnson's strong preference for mediation and persuasion over regulation and enforcement, especially in as potentially explosive an area as civil rights. As a master of backstage negotiation and compromise himself, he saw the Community Relations Service as a device for applying these skills on a grand scale.

This was, in principle, the same concept we had applied with considerable success in Operation Compliance. But the present undertaking was vastly different in scale and timing. The scheduled launching of the new council was only a few weeks off, by which time some two hundred prominent national leaders were to be recruited, briefed, and assembled in the White House Rose Garden for a presidential laying on of hands. And this was to be accomplished by a small, inexperienced staff whose mission was as yet only vaguely defined.

In one respect, we had too much help. As word of the impending affair spread, names of proposed invitees poured in relentlessly. Although the names came from a variety of top government officials, most of them reached us by way of the White House, usually with the blunt instruction: "Add the following individuals." Before it was over, the list of invitees far exceeded the originally proposed total of two hundred; more than five hundred prominent Americans received telegrams, signed by the president, inviting them to join him in the White House rose garden.

A few days before the appointed date, my already low spirits hit rock bottom when the departmental security chief called to say that he was sending us a batch of FBI files. It seemed that somebody had realized at the eleventh hour that the obligatory security checks had not been run on the president's invited guests. (Blessedly, this was not my responsibility.) Having hastily reviewed these hundreds of dossiers, the security chief was sending us those on which he was unwilling to sign off.

When the offending files were deposited on my desk, I was stunned by the size of the stack. Surely, I thought, that many of the nation's most illustrious leaders couldn't be security risks. My wonder grew as I read the names on the files. They included some of the best known and respected people in their fields.

Each of the folders bore a classified stamp and the inscription "THIS FILE CONTAINS UNEVALUATED DATA COMPILED BY THE FEDERAL BUREAU OF INVESTIGATION." Obviously, there had not been time for full field investigations of that many individuals. These were the so-called "raw" files—derogatory information casually collected, with little regard for reliability—maintained on almost anyone who had received significant public attention.

"Raw" was an apt description. The file contents were a hodge-podge of neighborhood gossip, clippings from newspapers and other publications, disparaging comments by disgruntled former spouses and employees, and allegations of one kind or another by unnamed informants. The file of one prominent corporate executive contained a detailed account of his quite commonplace marital troubles and his resulting separation from his wife, after which he reportedly cohabited for a time with another woman. The security implications of all this became even cloudier when the report concluded with a parenthetical note that later he and his wife were reconciled.

A distinguished lawyer's neighbor overheard him using obscene language and slamming doors in his house. Some of the subjects were believed to have belonged to radical campus organizations as college students in the 1930s. Another was said to have signed a petition to allow Henry Wallace's name to appear as a presidential candidate on the Arkansas ballot in 1948.

A few of the files contained allegations that might have warranted further investigation in the case of a candidate for top-secret clearance in the Defense Department. I saw nothing, however, that would justify excluding a prominent citizen from a thirty-minute audience with the president in the Rose Garden. And I saw a great deal that was both malicious and irrelevant.

I said as much to the security officer. He retorted that his job was to identify not only associations that might put the president in physical danger, but also those that might expose him to public embarrassment. I reminded him that all of the individuals he found unacceptable had received a personal invitation from the president to join him two days hence.

"Speaking of embarrassment," I said, "how would you suggest that the President retract his invitations."

"That's not my problem," he replied serenely.

Asking him to excuse me for a moment, I placed a call to the senior White House aide who dealt with security matters. When he came on the line, I read off to him the well-known names on the rejected files.

"What would you say," I asked him, "if I told you there's a security man in my office who says the President should rescind his invitation to these people."

"I'd say 'bullshit'! Put him on the line."

I handed the telephone to the security chief, who listened stolidly to what I assumed was an angry tirade. When it came to an end, he merely said, "I understand you" and hung up.

"Here's the situation," he said to me. "You and your friend at the White House want to go ahead with these people. I won't sign off on them. It's your baby. If Governor Collins wants to override me, that's his prerogative. If there are repercussions, it will be his ass, not mine, that's in a sling."

Governor Collins did override him. Nobody was disinvited, and the president survived undamaged. But my brief encounter with the security process left a sour aftertaste. It was a reminder of how little we had learned from the grim days of McCarthyism ten years earlier. I found it hard to accept that our government was incapable of achieving a reasonable balance between protection of the state and protection of the individual. Yet, then and now, abuses of the security system keep recurring with depressing regularity, and the millions of seamy "raw" files, now available at the touch of a computer key, probably go on accumulating.

President Johnson had escaped embarrassment. But when the affair was over and the distinguished members of the new council had gone home with the president's exhortations ringing in their ears, I was embarrassed enough for both of us. The convocation had perhaps been a ceremonial success, but in practical terms it was an abject failure. Many of those invited had come expecting to be deputized and given specific assignments in the civil rights effort. Instead, they got high-flown rhetoric and only general suggestions for action. Putting volunteers effectively in harness requires detailed planning and the capacity for professional supervision. The struggling new agency was not yet capable of either.

The Community Relations Service survived this early debacle. By the time I left it in December of 1964, however, it was clear that its mission would be different from that originally anticipated. There were, indeed, racial crises in the South for some time to come. But the feared wholesale rebellion against the Civil Rights Act did not materialize. Instead, there was gradual though sometimes surly compliance, except in the die-hard areas of the Deep South, where the racial status quo was maintained by custom, coercion, and when necessary brute force.

Such a community was Selma, Alabama, in early 1965. Local authorities there doggedly persisted in frustrating the attempts of black residents to become registered voters. The result was an historic confrontation between civil rights demonstrators and local and state police. Determined to focus national attention on their nonviolent cause, the demonstrators decided to defy the police by marching down the highway from Selma to Montgomery. Millions of Americans viewed on their television sets the vicious assault on the marchers by state troopers firing tear gas and wielding billy clubs. Not since the Birmingham brutalities had there been such a torrent of national outrage.

Martin Luther King hastened to Selma to announce that he would lead a resumption of the march on Tuesday, March 9. Among the many others who rushed to the scene was LeRoy Collins, representing the good offices of the Community Relations Service at the expressed wish of the president. The consequences for both King and Collins were destined to be painful.

Federal District Judge Frank Johnson had taken under advisement a request for an order prohibiting Alabama Governor George Wallace and his state police from interfering with the marchers. It was generally assumed that he would shortly issue such an injunction. On the strength of this expectation, Collins hastily negotiated an understanding between King and the police authorities that the marchers would cross the Pettus bridge and then, when confronted by the amassed state troopers, would declare themselves vindicated and turn back. At the crucial point, after a few suspenseful moments of uncertainty, King succeeded in turning around his bewildered followers, most of whom knew nothing of the privately reached agreement.

Judge Johnson subsequently issued his injunction, and the great symbolic march to Montgomery went forward. But many of the civil rights activists were slow to forgive King for what seemed to them a betrayal of the cause at the Pettus bridge.

Collins paid an even heavier price. He resigned from the Community Relations Service in June 1965 to serve for a time as Under Secretary of Commerce. Then he returned to Florida and sought election to the United States Senate. His opponent made the most of Collins's service as the federal government's chief race relationist, implying that he was a traitor to the South. The message was driven home by a widely distributed news photograph of Collins striding along beside Martin Luther King during the fateful march. A majority of white Florida voters was not ready to forgive a native son for what they regarded as defection to the black cause, and so he was defeated. Thus are the peacemakers blessed.

After Selma, the main focus of public attention and concern shifted rapidly from the traditional South to the big cities throughout the nation. There, pent-up black anger and frustration had begun to explode into massive rioting and destruction. Soon both the mission and leadership of CRS were adapted to this changing scene. A white skin and a southern accent, even when coupled with a passion for justice, were no assets in the ghettos of Los Angeles, Cleveland, New York, or Detroit. Collins's acting successor, Calvin Kytle, a native Georgian long committed to racial equality, had a short tenure. He was succeeded in December 1965 by Roger Wilkins, the nephew of the NAACP's Roy Wilkins. Shortly afterward, the agency was transferred to the Justice Department.

In 1989, CRS observed its twenty-fifth anniversary. Few Americans were aware of the occasion, just as few had been aware of the agency's existence over the preceding years. From the beginning, CRS labored under the legislative requirement that the details of its field activities be kept strictly confidential. This stern restriction inevitably consigned it to obscurity. Over the years, its small band of mediators has worked behind the scenes in scores of situations involving charges of discrimination and interracial or interethnic conflict. But its legally imposed veil of secrecy has denied it both credit for its successes and blame for its failures.

Under these circumstances, it is not surprising that CRS languishes as a tiny, virtually unnoticed appendage of the Justice Department. What is remarkable is that it has survived at all.

CHAPTER 12 ▪ *Yesterday's Sunshine*

PROSPECTS FOR BOLD federal action to advance civil rights never seemed brighter than in early 1965.

President Johnson had embraced the civil rights cause with a fervor that was almost disconcerting. Having been elected to a full presidential term in his own right, he exuded confidence. Not only had he won by a landslide; he had prevailed over ultra-conservative senator Barry Goldwater, a staunch opponent of the Civil Rights Act. Johnson regarded the widespread condemnation of the Selma brutalities as a mandate to press for a strong new voting rights act. He did so, in an emotional address to a joint session of Congress, which he concluded with the rallying cry of the movement, "We shall overcome!"

Although the effects of the Civil Rights Act and the new antipoverty programs were as yet limited, hope ran high that they would soon produce a profound transformation in the lives of black Americans. Some of the country's brightest and most innovative talent was busy in agencies throughout the government, translating the legislation into new regulations and programs.

No one dreamed that the end of the year would find the civil rights movement in disarray, the president and his administration in retrenchment, and racial attitudes hardening among both black and white Americans. For the moment the air was alive with promise.

During my absence from Potomac, the staff and consultants under Art Levin's direction had been hard at work on surveys, publications, conferences, and training sessions designed to help breathe life into the new legal requirements. All of the major titles of the Civil Rights Act were dealt with by one or more such activities.

Initially, Potomac published a brief "layman's summary" of the law to fill the need until the Civil Rights Commission's more comprehensive summary could be produced in early 1965.

Titles II and X: Public Accommodations

In the area of public accommodations, Potomac followed up its earlier work in Operation Compliance with two surveys updating the rapid spread of orderly compliance in previously segregated communities. The results were published under the reassuring titles *Americans Are Law-Abiding Citizens* and *Opening Public Accommodations to All*. Both publications stressed the economic consequences of a community's decision to drop racial barriers or to remain stubbornly defiant. By this time, even many segregation-minded politicians and business executives were publicly warning against the economic damage likely to result from die-hard resistance. We quoted them freely.

Law Enforcement

One governmental activity that we felt needed urgent attention, even though it was not dealt with directly in the legislation, was law enforcement. The history of American race relations is studded with examples of racial crises ignited or inflamed by unprofessional police practices. This has been true in all regions of the country, but the need for preventive action was especially acute in the South, where the Civil Rights Act had its greatest immediate impact.

Fortunately, Art Levin had extensive experience in staging community relations programs for police officials. On behalf of Potomac, he invited four other organizations with credibility in law enforcement circles to co-sponsor a national conference for high-ranking police officials. They were the International Association of Chiefs of Police (IACP), the University of Oklahoma's Southwest Center for Human Relations Studies and Southwest Center for Law Enforcement Education, and the Anti-Defamation League of B'nai B'rith. All four accepted. Most critical, of course, was the participation of the traditionally cautious IACP, which agreed to serve as principal sponsor, issue the invitations, and publish the conference proceedings.

By comparison with any previous effort of its kind, the conference was a huge success. On August 7 and 8, 1964, more than 130 police executives (an 80 percent acceptance rate) gathered at the University in Norman, Oklahoma, to discuss the Civil Rights Act and its implications for local law enforcement. By design, two-thirds of the attendees were from southern cities. Among the speakers were LeRoy Collins of the Community Relations Service, Atlanta Police Chief Herbert Jenkins and Quinn Tamm, president and executive director respectively of the IACP, and Assistant Attorney General Arthur Caldwell from the Department of Justice. Most important, discussion from the floor and in the smaller conference rooms was remarkably candid and constructive—not always the case when police officials were called on to grapple with sensitive issues of social change.

Not only did the IACP summarize the conference proceedings in its monthly magazine; it printed 250,000 copies of the full proceedings for distribution to every police chief and top city official in the United States. Potomac published a compact summary for distribution to a more varied audience.

Although we had no way of measuring the beneficial effects of the conference and its published products, many of the participants clearly found them helpful. Potomac and the other sponsoring agencies received a gratifying number of appreciative letters from police chiefs in both large cities and small towns across the South. It seemed reasonable to conclude that the conference had at the very least helped make it acceptable for police officials to confront the shortcomings of their profession in dealing with racially sensitive situations.

Title VI: Federal sanctions

During the long debate over the civil rights bill, the fiercest opposition had centered on the public accommodations and fair employment titles. We found it anomalous that Title VI, easily the bill's most far-reaching provision, drew comparatively little fire. It provided that no federal funds should flow to any public or private activity that discriminated on grounds of race, color, or national origin. Given the vast array of national, state, and local programs aided by federal money, this was truly a revolutionary new departure.

The enforcement of the sweeping new mandate presented a challenge not just to one or a few federal agencies, but to virtually all of them. Almost two hundred federal programs were covered. Collectively, they dispensed billions of federal dollars every year in support of education, agriculture, housing, health care, welfare, the National Guard, business and industry, interstate highways, and a host of other activities. In principle, every one of these dollars henceforth would carry with it the stern message: "No discrimination." In practice, however, even to make a respectable beginning in enforcement meant that scores of federal agencies had to develop new policies and regulations tailored to their particular missions.

An essential first step was to familiarize key officials of federal agencies with the requirements of Title VI. Since citizen complaints were the prescribed method of triggering enforcement, community organizations and public interest groups also needed to be informed about how the Title VI compliance process worked. To this end, Potomac published *The Federal Dollar and Nondiscrimination: A Guide to Community Action,* describing the coverage of Title VI, the federal agencies administering it, how to detect violations, how to file a complaint, and the like. This publication served as the standard guide during the lengthy period before agency regulations and official explanatory material were available.

Potomac also cooperated with the Commission on Civil Rights in staging a conference of federal administrators charged with implementing the new title, as well as representatives of the civil rights groups. The large gathering of bureaucrats in the Labor Department auditorium was awed by the powerful potential of this new weapon against discrimination. One administrator likened it to the atom bomb. "It's so powerful," he said, "I'm afraid we won't dare use it."

As those familiar with the ways of government realized, however, there was little danger that the ultimate penalty prescribed by Title VI would be lightly imposed. Few administrators were eager to contend with the political backlash that any major cut-off of funds was sure to provoke.

Title IV: Education

In the case of education, there were internal as well as external obstacles to meaningful enforcement. The Office of Education, with some three thousand school districts to bring into compliance, was given no new resources and none of the higher personnel grades needed for so monumental and complex a task. Moreover, policy-making authority in this area was ambiguous, divided as it was between Commissioner of Education Frank Keppel and Assistant Secretary of HEW James Quigley. Both were able and well-motivated men, but they were at loggerheads over enforcement strategy.

Thanks to Potomac's previous work with Keppel and his tireless assistant David Seeley, our collaboration in shaping the new compliance effort was welcome. But the magnitude of the task, the lack of resources, and the administrative obstacles combined to frustrate the best efforts of everyone involved. Segregated school districts responded to the impasse in Washington by submitting token desegregation plans, empty "assurances" of compliance, or in many cases nothing at all.

As it turned out, Potomac's most useful contribution was to facilitate the role of an ingenious expert consultant with whom both Potomac and the Taconic Foundation had close ties—Professor G. W. Foster Jr. of the University of Wisconsin Law School. For several years, with the aid of a grant from Taconic, Foster had been studying the complex evolution of case law on school desegregation; much of his information and insight was derived from discreet discussions with the operative federal judges themselves. He was ideally equipped, therefore, to help the Office of Education develop clear-cut compliance guidelines for the thousands of school districts affected by Title VI.

What followed was a remarkable example of how private skill and initiative can loosen the political and policy constraints that often inhibit decisive governmental action.

Foster and the small team of fellow consultants he recruited soon became increasingly dismayed by their inability to get guidelines formally approved and issued by the government. Many state and local officials were clamoring for guidance—not because they were eager to desegregate, but because they could get no new federal funds until their school districts were certified as complying with Title VI. The consultants were deluged with queries from school superintendents desperate to find out what kind of plans would shake the money loose.

Bill Foster was a frequent visitor at Potomac, where we commiserated over this wretched state of affairs. At one of our sessions, he laid out a daring strategy that just might, he thought, break through the logjam. His plan was simple enough, but loaded with explosive potential. It was to prepare a set of guidelines based on judicial precedents and get it published in the education section of the *Saturday Review* under his by-line. The document would have no official standing, but Foster's role as a consultant-insider would encourage the assumption that it was in line with official thinking.

The obvious drawback was that Commissioner Keppel might feel it necessary to repudiate the document, which would undermine the whole effort. Nevertheless, we promised Foster that, if the *Saturday Review* agreed to publish the article, Potomac would see that reprints were widely distributed.

The magazine ran the article in its issue of March 20, 1965, having prudently secured Keppel's informal assurance that he had no objection. The editors' note entered only the mildest of disclaimers: "Mr. Foster's memo has no official status and does not bind the U.S. Office of Education in any fashion. Yet there is no doubt that it reflects directly the thinking of the officials charged with the responsibility for enforcement of Title VI as it applies to education."

Potomac ordered eight thousand reprints. In distributing them, we were fortunate enough to gain the cooperation of an influential educational partner, the Southern Association of Colleges and Schools. Copies were mailed to every school superintendent in the South with an explanatory letter from Frank Dickey, director of the association. The Office of Education also requested several thousand copies to be used for "semi-official" guidance to the education officials who were demanding direction.

Foster's document having in effect won the endorsement of the Commissioner of Education, it was a foregone conclusion that issuance of an official version would soon follow. Quigley's fear that such a codification of minimum standards would bind the federal government to the lowest common denominator of enforcement had considerable merit. But his preferred alternative—negotiating with individual school districts for the most far-reaching plan obtainable in each case—was simply unrealistic. The staggering number of negotiations required and the political pressures to "unfreeze" the large new sums of federal aid to education made a single, standardized approach imperative.

The publication of formal guidelines did not, of course, launch a process of uninterrupted progress in school desegregation. Resistance, evasion, and de facto resegregation continued to present problems—and still do. Even so, the issuance of the guidelines was a significant landmark. It was the first step toward administrative—as contrasted to judicial—action against officially segregated school systems. As Gary Orfield observed in his informative history *The Reconstruction of Southern Education*: "The guidelines provided the standard operating principles that were to enable a small group of men to desegregate, in four months' time, far more districts than the Federal courts had reached in 10 years."[10]

Reviewing these events long after the fact, Bill Foster wrote in a recent letter, "Even now, nearly a quarter century later, I was shaken . . . that a major governmental policy was given critical shaping by extragovernmental activities."

Title VII: Fair Employment

The fair employment provision, which had been the center of so much wrangling during the congressional debate, appeared to have fallen off the White House agenda. While it was true that the provision was not to become enforceable until a year after passage, the president had been expected to appoint the members of the Equal Employment Opportunity Commission (EEOC) early, in order to allow ample time to gear up the new agency. Rumor had it that the delay was caused by difficulty in finding a sufficiently prestigious chairman. Early in 1965 Potomac distributed a summary of Title VII's requirements and opportunities, entitled *Fair Employment Is Good Business*, widely used by those seeking to prepare for implementation.

Finally named as chairman May 10, 1965, was Franklin D. Roosevelt Jr., the son of the former president who had created the wartime FEPC

more than twenty years earlier. The other commissioners were Luther
Holcomb, a clergyman from Texas, as vice-chairman; Samuel Jackson, a
lawyer and NAACP executive from Kansas; Aileen Hernandez, a human
rights professional from California; and Richard Graham, a progressive
businessman from Wisconsin who had served as Peace Corps director
in Tunisia.

With less than two months to go before startup, the commission was
under great pressure to get organized. In light of Potomac's history of involvement in the development of new federal programs—usually against
dauntingly short deadlines—it was not surprising that the commission
turned to us for help. Art Levin and I had our first meeting with Roosevelt and his senior aides on May 19, and then immersed ourselves in the
rush assignment for several weeks.

Having followed the evolution of the Civil Rights Act, we were well
aware that the EEOC had been dealt an exceptionally weak hand. Nomi-
nally, it had vast jurisdiction—beginning with all employers and labor
unions with one hundred or more workers and gradually extending
coverage to all those with more than twenty-five. When it came to enforcement powers, however, the new agency was virtually toothless. Its
intervention depended on the filing of properly notarized complaints of
discrimination. If the complaint came from a jurisdiction having a state
or local fair employment agency, the commission was required to refer
the complaint to that agency, which then had 120 days (60 after the first
year) to investigate and resolve it. If after that lapse of time the complaint remained unresolved, the commission took jurisdiction. Also, in
cases where a "pattern or practice" of discrimination was found probable, the commissioners themselves were authorized to file a complaint,
which would then remain under the commission's jurisdiction. Even so,
the commission had no enforcement powers. It could only seek voluntary compliance.

These constraints confined the commission's role to public education,
investigation, persuasion, mediation, and referral. If all efforts to achieve
voluntary compliance failed, the complainant could file suit in a federal
court or the commission could request the U.S. Attorney General to do
so. In either case, a lengthy effort to achieve voluntary compliance would
be followed by an even lengthier period of litigation.

Our recommendations dealt with the mundane, but essential, details of agency structure, functions, personnel, and so on. Our main concern, however, was to urge Roosevelt and his fellow commissioners to adopt the kind of policies and priorities that would make the most of their weak mandate. Our greatest fear was that the EEOC would be swamped by individual complaints and end up expending all its time and energy on paper-pushing and endless investigations. Therefore, we proposed that the EEOC keep a substantial part of its staff and resources free to pursue "affirmative action," in the broadest meaning of that term. This meant gathering and analyzing the kind of data that would show where remedies were most needed and could be most effective. It meant persistent efforts to enlist the top leadership of business, industry, unions, and employment services in wholesale improvements in recruitment, hiring, training, and promotion of women and minorities. Where public exposure and persuasion failed, it meant aggressive action to generate "pattern or practice" lawsuits that could result in systemwide changes.

In our discussions of the recommendations with the EEOC principals, we pointed out that complaints, while essential to credibility and fairness to the individual, would produce meager and long-deferred results; given the cumbersome procedures required by Title VII, few complainants would have the economic and psychological stamina to see the process through. We also cautioned that without clearcut division of staff responsibilities for the two approaches—individual complaints and broad-gauged affirmative action—the predictably large volume of complaints would soon crowd out the other functions.

The commissioners were skeptical. Not unreasonably, they believed that the effectiveness of the commission would be measured by its success in resolving individual complaints. Roosevelt also felt that we had an inflated notion of the number of complaints to be expected. He pressed us for a specific estimate. As I recall, the rough guess we came up with was four thousand the first year, with significant increases in the years following. Roosevelt found this so excessive as to be laughable.

Our estimate did, in fact, turn out to be off the mark, but not in the way Roosevelt expected. By the end of its first year, the EEOC had received more than eight thousand complaints. (Our prediction had not taken adequate account of the prodigious exertions to be expected of Herbert

Hill, the NAACP's indefatigable labor secretary.) In later years, the back-log would grow to monstrous proportions, not only monopolizing the staff's energies, as we had feared, but also rendering it demoralized and discredited.

Roosevelt was not around to cope with these problems; he resigned in less than a year to run for governor of New York. It remained for the agency's leadership many years later to begin to reverse the trend.

Civil Rights Coordination

The proliferation of these various civil rights functions and agencies, and the potential for duplication and confusion that would inevitably result from overlapping and fragmentation, had for some time worried people familiar with federal civil rights activities. As early as 1961, the members of the Civil Rights Commission were importuning President Kennedy to appoint a special assistant to ride herd on civil rights activities. Kennedy countered their demand by coolly announcing, apparently on the spur of the moment, that he already had such an aide in the person of Harris Wofford. (This was news to the bewildered Wofford, who was hastily summoned to the White House for the swearing-in ritual.)

When Wofford left the White House for the Peace Corps a year later, Lee C. White added civil rights to his already lengthy list of duties. White, a highly capable man who leavened his seriousness of purpose with a re-freshingly wry wit, continued to exercise this responsibility under President Johnson. But, by design, he served more as a trouble-shooter than as a coordinator.

Although the Leadership Conference on Civil Rights and others in the civil rights community periodically resurrected the proposal for a White House civil rights office, no president since Kennedy has even pretended to be interested. At least part of the explanation may be found in a comment once made by Lee White. He said, in effect, that any White House staffer who accepted an exclusive assignment to civil rights would be vol-unteering for a suicide mission.

All of this notwithstanding, the issue of coordination would not go away. On December 2, 1964, President Johnson dispatched a letter on the subject to Vice President-Elect Hubert Humphrey. After listing the array of new and established civil rights and antipoverty programs then in existence, the letter concluded:

> It is essential that the federal government speak with one voice to those reached by these programs. . . .
>
> I would like you, in the coming weeks, to consult on these problems with the appropriate members of my Cabinet who are most concerned . . . and others with particular assignments in this area. Within the time available, it would also be most helpful to discuss these matters with the appropriate state and local agencies, as well as the principal business, labor, civil rights, educational, and the other groups primarily affected.
>
> I hope that you will be able to give me specific recommendations on the coordination of these activities by the first of the year.

The president's announcement was greeted with enthusiasm by the civil rights forces. They had long argued for top-level coordination and direction of federal civil rights responsibilities, reflecting a serious programmatic approach rather than merely spasmodic reactions to racial crises. Naming the vice president as point man conferred a double benefit: it signified high priority, and it put in charge a man thoroughly committed to the cause. Throughout his political career, Humphrey had been a zealous champion of civil rights. As early as 1948, it was at his insistence that the Democratic platform included the civil rights plank that drove the "Dixiecrats" to secede from the Democratic party. There was no reason to doubt that he would bring the same energetic commitment to his new assignment.

As usual, the time available for consultation and planning was absurdly short—one month, and that spanning Christmas and New Year's. Within a few days, John Stewart of the vice president's staff had assembled a small task force to consult with public and private groups and submit recommendations to Humphrey. John Feild and I were asked to serve as nongovernmental members of the eight-member group. Feild, as a staff member of the U.S. Conference of Mayors, was to be responsible for liaison with state, county, and municipal officials. My assignment was the area of "community relations"—those governmental and private activities broadly concerned with racial and other intergroup relations.

Soliciting the views of public and private practitioners, although important, was the least complicated part of the job. No one expected the task force to come up with an exhaustive treatise on the many problems of federal civil rights coordination and how to resolve them. Rather, the crucial task was to devise the kind of coordinating machinery that would be both accepted and effective. The executive branch is not well suited for coordination of any kind, least of all coordination of touchy political issues. Cabinet officers are notoriously jealous of their authority. They do not take direction from other cabinet officers, or anyone else except the president. There is no way to force them to accept unwelcome changes short of constantly invoking the president's direct intervention.

The vice president is in a particularly awkward position. He has no power whatever by virtue of his office. He can and does, however, carry out special assignments by the president, relying on such authority as the president may delegate to him. This gave rise in our discussions to the question, Why shouldn't the president simply issue an executive order delegating to the vice president coordinating authority in the field of civil rights?

Burke Marshall, who was a member of the task force, laid this notion to rest in a succinct internal memorandum. He pointed out that such an arrangement would inevitably create an image of the vice president as a "civil rights czar," empowered to put into effect whatever civil rights policies he chose. Yet, in practice, he would be pressured to take steps that were ruled out by presidential or administration decisions beyond his control. In short, he would become a "whipping boy" for disgruntled advocates of all persuasions. Marshall further argued that the perceived role of "czar" would inevitably breed turf battles between the vice president and his staff on the one hand, and cabinet officers and theirs on the other.

After considerable debate and discussion, the reservations voiced by Marshall and others carried the day. In a memorandum of January 6, 1965, to the Potomac board, I summarized the recommendations that Humphrey had sent to Johnson the previous day:

1. There should be an executive order establishing a sixteen-member President's Council on Equal Opportunity composed of the heads of

departments and agencies most directly involved in civil rights, and chaired by the Vice President.

2. The Council should have an executive secretary and a small staff appointed by and working under the direction of the Vice President.

3. The Council would take over none of the operating respon-sibilities of the agencies. Acting mainly through its chairman, the Vice President, and his staff, it would set up working groups to effect necessary coordination among the agencies; it would have wide authority to require information and reports from the agencies; it would consult with interested public and private groups and in-dividuals; it would recommend to the President legislative and ad-ministrative changes in the civil rights program.

The rationale for this set-up, for better or worse, is that the office of Vice President does not have enough independent authority to enable him to function as a "civil rights czar." . . .

On the other hand, the assumption is that the [interdepartmen-tal] Council will meet seldom and will, in fact, delegate its authority heavily to the Vice President. Since Humphrey has already received various other major assignments from the President . . . it is clear that his coordination staff will carry the load on a day-to-day basis. They will work closely with designated departmental officials to get the basic job of coordination done. So a great deal will depend on the selection of staff. . . .

Although this initial report does not make recommendations for new types of coordination or administrative changes, it does iden-tify some of the major problems that must be dealt with. . . . In a nutshell, they are of two sorts: (1) how to keep the multiplicity of agencies from falling all over each other in the civil rights field; and (2) how to pull the diffused programs together for concerted attacks on particular civil rights problems (e.g., Mississippi) under some broadly conceived strategy.

The president approved the recommendations essentially as submit-ted, and the Council on Equal Opportunity was launched on a high tide of expectations. The crucial issue of staff leadership was resolved (as it had been once before in the case of the Voter Education Project) by the selection of Wiley Branton as director. He was succeeded at the Voter Education Project by Vernon Jordan.

As the next chapter will relate, Humphrey and Branton never got a chance to show what could be accomplished by this hopeful attempt to give force and cohesion to the federal civil rights effort. Nor would that be the only disappointment of the coming months. The race relations barometer had begun to drop. And one who listened intently could hear the distant rumble of thunder.

CHAPTER 13 ▪ *The Snows of Yesteryear*

ODDLY ENOUGH, an eloquent presidential call for racial equality heralded a series of events that ultimately splintered the civil rights consensus. The speech was delivered by Lyndon B. Johnson at the Howard University commencement on June 4, 1965. He said, in part:

> In far too many ways American Negroes have been another nation, deprived of freedom, crippled by hatred, the doors of opportunity closed to hope.
>
> . . . The American Negro, acting with impressive restraint, has peacefully protested and marched, entered the courtrooms and the seats of government, demanding a justice that has long been denied. The voice of the Negro was the call to action. But it is a tribute to America that, once aroused, the courts and the Congress, the President and most of the people, have been the allies of progress. . . .
>
> But freedom is not enough. You do not wipe away the scars of centuries by saying: Now you are free to go where you want, do as you desire and choose the leaders you please.
>
> You do not take a person who, for years, has been hobbled by chains and liberate him, bring him up to the starting line of a race and then say, "you are free to compete with all the others," and still justly believe that you have been completely fair.
>
> Thus it is not enough just to open the gates of opportunity. All our citizens must have the ability to walk through those gates.
>
> This is the next and more profound stage of the battle for civil rights. We seek not just freedom but opportunity—not just legal equity but human ability—not just equality as a right and a theory but equality as a fact and as a result.

He went on to cite the grim statistics that revealed a widening gap—in employment and income, in health and housing—between the Negro poor and the white majority. Then he added a note not often sounded in such litanies: "Perhaps most important—its influence radiating to every part of life—is the breakdown of the Negro family structure. For this, most of all, white America must accept responsibility. It flows from centuries of oppression and persecution of the Negro man. It flows from long years of degradation and discrimination, which have attacked his dignity and assaulted his ability to provide for his family."

He pledged that his administration would be dedicated to expanding efforts on "all these fronts—and a dozen more."

> But there are other answers still to be found. Nor do we fully understand all of the problems. Therefore, I want to announce tonight that this fall I intend to call a White House conference of scholars, and experts, and outstanding Negro leaders—men of both races—and officials of government at every level.
>
> This White House conference's theme and title will be "To Fulfill These Rights." Its object will be to help the American Negro fulfill the rights which, after the long time of injustice, he is finally about to secure.

The speech was widely acclaimed by influential blacks and whites alike, including the mainline civil rights leaders. It marked Johnson's finest hour as the "civil rights President"—and just about his last.

In time, the Washington rumor-mill let it be known that the speech had derived its content largely from a confidential research report authored by Assistant Secretary of Labor Daniel Patrick Moynihan. As the summer heated up, so did speculation about this mysterious report, titled *The Negro Family: The Case for National Action,* whose contents were said to be too explosive to bear public scrutiny. It was, in fact, intended only for inside consumption. Only one hundred copies had been printed, each one numbered in order to keep tight control of distribution.

In midsummer, it was officially confirmed that planning had begun for the White House Conference promised by the president and now scheduled for November. Several senior White House aides were meeting with social scientists and other specialists on the status of black Americans. There was no word, however, on the issues they discussed or on any specific plans for the conference that might have resulted.

That is how matters stood on July 20, 1965, when Pat Moynihan, at Stephen Currier's invitation, came to Potomac for a luncheon meeting with our board. Moynihan's erudition, patrician bearing, and Cantabrigian accent belied his origins in Hell's Kitchen, a poor neighborhood on New York's lower west side. Although he had a great flair for drama—the same one he later displayed as a United States Senator—on this particular day he was relatively subdued. He was quite forthcoming, however, about the hush-hush report that he had prepared for the benefit of key insiders in the administration.

With the aid of several large charts, he spoke in some detail about the points the president had touched on in his Howard address: the alarming, and worsening, status of disadvantaged black males; the growing gap between white and black unemployment rates; the increase in single-parent, female-headed black families; and his concern about indications that these and other abysmal conditions of ghetto life might have begun to "feed on themselves"—that is, to cease to respond to such traditional remedies as increased job opportunities. He was quite explicit about the historic and current causes of these disabilities—the destructive effects of slavery and segregation, the disastrous level of unemployment, the destabilizing impact of welfare programs that seemed designed to undermine the authority of black fathers and drive them away from their families.

When asked about the recommendations of the report, Moynihan replied that he had deliberately avoided detailed prescriptions. He wanted to focus attention as sharply as possible on the horrendous dimensions of the crisis and the need for national action commensurate with it. To leap immediately into a debate over remedies, he felt, would inevitably stir up controversy and detract from the shock value of the report. He left us with the impression that the White House Conference would be the appropriate forum to produce the kind of radical proposals the situation called for.

Moynihan's message was one of great urgency, but I do not recall that any of us viewed it as a political bombshell. Of course, we had not seen the actual wording of the report. Nor did we foresee the interpretations that the press would put on it.

I might have been more likely to anticipate the coming storm of criticism had I not already been exposed to Moynihan's findings. Almost a year before this, he and I had agreed to be among the contributors to a major issue of *Daedalus,* the journal of the Academy of Arts and Sciences, on race relations in America. (My subject was "The Federal Executive and Civil Rights, 1961–1965," and his "Employment, Income, and the Ordeal of the Negro Family.") All of the papers were read not only by the editors but also by all of the other contributors. The papers were then critiqued at a two-day working session. The discussants included eminent black scholars and activists, as well as whites who were wholly in sympathy with the civil rights struggle.

So it was that I had read and taken part in a discussion of Moynihan's paper several months earlier. His presentation at Potomac was simply an adaptation of the data and interpretations set forth in the *Daedalus* article. And, as I would soon learn, so was the "secret" Labor Department report that had inspired Johnson's Howard University speech, and about which Washington was all abuzz.

As was to be expected, numbered copies notwithstanding, the Moynihan report was soon leaked to the press, including the *New York Times,* the *Washington Post,* and various syndicated columnists. Their characterizations of the report differed in tone, balance, and emphasis, but all of them featured the disintegration of the poor black family, the declining status of the black male, and the "tangle of pathology" that threatened to become self-perpetuating in the black ghettos. They also uniformly reported that Moynihan's analysis was intended to set a new direction for federal policy and, to that end, would be the centerpiece of the forthcoming White House Conference.

Since the report itself was not publicly available, the newspaper accounts—especially the more lurid ones—were all-important in shaping public perceptions of its meaning and implications. The result was a tidal wave of criticism from blacks and white liberals and some embarrassing praise from conservative and racist quarters. Some of the critics, who admittedly had not read the report, prepared lengthy and detailed denunciations, some charging or implying that Moynihan was a racist.

Paradoxically, many of the harshest critics had been strong in their praise of the Howard University speech, which was inspired in large part by the Moynihan report. How many of those who rushed to judgment ever read the report itself (which was released some weeks later) is problematical.

The administration did not find it expedient to mount a vigorous defense of the report. It is true that, for various reasons, it would have been difficult to turn back the tide of criticism. By the time the report became publicly available, distortions and misconceptions of it had hardened into fervent convictions.

Moreover, in some respects the report was hard to defend. As a would-be "inside" document, it had been written with little regard for racial sensitivities or ways in which it might be misused to shore up racist attitudes. Unlike the Howard speech, it was not ennobled by compassionate rhetoric and inspiring promises. And unlike the *Daedalus* article, it was not buffered by the conventional language of scholarship. It was a stark, unadorned portrait of a people trapped in a brutal and dehumanizing "culture of poverty" that had perhaps become fatally resistant to customary remedial efforts. This encouraged those so inclined to lay the blame for black disabilities at the door of blacks themselves—the familiar ploy known as "blaming the victim."

Some critics, such as Bayard Rustin and Whitney Young, were at pains to repudiate charges of racism against the report and its author, but less rational reactions carried the day. The Moynihan report was destined to become merely a footnote to the history of political controversy. Some weeks before it was made public, Moynihan himself departed the federal government to run, unsuccessfully, for president of the New York City Council.

The controversy remained virulent enough, however, to damage the prospects for a harmonious and productive White House conference on civil rights. It was not the only complicating factor. The rapid escalation of the Vietnam conflict was beginning to take its toll on the national consensus. By the summer of 1965, Johnson had become obsessed with the undeclared war and was pouring into it vast amounts of manpower and money. The energy and attention of the president and many of his most effective and influential aides were diverted from domestic concerns to the involvement in Southeast Asia.

Yet another fateful development signaled that something was terribly amiss among America's black inner-city dwellers. On August 11, 1965 (only a few days after Johnson signed the new voting rights act), racial violence erupted in Los Angeles with a fury as sudden and terrifying as a tornado on a sunny afternoon. The Watts area of Los Angeles was suddenly transformed from a tranquil, if depressed, black neighborhood into a fiery maelstrom of rioting, looting, and blind destruction.

The violence, triggered by a routine traffic arrest, escalated into the most destructive civil disorder in the nation's history. When it was finally brought under control with the help of almost fourteen thousand national guardsmen, thirty-four persons (mostly black) were dead, one thousand injured, and nearly four thousand arrested. Close to one thousand buildings were looted, vandalized, or burned to the ground. Property damage was estimated at $40 million.

The American people were shocked. They would have been even more so could they have foreseen the violence that would explode in dozens of other cities during the "long, hot summers" to come.

The Watts riot, and the abysmal ghetto conditions widely believed to have spawned it, fed the resentment of civil rights leaders and advocates of the War on Poverty at what they viewed as the administration's cooling ardor for the battle against inequality. Many of them believed that this change of heart accounted for White House neglect of the promised fall conference on civil rights, announced with such fanfare only a few months earlier. Although the conference had been promised for November 1965, by the end of August there were still no signs of serious preparation for it.

At this point, someone evidently convinced the president that speedy, face-saving action was necessary. In late September, it was decided that the full conference would be postponed until sometime in the spring of 1966. The declared purpose of this continuance was to allow for a more deliberate preparatory process during which the many issues requiring consideration could be debated by experts and opinion leaders, codified in position papers, and otherwise predigested before the full conference was convened.

There would still be a meeting in November, called the "Planning Session," at which activists and experts would discuss the proposed format and substance of the main conference. (The number of participants originally contemplated was fifty; it soon escalated to two hundred.) Named as co-chairmen of the planning exercise were Morris B. Abram, a white southern attorney then practicing in New York, and William T. Coleman, an eminent black lawyer and civil rights advocate from Philadelphia. A. Philip Randolph was appointed Honorary Chairman. Berl Bernhard, who had left the U.S. Commission on Civil Rights to resume private law practice, was appointed executive director.

Bernhard promptly undertook to persuade two of his sometime collaborators to join him in a "troika" that would share responsibility for the staff operation. One was Carl Holman, then deputy staff director of the Civil Rights Commission, who had left a promising career as teacher and poet to serve as a strategist in the equal rights struggle. I was invited to be the third.

Bernhard made his proposal to us with characteristic candor and irreverent humor. It was an opportunity not to be missed, he said, to take part in one of the great kamikaze missions of our time. The liabilities that would confront the organizers of the session were obvious to both of us:

1. The dates set for the planning session were November 16–18, allowing a scant six weeks to commandeer a staff, solicit the views of a wide range of interested persons, select and invite the participants, devise an agenda, recruit specialists who could and would deliver background papers on such short notice, and make the necessary physical and logistical arrangements.
2. Disunity within the civil rights ranks was growing by the day. The extremists within SNCC and CORE had seized control of those organizations and, along with a group of black protestors who styled themselves "the wild men," were openly hostile toward the mainstream civil rights leaders. Even many of the latter were bitterly critical of the president and his administration for what was regarded as their diminishing zeal in the battle against discrimination and disadvantage.
3. There were clear indications that the president himself was in a resentful mood. Never one to suffer criticism gracefully, he was angered by black demands for more far-reaching and expensive domestic reforms at a time when he was trying to divert public attention from the huge financial drain imposed by the Vietnam buildup. From his point of view, black criticisms of his policies, the Vietnam involvement, the

Moynihan report, and the administration's ineffectual response to the Watts riot, showed rank ingratitude.

The deteriorating relations between the White House and the civil rights movement led to a bizarre set of events in mid-September. In a move intended to improve communication with the civil rights leadership, Vice President Humphrey invited a group of black leaders to join him, Wiley Branton of the president's Council on Equal Opportunity, and a few other government representatives for an afternoon cruise aboard the presidential yacht *Honey Fitz.* The invitees were hardly a radical lot; they included the NAACP's Clarence Mitchell, dean of the Washington civil rights lobbyists, Whitney Young, Martin Luther King Jr., and Andrew Young. Floyd McKissick of CORE was the only participant with any standing among the most disaffected elements of the movement. Nevertheless, the picturesque cruise on the Potomac ended up in a violent shouting match, in which the administration was denounced for its failure to pursue vigorous enforcement of the new Voting Rights Act.

A week later, the president abruptly ordered a wholesale shake-up of federal civil rights functions. Humphrey was stripped of his civil rights responsibilities. The President's Council on Equal Opportunity was disbanded. Henceforth, the attorney general would serve as the president's point man for civil rights. Wiley Branton was given a vague assignment as an "advisor" to the attorney general, and the Community Relations Service was also transferred to the Justice Department. Another independent agency, the president's Committee on Equal Employment Opportunity, was abolished. Its responsibility for overseeing fair employment by government contractors was lodged in the Labor Department. In a word, federal civil rights authority, having been greatly expanded, was restored to the conventional control of the mainline departments of the permanent government.

Given these turbulent developments, it was not hard to understand why the president's men found it prudent to delegate the management of the planning session to individuals who were not part of the administration. (Holman was a federal employee, but his agency was an independent, bipartisan commission, not officially under the direction of the White House.) If the hastily prepared Planning Session proved a fiasco, as seemed all too possible, the arms-length staffing arrangement would help shield the president and his immediate staff from embarrassment. It would not be the first time a president escaped criticism because he was seen as having been poorly served by temporary appointees.

Bernhard expected, quite rightly, that he would be heavily involved in managing the crises, controversies, and ticklish negotiations that were sure to arise. Holman was uniquely well equipped to relate to the volatile situation in the black community; he was a trusted adviser and confidant of virtually all the major black participants in the movement, young and old, militants and centrists alike.

My proposed role was to ride herd on the process by which the substantive issues would be defined and presented to the planning session. Somewhat to my surprise, I found myself attracted by this unpromising assignment. It was, despite all the negative circumstances, in line with Potomac's basic aim of building support for positive government action. The exercise might end badly for a number of reasons—inadequate commitment by the administration, dissidence in the civil rights movement, the poisonous byproducts of the Moynihan controversy, or sheer lack of time. But it seemed to me it would be even more regrettable if the planning session and subsequent conference went sour because the issues were not dealt with seriously enough. Fear of failure, embarrassment, or being "used" didn't strike me as acceptable reasons to refuse to help. So I accepted Bernhard's proposition.

The ensuing weeks were as frenetic as predicted. Some things, however, went more smoothly than one might have expected. For example, we were able to assemble in short order a volunteer staff, on loan from various federal agencies, that was remarkably competent and hardworking. We also found some of the ablest specialists in academic and organizational life willing to drop everything and devote themselves to the preparation of background papers against an unreasonably short deadline. They included economist Vivian Henderson, law professor Anthony Amsterdam, social psychologist Kenneth B. Clark, Judge William H. Hastie, fair housing expert George Schermer, and others of comparable distinction.

A major question was how to structure the planning session in order to achieve a reasonable balance among the many issues that needed consideration. The press and various other observers viewed this question almost entirely through the prism of the Moynihan controversy. They started from the assumption that the conference had originally been intended to center on the pathologies of black ghetto families. The overriding question, as they saw it, was whether or not the conference planners would stand by the original intent against the wrathful opposition of many black leaders and their allies. As some put it, even more colorfully, Would the president throw Moynihan to the wolves and use the rejection of his ideas as a pretext for downplaying the importance of the planning session and the ensuing conference?

To those of us involved in the exercise, these formulations seemed oversimplified. Under the best of circumstances, *The Negro Family* would have been unsuitable as the centerpiece of a White House–sponsored conference. It was never intended to be a public document. It was a bluntly worded in-house paper designed to shock policy-makers into an unaccustomed state of urgency. The problem was compounded by the emotionalism, distortions, and misconceptions that dominated the resulting public controversy. Unfair to Moynihan as it might have seemed, there was no point in deliberately creating a forum for bitter and divisive confrontation.

The objective as we saw it was to salvage as much constructive thinking and advocacy as possible from an essentially unpromising situation. This meant dealing with the broad range of problems that, interacting with each other, kept blacks and other minorities out of the mainstream of opportunity and achievement. The plight of the poor black family, critical as it might be, was not the root cause but the product of the complex web of discrimination and poverty in our society.

No doubt minority self-help and community initiatives would have to be among the remedies. But it was futile to suppose that lasting solutions could be found without strong leadership from government—government at all levels, but especially the federal government. It was equally futile to imagine that black leaders would be content to come together under presidential auspices only to be instructed in the responsibility of blacks to solve their own problems.

This was the rationale that led us to propose eight panels for the planning session: education, employment, family, housing, voting, health and welfare, community, and administration of justice. An agenda paper on each topic was commissioned. Consultants served as advisers, reviewers, and on occasion collaborators of the principal authors of the papers. The most sensitive of the papers, naturally, was the one on the family. The author was Dr. Hylan Lewis, a highly regarded sociologist at Howard University who had done extensive studies of black families in Washington, D.C.

Having known and worked closely with Lewis when we were both in Atlanta, I rightly assumed that his commitment to high scholarly standards would prevail over the polemical fever that gripped so many participants in the Moynihan controversy. He wisely avoided any direct references to the Moynihan report and the debate it had engendered. His analysis differed from Moynihan's in some respects. It was notably more temperate, less dramatic, and more heavily qualified in its conclusions. But these were differences more of tone and emphasis than of substance. Rhetoric aside, the two reports had much more in common than in contradiction.

Although it was apparent from the beginning that not all of the agenda papers would be as thoroughgoing as Lewis's, there seemed little doubt that they would be completed on time and in competent fashion. We concluded with relief that at least there would be no paperwork crisis.

The human geometry of the conference was more ticklish by far. All of the interested parties were resentful and suspicious. The president feared that the planning conference would end up as a forum for attacks on his policies and egregious demands on the federal purse. The more militant blacks suspected a plot to assemble apologists for the White House and its presumed preference for private and self-help initiatives. The mainline civil rights leaders were angered by the White House failure to grant them a central role in the initial planning of the session. The hastily inducted planning staff saw itself as charging full tilt through a fog-shrouded minefield.

A first order of business was a hurriedly arranged meeting with representatives of the civil rights organizations. It took place on October 21 at the offices of the NAACP Legal and Educational Defense Fund in New York. Bernhard, Holman, and I, accompanied by Clifford Alexander of the White House staff, represented the planning conference. It was not a summit meeting. Most of the top civil rights leaders had sent a deputy or other senior staff member. Bayard Rustin, representing A. Philip Randolph, was the most incisive—and most insistent—of the group. He went straight to the heart of the matter.

"What I want to know is this," he said in his clipped, proto-British style, "Who is making policy?"

It was the right question, and—since we were poorly positioned to give an unequivocal answer—one that Rustin would raise more than once. To reply that co-chairmen Abram and Coleman were the definitive policy-makers would seem to belittle the president. (After all, it was a White House conference, personally decreed by Lyndon Johnson.) On the other hand, to state flatly that the president was making policy would be both imprudent and deceptive. Imprudent because it would certify the president as the appropriate target of all complaints and deceptive because the conference had been deliberately structured to limit the president's direct involvement.

The truth was that the answer to Rustin's question had deliberately been left ambiguous. The co-chairmen were the official arbiters of policy. But the president, represented by his aides, wielded an immutable veto power over any and all decisions. Our efforts to explain this in tactful language inevitably were seen as evasive.

Nevertheless, the discussion was generally amicable. It was also productive in several important respects. It gave us a chance to debunk unfounded rumors that had gained wide circulation. For example, we could honestly reassure the group that there was no thought of limiting the agenda to a discussion of black family instability or self-help remedies or purely private initiatives. Nor was anyone proposing to stack the meeting with compliant participants who would obligingly rubber-stamp a set of bland recommendations. I believe our citing the names of the agenda paper authors we had recruited did more than anything else to relieve the air of skepticism on which the discussion had begun.

We received, in return, some useful suggestions. James Forman of SNCC, for example, stressed the importance of including community activists in the planning session. SNCC later followed up with a list of proposed "grassroots" participants, most of whom were added to the invitation list. Others also had suggestions to make about the range and diversity of attendance. So much so that by the end of the discussion, it was clear to us that the originally contemplated limit of fifty participants would have to be substantially raised.

Perhaps no aspect of the conference preliminaries consumed as much time and attention as the invitation list. Even after the decision was made to expand attendance to two hundred, only a fraction of the individuals who merited consideration could be invited. The dilemma was sharpened by the dissident climate of the times. The staff was determined to assemble as authentically representative a group as possible. In a period of growing militancy and disaffection in the black community, and mounting anti-Vietnam sentiment among both black and white liberals, this was not an easy goal to achieve. Our mentors at the White House were understandably leery of a public relations disaster and the Johnsonian wrath it would surely provoke. We shared their apprehension but felt that the risk had to be taken if the planning session was to have any credibility.

The president's aides with whom we mainly worked—Lee White, Clifford Alexander, and later Harry McPherson—could not have been more congenial. I found them, in their somewhat different roles, unfailingly considerate, supportive, and appreciative of the humor as well as the hazards of the situation.

Their job was not an enviable one. As the president's representatives, they were expected to see to it that the session did not blow up in his face. Yet there was no defensible way to stage a meeting of this kind that would give no offense to the president. In one of our frequent meetings with Lee White, I remarked on this dilemma. "Surely," I said, "the President understands that."

"Oh, he understands all right," White replied. "But it's like a man on death row who understands he's going to be executed. That doesn't necessarily mean that when the time comes he'll go quietly."

When the time did come, on November 16, Berl Bernhard opened the meeting at the Washington Hilton on a note of gallows humor.

"I want you to know," he told the conferees, "that I have been reliably informed that no such person as Daniel Patrick Moynihan exists."

Bernhard's humorous intent was lost on the representatives of the press, Moynihan's partisans, and presumably Moynihan himself, who was not only alive but conspicuously in attendance and much in demand by press interviewers who roamed the hotel corridors. Typical of their reaction was a scathing article by columnist Mary McGrory titled "Moynihan Conspicuously Ignored: The Non-Person at the Conference."

Not surprisingly, the press reports of the planning session were preponderantly unfavorable. They were based mainly on interviews with disgruntled delegates and unnamed "government" or "White House" sources. As usual, the ubiquitous Evans and Novak came up with the direst account of the two-day event. In a column headed "Civil Rights Disaster," they reported:

> Nothing in the glittering two-year history of President Johnson's Great Society has failed so dismally as his White House Conference on Civil Rights last week. . . .
>
> The gap between the civil rights movement and the Johnson administration is wider than ever.
>
> A carefully planned effort to inject a new realism regarding the plight of the Northern Negro was a failure. The reason: Shrill cries of Negro militants continued to drown out cautious attempts by more thoughtful Negro leaders to make a hard-headed appraisal of America's agonizing social problem. As a result, the country is farther than ever from even defining the boundaries of the problem. . . .
>
> Sweeping the problems posed by the Moynihan report under the table, Negro leaders at the conference insisted that the Federal government and the Federal government alone could relieve the torment of the urban Negro. . . . Some disillusioned liberals hint darkly that radical white elements are at work, prodding Negroes to seek the unattainable. . . .
>
> Thus what was boldly conceived at the White House as a fresh new look became a tired rehashing of old slogans. It will happen again at the full-dress conference unless the White House comes up with a new cast of characters willing to leave their dogmas at the door.

A *New York Times* report, written by its highly respected correspondent John Herbers, reached a similar (though more temperately expressed) conclusion:

Drastic remedies were suggested at the conference. A. Philip Randolph, the honorary chairman, proposed a $100 billion "freedom budget" to eradicate slums, over a period of years and provide employment.

There were several proposals for replacing welfare payments and their resultant unintended encouragement of broken homes, with a guaranteed income that "would not discourage work."

But there was no new "handle," no suggestion for winning the "understanding heart" that President Johnson has said is needed for Negroes to become first-class citizens.

The conference was billed as an idea generating session for a fuller conference next spring. Some of the ideas brought out will receive consideration. But mostly it's back to the drafting board for the White House.

Allowing for variations in style, this was the tenor of most reporting on the planning session. The $100 million Freedom Budget proposed by Randolph was commonly cited as an example of the unrealistic demands of the blacks in attendance. Most of the reports, however, failed to mention that the Randolph proposal was not adopted by the conference. Even if it had been, would that have been any less realistic than President Johnson's commitment to the laudable but unlikely goal of "not just equality as a right and a theory but equality as a fact and as a result"?

The general disenchantment with the planning session did not really stem from any extraordinary display of demagoguery, willfulness, or irrationality on the part of the participants. It is true that the plenary sessions were marked by a certain amount of bombast and table-thumping—about the same in kind and degree as occurs in a congressional debate on a highly charged issue. On the other hand, the working sessions went about their assignments in an orderly and serious manner. As is true of most White House conferences, the resulting recommendations stressed the role of the federal government and called for actions that had already emerged in public advocacy and debate. Some of the recommendations were later instituted and others were still being debated years later—proposals for welfare reform, early childhood education, magnet schools, job training and employment programs, penal reform, low-income housing, and the like. Few of them were novel, but few also were without merit. White House conferences do not shape budget priorities, resolve political problems, or originate new solutions to complex social problems. They provide an opportunity for delegates to air their concerns and to express approval or disapproval of proposals that have already gained public currency.

The critics gave the planning session bad marks because it did not—in the words of the anonymous government spokesman—come up with "a new handle." The kind of handle hoped for varied from one faction to another. The press liked the Moynihan formulation, which offered freshness, drama, and controversy; yet the conference, unforgivably, refused to make it either the centerpiece or the target of the proceedings. White Americans generally were tired of racial controversy and black demands; it was high time, they felt, for blacks to stop protesting and start helping themselves. The Johnson administration wanted a new theme that would satisfy the blacks, disarm the whites, impose few demands on the overburdened treasury, and thus enhance the president's popularity. Black activists and their white sympathizers wanted tougher civil rights enforcement and other federal interventions on a large (and inevitably costly) scale.

The problem was not that the planning session was too radical but that it was entirely too conventional to please any of its assorted critics. And so expectations shifted to the prospective June 1966 conference and a more determined search for the elusive new handle.

THE PRESIDENT AND HIS MEN took steps to assure that the June White House Conference would be a less contentious occasion than the planning session. In February, the White House unveiled a new policy group charged with setting the ground rules and agenda of the conference. This was a blue-ribbon council of thirty members headed by Ben W. Heineman, chairman of the Chicago and Northwestern Railroad Company.

Among the council members were the chief executives of several of the nation's largest corporations, leaders of the major civil rights organizations, the head of the AFL-CIO, and several prominent educators and churchmen. Stephen Currier, as president of the Taconic Foundation, was one of those appointed. The vice chairmen were Walter Fauntroy, Washington director of the Southern Christian Leadership Conference, and Edward C. Sylvester, director of the Office of Federal Contract Compliance.

The planning session was tactfully saved from oblivion by the inclusion of its principals in the new apparatus. A. Philip Randolph continued as honorary chairman. Former co-chairmen Abram and Coleman were appointed to the council, Berl Bernhard was named special counsel, and Carl Holman and I were designated special consultants. Clifford Alexander of the White House staff devoted what must have been the lion's share of his time to the conference planning activities.

By the standards of the day, the council was indisputably an "establishment" group. (The sole concession to the dissidents was the inclusion of Floyd McKissick of CORE.) The appointment of a big-business executive as chairman was viewed by critics on the left as evidence of a determination to impose conservative control. But Heineman hardly conformed to the Daddy Warbucks stereotype. He had, for example, long been a staunch supporter of fair housing—a commitment that he actively pursued in the desegregated Chicago neighborhood where he lived.

The main focus of my part-time role as consultant was, as in the planning session, to help oversee the preparation of the background papers and the council's overall statement and recommendations to the conferees. I also sat in on council meetings, which reviewed staff proposals for the conference agenda and procedures.

Most memorable, however, were the freqent informal sessions in which Chairman Heineman, the vice chairmen, and the principal staff members mulled over questions of strategy. Under Heineman's persistent prodding, we explored alternative approaches and their possible consequences with a thoroughness that the National Security Council might have envied.

Security was, in fact, a major concern. In early 1966, protest groups were rapidly shedding the constraints of nonviolence and civility that prevailed in the first years of the decade. Both the growing black power movement and the anti–Vietnam War demonstrations were adopting the rhetoric, and sometimes the tactics, of guerrilla warfare. As so often happens, the authorities' tendency to overreact to these provocations only made matters worse.

It was not surprising, therefore, that Heineman's strategy sessions devoted much attention to security matters. Not the least of these was the question of whether, when, and how the president should appear at the June conference. It was generally agreed that there should be no prior announcement or confirmation that he might show up. This uncertainty, it was felt, would make it difficult for ill-wishers to plan a demonstration large and rowdy enough to endanger or discredit the president. It would also allow the president to defer a final decision on his appearance until the last minute, guided by an on-the-scene appraisal of the risks involved.

This cautious planning was not without justification. The horror of John F. Kennedy's assassination was still a vivid memory. Much less traumatic, but still unsettling, was an ugly event that occurred even as the conference was being planned. A community action conference sponsored by the Office of Economic Opportunity (the antipoverty agency) had grown so raucous and threatening that the federal officials on the platform were obliged to flee ignominiously through a rear door. The thought of the president suffering a similar humiliation made the planners' blood run cold.

Even so, as our discussion turned to more and more bizarre stratagems for smuggling the chief executive into and out of the hotel ballroom, I was overcome by a sense of the ludicrous. I remarked to the group that as a boy I had been awed by a mechanism used in Atlanta's ornate Fox Theater. It was a platform that rose magically through the floor of the orchestra, bearing aloft the organist and his huge, blaring instrument. Perhaps, I suggested, we could have this device shipped to Washington and installed in the ballroom for the president's entrance.

"It's one thing to be prudent," I concluded, "but it's another to be pusillanimous."

This quaintly pedantic statement startled me as much as it did everyone else. At any rate, it relieved the tension. Led by Ben Heineman, we all roared with laughter. I still have two memorabilia of the conference of which I am especially fond. One is a letter of commendation from Lyndon Johnson for my work during "a period, I know, as full of peril as promise." The other is a telegram from Ben Heineman promising to be ever mindful of the distinction between prudence and pusillanimity.

Another nettlesome issue was the type of ground rules to be prescribed for the conference. Part of the concern grew out of apprehension that the session might degenerate into a shouting match over the Vietnam War. That issue had already begun to create discord within the civil rights movement. Martin Luther King's decision to denounce the war as an immoral use of American might had drawn fire not only from certified hawks, but from Roy Wilkins and other prominent civil rights advocates as well; even most of those who abstained from public criticism of King privately deplored his outspoken opposition to the war. They did so not because they approved of the war, but because they feared that a fusion of pro–civil rights and antiwar advocacy would dilute the civil rights message and alienate many sympathizers. They felt that King, as the nation's emblematic leader of the equal rights struggle, owed it to the cause to stick to his knitting and leave the Vietnam issue to others. They had no wish to see as choice a forum as a White House conference diverted from civil rights priorities to divisive issues of foreign policy.

There were also purely procedural problems. Could a one-time assembly of more than two thousand participants from widely diverse backgrounds, convened for only a two-day period, cope with parliamentary procedures that occupied legislative bodies for weeks or months? Clearly it could not. Yet demands were already emerging for the right of delegates to vote on the issues and to introduce resolutions from the floor. Militant spokesmen were charging that the conference planners were intent upon muzzling the delegates and forcing them to rubber stamp the administration's agenda.

The conference plan approved by the council rejected as unworkable the demands that resolutions and formal voting be permitted. It did, however, attempt to provide an opportunity for all delegates to be heard and to have their views considered for inclusion in the council's recommendations to the president. To this end, every delegate was assigned to one of twelve discussion groups of roughly two hundred participants each. The proposed starting point of their discussions was a one-hundred-page document entitled "Recommendations of the Council to the Conference." The recommendations were grouped in four major categories—Housing, Economic Security and Welfare, Education, and Administration of Justice. Each discussion group would discuss all four areas, and each discussion would be transcribed verbatim. The transcript would then be the basis for summaries of the conferees' comments and proposals in the report to the president.

As predicted by the doubting Thomases, the council's report urged a number of voluntary affirmative actions by state and local governments, private institutions, and local citizens' groups. Contrary to those predictions, however, even die-hard skeptics were surprised by the liberal tenor of the council's recommendations for mandatory action— by the federal government. Among them were the following, briefly described:

• Establish "Domestic Peace Corps" programs for rural residents in economically depressed areas that would, among other things, "facilitate the economic and social adjustment of rural Negroes migrating to the city."

- Develop federally financed jobs in public works and services to "solve the Negro unemployment crisis." Such jobs "must be available for Negroes at their existing level of skill attainment."
- Federalize the state-operated Public Employment Services in order "to strengthen program standards, eliminate discrimination in referral of applicants to jobs, and to raise the quality of services, such as intensive counseling, furnished to applicants."
- Set national standards, by federal action, for the level of public assistance benefits paid by the states, raising benefits to furnish a standard of living compatible with health and decency. Enact legislation to permit operation of public welfare programs by the federal government in states which could not or would not meet federal standards.
- Accept the government's responsibility for guaranteeing a minimum income to all needy Americans through "last-resort employment" for those able to work and improved public assistance for those who were not.
- Equalize public school expenditures among the states, within states, and within school districts—where necessary, in the poorest states, by substantially increased federal aid to education.
- Make federal education grants contingent on the recipient communities' adoption of effective area-wide "workable programs" to reduce racial concentration in the schools.
- To speed school desegregaton as required by Title VI of the Civil Rights Act, "the Office of Education must provide for a much enlarged technical staff, insist that compliance meet both the letter and the spirit of the law, and develop more prompt and efficient machinery for withholding or terminating Federal aid where reasonable compliance efforts have failed."
- "Both schools and other agencies . . . should add pre-kindergarten programs wherever they are needed to offset disadvantage, making use of early childhood development research."
- "Federal legislation designed to increase the rate of production of new houses to 2,000,000 units per year. Half of such units should be reserved for moderate and low-income families."

- "In areas in which the local governing bodies are not meeting their responsibility to provide housing for all segments of the population, the nonwhite and the poor, the Federal Government should take direct action to provide the housing needed."
- Enact federal legislation to provide strong criminal penalties for those who "injure, intimidate, or interfere with persons because of their race, color, religion, or national origin" while seeking to exercise their civil rights.
- Enact federal legislation to enable persons who suffer injury or loss as a result of civil rights activities to seek compensation in a federal court or administrative tribunal.
- Enact federal legislation to afford more adequate criminal sanctions against state and local officials who deprive citizens of constitutional rights.

Many of these and other recommendations submitted by the council to the 1966 conference would be regarded even twenty-five years later as radical extensions of the federal government's authority. It is a commentary on the public mood, then and later, that many advocates at the time felt the council's proposals did not go far enough.

Shortly before the conference began, Ben Heineman issued a defense of the procedures decreed by the council:

> To establish this session with 2,400 persons on a parliamentary basis would be undemocratic in itself. This is true because it would not allow people to make their views known. A fair and desirable substitute is to make a complete stenotype transcript of the proceedings, all of which would be considered in drafting recommendations to the President. With such an arrangement persons who are not familiar with parliamentary procedures and are unskilled in competitive debate would have an opportunity to participate in the conference.

Despite these assurances, expressions of dissatisfaction continued with sufficient vigor to convince the policy makers that a compromise was necessary. On the eve of the conference, an emergency council meeting modified the ground rules to allow resolutions to be introduced and voted on in the final sessions of the discussion groups.

Anxiety ran high among the conference planners as the delegates swarmed into the regal lobby and public rooms of the Sheraton Park Hotel. Their uneasiness soon began to ebb as it became evident that the delegates took a serious view of the business of the conference. They came prepared to speak bluntly of their grievances and frustrations, but they were in no mood to tolerate disruptive tactics. Attendance in the discussion groups was sporadic, a shortcoming common to most large conferences, where sociability in the corridors and hospitality suites is a powerful lure. Yet, as the transcripts revealed, most of the delegates voiced their complaints and proposals with a simple decorum that seemed downright old-fashioned in that raucous era. As contrasted with the planning session of the previous fall, the conference was attended mainly by people unsophisticated about the intricacies of legislation, regulation, and bureaucracy. They ratified, and occasionally enlarged on, the council's recommendations. But mostly they spoke of black-white relations in terms of their own daily lives and home communities.

The emotional debate over the Vietnam conflict that some had predicted never surfaced. The lone resolution on that issue, introduced by Floyd McKissick, was resoundingly defeated on grounds that it was not germane to the purposes of the conference.

As the appointed time of the concluding dinner neared, only a handful of insiders knew whether or not the president would appear; in fact, no one knew for certain until about an hour beforehand, when the decision was finally made. Meanwhile, the only sensible course for the staff was to operate on the assumption that the president would be there. Accordingly, tight security procedures were prescribed. One or more staff members were posted at each entrance to the huge ballroom where the dinner would take place. They were charged that, without exception, no one should be admitted without first displaying his or her personal invitation. This instruction was rigorously applied, sometimes with unfortunate results. One awkward instance involved Willard Wirtz, the highly respected secretary of labor, who had neglected to bring his invitation. Told by a dutiful doorkeeper that despite his high rank he could not be admitted, he shrugged philosophically and headed for the hotel exit. Luckily Berl Bernhard was near enough to witness Wirtz's departure. He chased Secretary Wirtz down and led him back to the ball-room entrance to receive apologies from the red-faced staffer.

Harry McPherson, in *A Political Education,* vividly describes the evening's climax:

> On the last day we spent a lot of time debating whether the President should address the closing dinner. A hostile demonstration was still a possibility; though it could only come from a tiny minority, it would, given the laws of reporting, dominate the news—like the red paint thrown on his car in Sydney. The impression would be left that the group for which he had done so much, and promised so much, had repudiated him; and that would hurt the Negro's cause no less than him.
>
> Around six o'clock the chances for peace seemed good, and I shaped up a draft I had prepared a few days before. Johnson's entry into the hall set off a tremendous ovation. . . . On and on they chanted, "LBJ! LBJ!" and once—following his extemporaneous pledge to "give my days—and such talents as I may have—to the pursuit of justice and opportunity for those so long denied them," they were back on their feet and shouting. The trump card was his introduction of Thurgood Marshall, who told the crowd—his crowd, for whom he was exemplar and father figure: "Thirty years ago when I started in this business, you just didn't hear things like that." When Johnson left, I followed him out to congratulate him. In the light of his car his eyes were large and his face almost incandescent with the pleasure of an unexpected and flawless triumph. It was about the last one he would have.[11]

After the dinner, I encountered Martin and Coretta King in the hotel lobby. Although it seemed to me Martin looked even more somber than usual, he greeted me in his customary courtly fashion. We exchanged a few remarks about the conference and the warm reception accorded the president. Neither of us mentioned what was uppermost in my mind and probably his as well: this time, it was he who was the "non-person" at the conference. Whether accurate or not, the general assumption was that this was his rebuke for criticizing the president's Vietnam policy. Throughout the two-day meeting, he had been asked to play no honorific role, to make no speech or statement of any kind, not even an invocation or benediction. At the dinner, he was seated at the head table, but after the routine introduction of head table guests, his name was not spoken again. For the emblematic leader of the civil rights movement, this was a conspicuous snub. As he and his wife left the hotel, I wondered what he was feeling.

Civil rights chroniclers invariably characterize the Johnson White House Conference as a foredoomed and tempestuous affair whose reports were deposited unread on dusty archival shelves. That's not quite the way it was. An interdepartmental committee, chaired by Harry McPherson and Clifford Alexander, was set up to superintend the conference followup. As an ad hoc staff member of the conference, I was sporadically involved in this process. The various government departments and agencies were asked to submit their comments on the proposals in their respective areas of responsibility. Their responses, expectably, dwelt heavily on objections and obstacles to the recommended actions. For this and other reasons, the process went slowly and produced only minor results. McPherson has explained why he soon grew skeptical about the usefulness of the followup effort:

> After our [the followup committee's] first few meetings, I began to wonder about the recommendations. If they were so sensible, as both the conference and the committee seemed to think, why hadn't they been adopted before? Because of political objections—in Congress; in the states, through which most benefits for the poor were disbursed; in the departments themselves, where secretaries and bureaucrats competed for control over the administration and direction of remedial programs; in the White House, where money was tight and already committed.[12]

This is another way of saying that the times were not propitious—and, indeed, they were not. Yet one may wonder what might have been possible if Johnson had rid himself of the incubus of Vietnam and run successfully for another term. As it was, he was able to score one more substantial civil rights victory—passage of the fair housing legislation following King's assassination in 1968.

The intensity of Johnson's preoccupation with the Vietnam controversy was dramatically displayed at a sequel to the White House Conference several weeks later. A group made up of council members and senior conference staff was invited to the White House for an audience with the president. This was supposed to be a brief ceremonial occasion at which the president would receive the final report and thank the group for their labors on behalf of the conference.

In keeping with the intended brevity of the affair, no seating had been arranged. We stood in a semicircle around the president while he paced restlessly about. It was clear from the start that his mind was on something other than civil rights. After a few perfunctory remarks about the White House Conference, he launched into an impassioned soliloquy about criticisms of his Vietnam policy. On this theme he held forth for the better part of an hour, pausing only for an occasional swig from a bottle of soda.

He denounced the critics who would have him abandon Southeast Asia to the forces of communism, the heedless demonstrators and flag-burners, the ruthless enemy. The need was urgent, he declaimed, for thoughtful citizens to stand behind their president and the brave servicemen fighting in far-away jungles. Most emotional of all were his ruminations about the lonely and agonizing burden of decision that rested upon him. He was comforted, he said, by the example of Abraham Lincoln, who held fast to his resolve in spite of the abuse and derision heaped upon him by his detractors.

While this painful monologue ran on, anxious aides consulted their watches and tried in vain to attract the president's attention. Meanwhile, the small captive audience shifted about uneasily. The absurd image that flashed through my mind was that of a group of tourists confronted by a dancing bear with one leg caught in a trap. I silently reminded myself that millions would give their eye-teeth to spend an hour at the elbow of the nation's president, however agitated he might seem. Yet I could feel only disappointment, embarrassment, and a desire to be gone.

As we trooped silently out of the White House, I pondered my excessively negative reaction to the president's impromptu performance. It could not be explained simply as antipathy for his stance on Vietnam. Although my misgivings had escalated along with the war itself, they had not yet hardened into dogma; I still nurtured a forlorn hope that our leaders would bring an end to the conflict before the country was totally poisoned by dissension. No, my discomfort had another cause, and suddenly I realized what it was—I had found myself reacting to Johnson with something like the disdain for him that I deplored in so many liberal intellectuals. I was irked both at my reaction and at Johnson for conjuring it up.

In the years since he left the presidency, much has been written about Lyndon Johnson, the greater part of it uncomplimentary. He has been depicted variously as a boor, a bully, a womanizer, an election stealer, a near paranoiac, and a shameless deceiver of the American people. The evidence that he was, at one time or another, each of these things is depressingly persuasive. Yet a good many Americans, myself included, are nagged by the suspicion that he is the most underrated of our presidents. It is not so much that his flaws have been exaggerated as that they have been allowed to eclipse his virtues and the achievements of his presidency. No one can reasonably deny that his accomplishments in the area of civil rights were as monumental as they were unprecedented. And although it is not fashionable to say so today, the scorn hurled retrospectively at his "war on poverty" (especially by his Republican successors) is supported more by ideology than by hard evidence. The critics conveniently ignore the fact that the proportion of Americans living in poverty declined sharply during the Johnson administration, reaching its lowest point of the post–World War II era. (Since then it has steadily increased, rising most steeply in the Reagan-Bush years.)

Johnson was without doubt a seriously flawed leader. His faults, like his aspirations and everything else about him, were outsized. It should be remembered, however, that unlike most of his successors he did not look comfortably the other way while poverty and inequity took a fearful toll on the least-favored members of our society.

CHAPTER 15 ▪ *Visions of Urban America*

STEPHEN CURRIER WAS a man in a hurry. His agenda was as extensive as it was ambitious, and he pursued it with impatient energy, yet always with meticulous attention to details. Many, though not all, of the issues that engaged him and Audrey were reflected in the grant-making activities of the Taconic Foundation. In addition to civil rights and race relations, these included the special needs of children from disadvantaged backgrounds; education, job training, and employment opportunities for minority youths; low-income housing and community development; and urban planning. Some concerns, such as the arts, the Curriers chose to deal with outside the foundation framework, through direct giving and personal involvement.

Spurred by his feelings of urgency about a wide range of urban problems, Stephen Currier focussed his own efforts through the consolidation of two major agencies long concerned with urban issues: the American Planning and Civic Association (APCA) and Action To Improve Our Neighborhoods (ACTION). So it was that in 1965 the Potomac Institute acquired an organizational sibling called Urban America.

The organization's mission, broadly defined, was to "improve the quality of life" in America's cities. More specifically, this meant that, in tackling the cities' problems, Urban America would seek solutions that enhanced the well-being of all their residents. Writing at the end of 1966, Currier spelled it out this way:

> Ours is a broad concern: that our new communities be built and our old ones rebuilt according to progressively higher standards of excellence—standards which are as respectful of human values as they are reflective of our expanding technology.

We provide a forum for the expression of divergent views, at the same time exercising the right of advocacy. While most of our activities are educational, centered around research and discussion, we also offer direct assistance to local communities. We seek to bridge the gap between the layman and the expert, between the planners and the do-ers, between the private and public sectors. . . .

We regard the city as an organism, in which the physical, social and economic are inextricably related. We work, therefore, to see that all three elements are properly considered in the development of any comprehensive plan. We believe that people affected by the planning process should be involved in the planning process. We are equally convinced that no plan should be considered complete unless there is a mechanism to carry it out. To help communities set up the appropriate mechanisms is one of our primary objectives.

For problems so complex they seem almost overwhelming, we do not pretend to have all the answers. We do, however, mean to raise the right questions.

Currier had picked a tumultuous time to launch a new venture with these bold aspirations. The catastrophic Watts riot of 1965 was the precursor of scores of big-city ghetto explosions in successive summers. The Great Society initiatives aimed at improving inner-city conditions— notably the antipoverty and model cities programs—were soon afflicted by public controversy, reduced funding, and declining political support. The anger and dissension generated by the Vietnam conflict and growing black alienation made it increasingly difficult to build the broad popular consensus needed to fuel effective remedial efforts.

Despite these liabilities, as Urban America began to take shape, it attracted strong and diverse participation by business and financial executives, the churches, mayors and other public officials, planners and developers, journalists, architects, labor leaders, and other influential citizens. It was also able to supplement initial funding from the Taconic Foundation with contributions from other foundations, corporations, and individuals. And, finally, it attracted a professional staff of impressive talent and experience.

All of this was not accomplished overnight. Currier's involvement began in 1962 when he first worked with leaders of APCA to energize its focus on urban problems, leading by 1964 to a changed name, Urban America. Meanwhile, Andrew Heiskell, chairman of Time, Inc., approached Currier in his search for a nonprofit home for *Architectural Forum*, an illustrious Time, Inc. publication. Heiskell was also chairman of ACTION, and the two men saw a natural alliance between ACTION and Urban America; a merger took place with Currier as chairman of Urban America and Heiskell as a key board member. At Currier's request, Potomac board member and urban planner, Philip Hammer, shepherded the transformed organization from his Washington office during the transition period, and Herbert Franklin then came from ACTION to open an office for Urban America in the capital. The first fifteen months were devoted largely to perfecting the organization, defining its program priorities, and recruiting staff. But by mid-1966 Urban America was very much a going concern. Among its accomplishments were:

- Assuming the sponsorship of *Architectural Forum*, the premier publication in its field.
- Development of five centers of program activity: The Business and Development Center aimed at involving the resources and leadership of the private sector in efforts to enhance the quality of urban life, especially for the poor and minorities; its outreach was aided by a National Action Council of one hundred prominent business and professional leaders. The Urban Policy Center promoted research and consultations to encourage public policies favorable to improvement of the cities. The Urban Design Center promoted the inclusion of design professionals and issues in the urban decision-making process. The Non-profit Housing Center offered expert advice, information, and technical assistance to nonprofit sponsors of low- and moderate-income housing. The Information Center was responsible for Urban America's publications program, including its new magazine *City;* it also served a nationwide constituency of editors, reporters, and other media professionals.
- Recruitment of a top quality forty-member staff in the Washington headquarters. (*Architectural Forum*, which remained in New York, had a staff of more than twenty.) In mid-1966, Bill Slayton, having resigned

as federal urban renewal commissioner, was named executive vice-president and assumed direction of the staff operation.

In September 1966, Urban America staged a major "coming out" party. A year in the planning, the three-day national conference was attended by one thousand delegates, including such notables as the vice president, governors, mayors, cabinet members, heads of major corporations, architects, planners, developers, leaders of minority organizations, and a variety of specialists in urban affairs. While the agenda was heavily weighted toward working sessions, the conference had its gala aspects— an opening session on the Washington Mall under striped tents featuring a large model of plans for rejuvenating the Mall and Pennsylvania Avenue; striking exhibits of both urban squalor and superior design projects; and a White House reception hosted by Lady Bird Johnson.

The object of all this panoply was not showmanship for its own sake. It was meant to focus major public attention on the goal of vibrant and livable urban areas. For Stephen Currier, the occasion marked a personal turning point of great significance. His almost obsessive insistence on privacy and anonymity began to give way to a new willingness to play a public role commensurate with the size and importance of his undertakings. From that time onward, he was increasingly at ease in press conferences or on the podium as spokesman for the issues about which he cared so deeply.

During the following years, the Potomac Institute and Urban America had a close collaborative relationship. The linkage was personal as well as professional, since Stephen Currier, Bill Slayton, Philip Hammer, and I played an active part in both organizations. I especially enjoyed my association with Urban America's Information Center and its talented director, Don Canty. He left the staff of *Architectural Forum* in mid-1966 to assume responsibility for Urban America's information and publication programs. One of the most important of these was the launching of the new periodical *City*.

Not long afterward, I was invited to serve on the magazine's five-member editorial board. I soon perceived that Canty, who was an accomplished (and supremely confident) writer and editor, neither needed nor particularly wanted a board. He was passionately committed to the proposition that the editor had an absolute right to decide what the magazine should publish. Although the editorial board members fully understood this, we maintained the polite fiction that our discussions had some policy significance. This suited me fine, since the discussions were lively and informative enough in themselves to need no further reason for being.

By far the most ambitious joint activity of Potomac and Urban America was the effort to create a nationwide coalition to champion the neglected needs of the big cities. By the summer of 1966, almost every major metropolis in the country was in danger of uncontrollable rioting, arson, looting, and senseless violence of every description. Following the Watts riots of the previous year, President Johnson had appointed a blue-ribbon committee, commonly called the "Kerner Commission" after its chairman, to determine the root causes of the disorders and recommend remedial actions.[13] But the commission's deliberations would take more than two years. Meanwhile, the epidemic of racial tension and violence continued to spread. The nation's leaders did little more than deplore the rioting and hope that the police and military could quell it—or at least contain it in the decaying inner-city areas. Aside from the devastation wrought by the riots themselves, there was a growing danger of a white backlash that could only worsen the situation.

Paul Moore, then the Episcopal Suffragan Bishop of Washington, D.C., was deeply dissatisfied with the flaccid response to a national crisis of tragic proportions. One evening in early October 1966, I attended a reception at his home. Bill Slayton was also there. In the course of the evening, Moore took the two of us aside and gave vent to his feelings of frustration. It seems he had been trying to persuade his fellow churchmen to take the lead in initiating a broad-based campaign for major improvement in living conditions and economic opportunity in the inner cities. His pleas had fallen on deaf ears, however, and he had concluded that further effort in that quarter was hopeless. Surely, he said, there is some influential institution or organization that will take the initiative on this. He urged us to try to come up with an alternative approach.

A few days later, I flew to New York for a meeting of the Taconic Foundation board. It was customary on these occasions for Currier to invite me into his office for an hour or so of shoptalk. I decided to use this opportunity to try out on him a few ideas that Paul Moore's lament had stimulated. My suggestion was roughly as follows: The leadership groups with the largest stake in the viability of the cities were mayors and other local officials, business, labor, civil rights and minority organizations, and religious bodies. It would be highly desirable if an initial call for formation of a broad-based coalition came from a group of influential mayors. As founder and president of Urban America, Currier was working closely with just such individuals; he had recruited many of them to the board and National Advisory Committee of Urban America. Why not involve them in a few meetings under the auspices of Urban America to consider the idea?

Currier thought the suggestion was worth exploring. During succeeding weeks, we discussed it with Bill Slayton and other associates in the Taconic Foundation and Urban America. We also gained the cooperation of the U.S. Conference of Mayors and the National League of Cities. It was decided that the next step should be to convene a group of mayors who might serve as the nucleus of a steering committee.

On January 9, 1967, eight big-city mayors gathered, at Stephen Currier's invitation, in Washington. It was a high-powered group, including Joe Barr of Pittsburgh, John Lindsay of New York, Jerome Cavanagh of Detroit, Theodore McKeldin of Baltimore, T. G. Currigan of Denver, Robert King High of Miami, Henry Maier of Milwaukee, and Harold Tolefson of Tacoma. Also attending were representatives of mayors of seven additional cities—Atlanta, Boston, Chicago, New Haven, Philadelphia, Portland (Oregon), and San Francisco.

The mayors responded enthusiastically to Currier's opening statement, in which he summarized his views on the plight of the cities and the acute need for a national coalition to carry the message to the public. The timing of the meeting was fortuitous. Congress was to reconvene the following day, and the air was thick with rumors of drastic cuts in federal support of the War on Poverty, the Model Cities Program, and other Great Society initiatives. The mayors voiced their fears that President Johnson might be willing to trade away funding for his domestic programs in return for support for the Vietnam War. The danger that summer would bring a resumption of urban violence also figured prominently in the discussion.

At a press conference following the meeting, Currier announced that the mayors had resolved to work with Urban America to enlist other mayors, business leaders, "and many other interests" in a new urban coalition. As evidence of their eagerness to advance the project, the mayors asked Currier to reconvene the group for further planning within three weeks, which he agreed to do. We had no way of knowing that, when the time came, Stephen Currier would not be with us.

CHAPTER 16 ▪ *Darkness at Noon*

ON TUESDAY, JANUARY 17, 1967, a small chartered plane bearing two passengers rose from the San Juan, Puerto Rico, airport. It was bound for the island of St. Thomas, a scant seventy miles away. Thirty minutes later the pilot, John B. Watson, radioed a routine request for permission to fly over Culebra Island, then used by the Navy for restricted exercises. He was equally routinely instructed instead to fly around the island. He was not heard from again. The Coast Guard later concluded that the plane, flying by night at a very low altitude, ran into an area of strong unanticipated (but later verified) tropical turbulence. Violent buffeting probably caused it to hit the water and submerge.

The passengers were Stephen and Audrey Currier. That morning, they had departed from Boca Raton, Florida, where they had attended an Urban America conference. They were looking forward to joining their young son Michael in St. Thomas for a ten-day cruise aboard their yacht *Sandoval.*

I learned of their disappearance the following morning by way of a telephone call from Taconic board member Lloyd Garrison. The dreadful news left me too numb at first to grasp what the pained voice at the other end of the line said next. Then I comprehended that there was at least a possibility that the Curriers might be found alive, since there was a life raft aboard the chartered plane. The Coast Guard was initiating an air and sea search of the area along the plane's flight path. It was essential, he said, that we have observers on the scene to monitor the search effort. He hoped I could go.

The prospect of doing something useful was a welcome antidote for my sense of shock and helplessness. I agreed at once to fly to New York and join John Simon and Dorothy Hirshon on a night flight to Puerto Rico.

We arrived in San Juan at daybreak. Dorothy left us to give aid and comfort to Michael. John Simon and I made our way to the Coast Guard headquarters for a meeting with the commanding officer, Captain Thompson. He gave us a sympathetic reception and briefed us on the details of the search. He informed us that two Coast Guard planes, two helicopters, a Civilian Air Patrol plane, a Coast Guard cutter, several patrol boats, and the *Sandoval* were scouring the sea between San Juan and St. Thomas. He also spoke of the limitations of the search. There were two major problems: the size of the area to be covered and the type of Coast Guard aircraft available.

The search area was not just a narrow strip between San Juan and St. Thomas. A life raft or wreckage might already have drifted a hundred miles or more, and the area grew larger with every passing hour. Depending on the prevailing currents in the Caribbean, in a few days the surface to be scanned could stretch westward to Cuba and eastward to Antigua. The number of planes assigned could not come close to overflying so large an expanse within a reasonable time. Moreover, the planes available were designed for high speed. The need was for aircraft capable of flying slowly, virtually hovering over the water, allowing spotters time to identify relatively small objects floating below.

In response to our prodding, Captain Thompson asserted that he simply could not spare more planes for the search. The nearest Coast Guard planes capable of low speed were based in Newfoundland; flying them to San Juan was simply not practicable.

Since the Curriers and their families had the resources to charter private planes, three Piper Aztecs were flown in from Florida—the first of a small fleet of private planes to join the search. Captain Thompson accepted this turn of events with good grace but also with misgivings. He urged us not to add to the influx of private planes, citing the dangers posed by incompatible radio frequencies and the possibility of more crashes, requiring in turn more rescue efforts. We replied that so long as there was a possibility that the Curriers were alive, we had a responsibility to see that the most effective possible search was mounted.

Confronted by two unpalatable alternatives, the captain finally yielded the argument. The ponderous "geese" were flown in from the north. At its peak, the search force consisted of some forty planes, as well as a number of boats, ranging over an area the size of Texas. Meanwhile, John and I were joined by several welcome volunteers from the States, including Peter Berle of Lloyd Garrison's law firm. By virtue of his military experience, as well as intelligence and sound judgment, he was well equipped to coordinate the flights of the chartered aircraft.

During the hectic days and sleepless nights that followed, our gloom and anxiety were periodically lightened by flares of short-lived hope. These false alarms left us with a mounting sense of irreparable loss. By the end of a week of intensive search, there was little more John Simon and I could usefully do in San Juan. We prepared to return to the States, leaving Peter Berle to look after the continuing but vain activity. John was especially needed on the home front. He and his wife Claire had been named in the Curriers' will as personal guardians of the three Currier children—a contingency to which the Simons had consented, never dreaming that it would ever materialize. It was a daunting responsibility.

Before departing, John and I made a farewell call on Captain Thompson. In the course of the conversation, he volunteered a startling explanation of his initial reluctance to extend the search. The background for his revelation went back three decades. In the late thirties, the pioneering woman aviator Amelia Earhart had embarked in a small plane on a flight around the world. On the longest and most desolate leg of her flight, across a wide expanse of the Pacific Ocean, her plane disappeared.

In the suspenseful days that followed, the most massive and widely publicized search of all time ranged over the wastes and tiny, mostly uninhabited islands of the Pacific. Despite the deployment of a huge armada of planes and ships, no conclusive evidence of Amelia Earhart's fate was found.

The public disappointment that followed the fruitless search soon degenerated into angry scapegoating. The Coast Guard officer in charge of the effort was pilloried in the press and other public forums for a monumental waste of taxpayers' money. He narrowly escaped demotion, or worse, before the storm of criticism subsided. In any event, his experience was an object lesson for him and for others who would come after. One of those was Captain Thompson himself, for, as he told us, the commander of the ill-fated search for Amelia Earhart was his father. The search for the Curriers, however, had no adverse consequences for Captain Thompson.

The night flight from San Juan to Washington enabled me, for the first time, to ponder in solitude the full extent of the tragedy. I thought of the pitifully short time the Curriers had to pursue their vision of a generous and beneficent society. I thought of their small children—Michael (5), Lavinia (9), and Andrea (10)—struggling to comprehend that their parents had suddenly and unaccountably vanished from the face of the earth.

The death of Stephen and Audrey was a shattering blow to family, friends, and others who knew and prized them. But it was more than a personal bereavement. It was a grievous loss for all those whose lives had been enriched as a result of their generosity and commitment. Beyond that, it was devastating for a host of people who had never even heard of the Curriers—people who lived in the shadow of the poverty, oppression, and neglect that Stephen and Audrey sought to remedy.

Stephen was thirty-six, Audrey thirty-three. In the brief period allotted to them, they accomplished more than many others had even attempted. Given a full life-span, how much more might they have achieved? As it was, they left a considerable legacy—the changes they set in motion, the good causes they enabled, the individuals whose lives they touched, the foundation they created to extend the reach of their commitment.

As Lloyd Garrison said of the Curriers in his eulogy, "They enlarged our hearts to the measure of their own . . . and they left much for us to do."

WITH THE DEATH OF Stephen and Audrey Currier, the chapters of *The Potomac Chronicle* entirely written by Harold Fleming come to an end. At the time of his own death in 1992, he had completed the manuscript through his description of the harrowing search in Puerto Rico. It is ironic that his personal account of the history of the Institute was cut short at the point in the narrative of the deaths of Stephen and Audrey Currier, who had created it.

The remainder of the history of the Potomac Institute has been completed by his wife, Virginia Fleming, on the basis of his notes and conversations. It incorporates much of Fleming's writings, reflections, and speeches, as well as internal memoranda he prepared for his Potomac colleagues and board members.

In the weeks that followed the Curriers' disappearance, the Taconic Foundation board, led by senior trustee Lloyd K. Garrison, struggled to define its future course. The foundation's contributions to civil rights groups, improved race relations, and child welfare and mental health had largely been financed by annual grants from the Curriers to the foundation. These grants now ended, to be replaced with endowment funds from the Currier estates—funds that would support foundation operations at only one quarter of the previous level. The tragedy, which seemed to put an abrupt end to their long-range plans, caused a great deal of anxiety and uncertainty among those who had earned Taconic support in the past. As the Currier estates were gradually settled, the board set out to establish policies that would carry out the Curriers' intentions, albeit with more limited resources. John Simon was elected the foundation's new president, and Jane Lee Eddy was asked to continue as executive director.

The two largest organizations that had been founded by the Curriers as vehicles for realizing their vision of racial justice—the Potomac Institute and Urban America—had sufficient funds to keep going through the rest of 1967. In succeeding years, Potomac earned grants from the Taconic Foundation on the basis of its performance and an annual proposal that covered the small staff and basic operating costs. Major projects were generally funded through applications to other private foundations.

The Potomac Board of Directors unanimously elected Harold Fleming as president, a position he held until his retirement in 1987, two decades later. Arthur Levin was named executive vice president. Despite the loss of Stephen Currier's active participation, they were determined to carry on the work to which both he and his wife had been committed.

■ PART TWO

CHAPTER 17 ▪ *Consolidating the Gains*

THE SOUTHERN CIVIL RIGHTS movement had won tremendous victories: the Civil Rights Act of 1964 and the Voting Rights Act of 1965.
But what would Washington do with these new powers, these new defi-
nitions of rights? When laws expressing great shifts in national purpose
are passed, putting them to work to change society and institutions is
another story. Those great acts had to be translated into enforcement:
staffing agencies, spelling out regulations, meshing federal, state, and local
responsibilities. All of this would have to be done well, and done in a spirit
faithful to the intent of the laws.

This is what Potomac set out to assure. This was the next step in
its founding mission of furthering positive government action on civil
rights. The institute would assist federal offices when it could, monitor
them closely, pressure them when necessary, lessen political barriers when
possible, and seize opportunities to make the acts work to serve people
who believed they were "free at last".

In retrospect, the years from 1965 to 1968, when a host of federal agencies looked to Potomac for detailed advice about implementing the new
acts, can be seen as the high-water mark of the institute's positive influence on federal agency operations. Although the national commitment
to civil rights was never as courageous or far-reaching as it should have
been, it became more so during the 1960s. The federal government was,
within limits, an active ally. The contrast is compelling between those cooperative years and the later years, when the civil rights forces spent massive energies simply to maintain long-standing policies of fairness and
equal treatment.

Whether in relatively harmonious work or in the later rear-guard
actions, however, the importance of this concentration on administra-

tive and regulatory enforcement of the newly won civil rights legislation should not be underestimated. As activists in related fields such as
women's rights, consumer rights, or environmental issues have also come
to understand, the intent of any law can be realized or vitiated by administrative practices. Potomac's contribution to administrative enforcement
of civil rights was an early example of what are now numerous nonprofit
public interest groups keeping watch on the federal executive branch. The
institute and its colleagues provided an essential link between grassroots
civil rights leaders in the field and the federal agencies who made the
rules by which all were bound.

Many working partnerships between Potomac and a diverse assortment
of federal agencies flourished during the middle years of the 1960s. Institute staff collaborated with the Department of Justice on a range of
civil rights issues, including voting rights, school desegregation, state
and local police violations, public accommodations, and interstate travel.
Under its auspices, Justice Department officials were brought together
with victims of discrimination and others working at the local level, and
Potomac served as a Washington clearinghouse for many of the private
groups working in the South.

Potomac was also directly involved with other agencies that had civil
rights responsibilities, particularly the Department of Health, Education
and Welfare (HEW), the Department of Commerce, the Office of Economic Opportunity and even the Selective Service.

Arthur Levin spent more than a year serving on an HEW task force
charged with working out ways to implement Title VI of the Civil Rights
Act, the provision that carried the threat of denying federal support to all
public institutions that failed to comply with the new act. The scope of
this mandate was unprecedented, and some of the heaviest compliance
responsibilities fell to HEW, which had oversight of schools, hospitals,
and nursing homes. The reporting requirements alone were overwhelming. To no one's surprise, institutions threatened with the potential loss
of major government support wasted no time in mounting campaigns to
weaken any possible enforcement mechanism.

HEW Secretary John Gardner and Peter Libassi, his special assistant
for civil rights, recruited Levin to help examine the Secretary's Office of

Civil Rights and the main HEW divisions: the Public Health Service, the Office of Education, the Social Security Administration, the Welfare Administration, and the Vocational Rehabilitation Administration. The task force took on thorny problems: Should actual field reviews of private agencies be required? How extensive should they be? How should complaints be handled? What constituted fair hearings for agencies found in default? How and when should sanctions be applied? What were HEW's training and staffing needs?

Gradually, much of the recommended new implementation machinery was put in place. This proved to be just the first stage, however, in the long struggle by Potomac Institute and other civil rights organizations to pressure the agency to realize the promise of Title VI.

Two other weapons in the War on Poverty were the Public Works and Economic Development Act and the Appalachian Regional Development Act. Between them, the laws mandated the infusion of massive federal funds—more than $1 billion annually—into depressed areas. Most of the money going to targeted "redevelopment areas" was to be used for public works such as water and sewer systems, access roads and industrial parks; some was for business loans and technical assistance grants.

The Economic Development Administration (EDA) in the Department of Commerce was responsible for implementing the legislation. Percy Williams Jr., special assistant to Assistant Secretary of Commerce Eugene P. Foley, asked Potomac to take on another task force assignment. Arthur Levin served as director, with staff work provided by James Gibson, Kenneth C. Jones (an outside consultant), and Commerce Department staff members.

Potomac's report to Foley in May 1966 pointed out that although the intent of the act was to provide economic well-being for the people who lived in depressed areas, EDA had thus far emphasized the development of industry. The task force urged EDA to refocus on its basic mission and stressed the need to link economic development resources with other manpower development programs. Not only was sharing the "benefits of federally assisted economic development and growth by all the people of a designated area, particularly minority groups . . . mandatory under Title VI of the Civil Rights Act of 1964" but it also made good economic sense. Foley accepted all the recommendations.

The Office of Economic Opportunity (OEO) under Sargent Shriver's direction also sought out Potomac. In 1965, institute staff helped the Job Corps Community Relations Division in its efforts to integrate its trainees into the social and cultural life of the communities in which they worked. Early in 1966, Sam Yette, Shriver's special assistant, enlisted Potomac staff in discussions of OEO's civil rights program. He wanted to be sure the agency met the minimum legal requirements, but was also very concerned that the War on Poverty have a significant effect on the lives of minorities.

The institute readily agreed to do a formal study of OEO's civil rights functions, organization and procedures. It covered all programs, including the Job Corps, Rural Poverty, National Youth Corps, VISTA, Community Action Program, Head Start, Legal Services, and Upward Bound, and examined federal and local employment practices, volunteer and enrollee recruitment, composition of local boards and committees, contract compliance, complaint procedures, and Title VI compliance.

While doing the study, Potomac began to question whether the usual governmental practice of construing civil rights in narrow, legalistic terms of "controls," "enforcement," "complaints," and "compliance" made sense within the context of the poverty program. The final report recognized OEO's substantial and in many cases unprecedented accomplishments, and the freewheeling approach that made these possible, but it also spelled out some of the complex problems inherent in empowering minorities and poor people. It concluded that under the Economic Opportunity Act of 1964 and the Civil Rights Act of 1964, "Civil rights must include the right of full participation in the working of our society, without exclusion, without denial, without discrimination. This does not mean legal equity or equality in the OEO program alone; it means the right to share fully and equally in American society. . . . It is only within this broader context that the next and the more profound stage of the battle for civil rights can be waged."

The report's recommendations followed the same broad themes: the OEO Office of Civil Rights, rather than serving a routine compliance function, should be upgraded to a fundamental policy review role. Projects had to be carefully reviewed to assure that they did not foster segregation of groups from each other or from the majority community.

OEO's civil rights staff should initiate relationships with their counterparts in other federal agencies, both in Washington and locally. Staff and funds should be directed to launch programs in unserved rural areas. Although Shriver apparently found these conclusions more far-reaching than he anticipated and chose not to publish or release the report, he received it cordially and did incorporate a number of its recommendations into agency policy.

Finally, as the Vietnam War brought the operation of the Selective Service under intense national scrutiny, Potomac took on an assignment to determine how the military draft could treat minorities more equitably. In September of 1966, President Johnson appointed a National Advisory Commission on Selective Service chaired by Burke Marshall, who had by now left his post as Assistant Attorney General for Civil Rights to become General Counsel of IBM. The commission's task was to examine long-range principles for governing the selective service or other systems of national service. Potomac's research associate Margaret Price first gathered information on military service by race. The Institute then convened a group of specialists on civil rights, civil liberties, and manpower issues to analyze the inequitable effects of current admission standards, the composition of local draft boards, local quotas, and student exemptions. Their brief report to the commission emphasized the importance of a fair national lottery with exemptions only for conscientious objectors and those totally unfit to serve.

But even as the Potomac Institute recommended ways to make civil rights concerns an integral part of the operation of the military draft, the bitterness engendered by the Vietnam War had become a major factor in changing the whole governmental context in which it worked.

CHAPTER 18 ∎ *Slouching toward a Divided Society*

THE PROJECT THAT HAD captured the interest of Stephen Currier just before his death was well under way in early 1967: to create an effective coalition of mayors and business, civil rights, religious and labor leaders which would address urban decay and neglect. But the rapidly changing social and political realities would limit its possibilities before many months passed.

In January, a potent group of big-city mayors convened by Currier had agreed to seek a strong national commitment to help cities deal with poverty, the pressing need for urban redevelopment, and the challenge of providing equal opportunity to their citizens. The new group was called the Urban Coalition. Following Currier's death, Andrew Heiskell, chief executive officer of Time, Inc., was persuaded to become chairman. He and Walter Reuther, president of the United Auto Workers, did a remarkable job of pulling together disparate groups to tackle the coalition's work. The executive committee chose to begin with an immediate response to the frightening epidemic of urban riots that seemed to paralyze the country during 1967's "long hot summer": a Washington convocation that would rouse the nation to action.

The convocation gathered leading business, labor, religious, and civil rights figures of great prestige to meet with the mayors of virtually every major city. As Whitney Young, president of the Urban League, commented, "The people gathered in this room have the power, the resources, to turn this country around." He also noted, "There has been much discussion in the past few weeks and months that established Negro leadership has failed and has lost its influence. Historians will point out differently. They will point out that it is a miracle that established leadership has for so long a time enjoyed the support of Negro citizens—living as they are in squalor, poverty and unemployment while still retaining their hope and faith in the society."

A ringing call to action emerged from the convocation: "We believe the American people and the Congress must reorder national priorities, with a commitment of resources equal to the magnitude of the problems we face." The nation must "end once and for all the shame of poverty amid general affluence." Congress must "move without delay . . . on additional civil rights legislation, adequately funded model cities, anti-poverty, housing education, and job-training programs." The country must put at least one million of the presently unemployed into productive work as soon as possible, and produce a million housing units for lower-income families each year.

As staff generated followup programs, the coalition gradually spun off from Urban America and opened its own office. The Potomac Institute worked with a number of local coalitions organized across the country, seeding project ideas and distributing useful information. Fleming assisted William Slayton and Don Canty of Urban America to organize a massive publicity and information campaign by the National Advertising Council.

By February 1968, the Urban Coalition had become a fully independent organization. Heiskell recruited John Gardner, until recently secretary of Health, Education and Welfare, to become chairman of the new organization, bringing the promise of significant leadership and resources. He was in turn succeeded by Carl Holman, a highly respected civil rights leader.

From these beginnings grew in the long run a new engagement with social justice on the part of the business community. But the determined hopes of 1967 soon gave way to the tensions of 1968. Urban crime and disorder, the Vietnam War, the alienation of the student generation, and stubborn resistance to real integration in schools, employment and housing overwhelmed the cries for justice. Violence in the ghettos and on campuses took an increasing toll on Lyndon Johnson's domestic agenda, and on his own equilibrium. Both the president and Congress seemed to give investment in the war and the space program a higher priority than urban and social programs.

The Ninetieth Congress briefly considered a bold response to the riots proposed by Senators Javits and Clark. It would have added $300 million to the antipoverty bill to restore small businesses hurt by riots and create emergency jobs. The legislators settled half-heartedly, however, on a weak compromise appropriation. By 1968, political disarray and backpedaling on social goals were the order of the day. Vietnam had undermined the psychic and social health of the country more grievously than any conceivable merits of our involvement there could justify.

Northern resistance to real desegregation had by now become an intractable fact of life. As Fleming noted in speaking to civil rights groups, "The veneer of racial liberalism looked solid when the evils of the Old South were dramatically brought into the open. But it cracked badly when the issues came close to home, when the sordidness of the big city ghettos threatened the complacency of the suburbs. . . . In the immortal words of Walt Kelly, 'we have met the enemy and he is us.'"

The unity of the civil rights movement had always been fragile; now it was fracturing. Its older generation of leaders could no longer maintain order in the face of an apparent retreat on the part of white America.

Many of the emerging black leaders distrusted white intentions and challenged both the goals and tactics of the old-line civil rights organizations. Martin Luther King Jr.'s opposition to the Vietnam War, which he announced early in 1967, antagonized some of his former allies who thought his stand diluted the strength of the movement. And as more blacks listened to those who preached violence, more whites demanded sterner law enforcement.

In Fleming's view, white "backlash" was an irrational and self-serving response to the new militancy of young black organizers:

At a time when most Negro Americans are impotent to improve their lots, a few cries of "black power" are regarded not as wistful sloganeering, but as a dire threat to national security. Whatever one may think of Stokely Carmichael's ill-tempered advocacy of self-help, it is absurd that he can be so widely depicted as the explanation—and even justification—of the "white backlash," the emergence of non-entities and incompetents into political prominence, the disarray of the civil rights movement, the relapse of white liberals, and the decline of progressivism generally. I am surprised that he has not yet been seen as the cause of high food prices and smog.

So long as many white Americans persist in treating the irrelevancy of color as a badge of inferiority, so long will Negro Americans organize and act as a group to combat prejudice and its blighting effects. These responsible efforts deserve our respect and our active support.

The pyrotechnics of Black Power may seem to blot out all hope of accommodation on the philosophic level, but I doubt that the same is true on the pragmatic level. . . . As I read them, [young black militants] earnestly want to build new community institutions, conceived and run by black people, that will command respect because they really work. . . . Their message to whites goes something like this: "Why should we respect you? If you have power, you have misused it; if you are powerless, you are irrelevant." It is unkind, but hard to argue with.

Some things said or done in the name of the new Blackness must, I believe, be challenged. One cannot, it seems to me, remain silent when demands are made that black separatism be mandated by law or regulation. . . . The principle that the civil liberties of friend and foe alike must be respected may seem an irrelevant middle-class luxury to the young, the poor, the alienated; but others cannot be excused for not seeing it as a necessity, to be defended against dilution by anyone.

Although some of us older heads may be disturbed by the excesses of youthful revolt and repelled by black imitations of white racism, we would do well to keep our antennae up and our volume down. It may just be that out of the ugliness of alienation and anger some hopeful new things are about to be born.

But in 1968 there was little evidence of hope. President Johnson appointed a National Advisory Commission on Civil Disorders chaired by Governor Kerner of Illinois to examine, and perhaps recommend a way to defuse, the urban chaos. Its report cited as root causes of civil disorder the exclusion of blacks from economic life, and the massive concentration of poor blacks in urban ghettos where they were segregated into substandard housing and schools. It warned that the nation was "moving toward two societies, one black, one white—separate but unequal." Its language was direct: "What white Americans have never fully understood—but what the Negro can never forget—is that white society is deeply implicated in the ghetto. White institutions created it, white institutions maintain it, and white society condones it. The consequence is a greatly increased burden on the already depleted resources of cities, creating a growing crisis of deteriorating facilities and services and unmet human needs . . . [S]egregation and poverty have intersected to destroy opportunity and hope, and to enforce failure."

"To pursue our present course," the report concluded, would lead to "continuing polarization of the American community and, ultimately, the destruction of basic democratic values".

Yet the bitter march of events was overwhelming. On April 4, Martin Luther King was assassinated in Memphis. Shock and sorrow swept the country as the news media played and replayed the prophetic words of his final speech. Blacks gave way to grief and rage. Violence broke out in more than 150 cities, nowhere more shockingly than in Washington, D.C. Television cameras sent around the country and the world scenes of the White House barricaded by a ring of buses and the night sky over the nation's capital lit by the flames of over seven hundred fires.

The Democratic party seemed on the verge of uniting under the leadership of Robert Kennedy, who was beginning to speak out passionately on issues of human rights and urban blight. But his assassination in June, on the night he overwhelmingly defeated Vice President Hubert Humphrey and Senator Eugene McCarthy in the California primary, set off another wave of national outrage and mourning. It led ultimately to the disastrous Democratic convention in Chicago. Young protesters were bloodied in a confrontation that turned into what an investigating commission described as a "police riot." Middle-class Americans soon thereafter voiced their grievances against higher taxes, inflation, "moral decay," unruly students, rising crime, and public disorder by electing Richard Nixon to the presidency in November.

Civil rights achievements in the decade of the sixties were dramatic: the end of legal segregation and the legally supported dual school system in the South, free access to public accommodations, and legal protection for the right to vote. But in fact they only set the stage for a possible future. Measured in economic and social terms, equity was not yet visible. Census data in 1970 made it plain that statistical gains in black well-being were outdistanced by white gains.

To many Americans, however, the years of civil rights protest, capped by legislative victories, seemed sufficient. Presidential leadership on civil rights evaporated. It would not return in any significant way during all the remaining years of Potomac's work.

CHAPTER 19 ■ *Riding Herd on Federal*
Retrenchment on Civil Rights

ANY PROGRESSIVE VISION Nixon may have harbored of improving
social services or promoting civil rights soon gave way to his political
agenda—the courting of conservatives in both political parties, especially
in the South. His urban affairs adviser, Daniel Patrick Moynihan, suggested (in another famous memorandum leaked to the press) that race
relations might benefit from a "period of benign neglect."

It soon became clear that White House policy went beyond mere neglect. As Fleming wrote to the Potomac board in 1969:

> With the advent of the present administration, the use of govern-
> mental power to advance equal opportunity has not merely con-
> tinued to decline, it has increasingly been used repressively.
>
> Not all of these regressive attempts have succeeded—in part,
> ironically, because of resistance in Congress, which was the last of
> the three branches to move affirmatively in this field. But the nega-
> tive trend continues as the hallmark of the Southern/Suburban
> Strategy.
>
> Partly as cause and partly as effect of these Federal divaga-
> tions, public perceptions of America's race problem have radically
> changed. . . . What was once seen as a predominantly Southern prob-
> lem has come to be seen as a primarily urban problem, most acute in
> the ghettos of the North and West. Overt discrimination and segre-
> gation now figure less prominently in public discussion, while the
> "culture of poverty" and "institutional (i.e., indirect) racism" are
> more commonly viewed as the heart of the matter. . . .
>
> During the Potomac Institute's brief life span, the level of "ex-
> pectation" has gone from an excessive high to an abject low. The

attempts to render the "establishment" responsive to the needs of minorities and the poor not long ago was viewed as the essence of meaningful organized effort. Now, for many, it is a contemptible diversion. . . .

But all is not occasion for hand-wringing and lamentation. Unmixed curses are as rare as unmixed blessings, and for every negative trend there is a positive counter-trend. The Administration's Agnewisms, Mitchellisms, Carswellisms, and even Moynihanisms, may yet succeed in creating new life in a liberal black-white coalition that was all but suffocated by the Democratic Administration's embrace. By virtue of the very fact that they are threatened, school desegregation, Title VI of the Civil Rights Act, the fair housing title, and other fundamental issues are attracting renewed visibility and support. . . .

There is some justification for the assumption that Potomac . . . need not want for opportunities that are worth the effort.

A sign of the times was the rapid proliferation of Washington-based advocacy groups, almost an "administration in exile." Potomac, of course, was already there. Its life and work, however, would be changed. The administration would not now be staffed with friends (dropping by for fiveses), reliably returning phone calls, keeping doors open.

Riding herd on executive action to weaken civil rights enforcement— soon commonly referred to as administrative repeal of civil rights— meant in Fleming's view "being attentive to the possibilities of new (and previously unperceived) combinations of talent, resources and self-interest that can fruitfully be brought together around one of the issues of our current concern." One of these combinations, in which Potomac played an important part, was a working collaboration organized by the venerable Leadership Conference on Civil Rights with staffing by a new group—the Center for National Policy Review (CNPR).

The Leadership Conference was a long-established and successful partnership of more than 125 national organizations concerned with civil rights. Under the indomitable leadership of attorneys Joseph Rauh and Clarence Mitchell, it had over many years kept the heat on Congress and the executive branch on every aspect of civil rights.

The Center for National Policy Review, on the other hand, was in 1970 a brand new non-profit organization established by William L. Taylor, who had served as the general counsel of the U.S. Commission on Civil Rights and an attorney for the NAACP Legal Defense Fund. CNPR relied on law students and a small staff to keep a close watch on regulations implementing civil rights statutes and to conduct research on major legal cases. In the process, it served as a training ground for many young lawyers who went on to work in civil rights and other public interest activities. Beginning in 1974, Fleming served on CNPR's advisory board, and later became its chairman, an office he held until it closed its doors in 1986.

CNPR joined forces with the Leadership Conference in the early 1970s to monitor systematically the performance of executive agencies in enforcing civil rights mandates. It was a necessary but often tedious and unrewarding job. Several task forces made up of Leadership Conference members and other private organizations acted as watchdogs, commentators and negotiators with agencies that were delinquent in their compliance activities, or even totally inactive. Their mission received major support from the Ford, New World, Stern, and other foundations.

Using tax-exempt funds to monitor public expenditures and program performance was at the time a new strategy. As Fleming noted, "The issue is one of accountability. Business, professional and trade associations, unions and other special interest groups have long employed lobbyists as watchdogs and advocates of their interests, in both the legislative and executive branches. Ordinary citizens have no comparable means of exacting accountability in terms of the broader public interest."

Many of those who worked on education or housing issues, including Arthur Levin, found little response. But not all the Nixon officials Potomac worked with behind the scenes were hostile. At the Office of Management and Budget (OMB), Director George Schultz and his deputy, Frank Carlucci, welcomed the new channel of communication with the task force on civil rights oversight chaired by Fleming, with the assistance of CNPR attorney Mort Sklar. Schultz issued an internal directive requiring OMB personnel to make civil rights concerns an integral part of the agency's management of all federal operations. The president's Domestic Affairs Council created a Civil Rights Committee which Schultz chaired.

One of the toughest issues OMB had to deal with was the perennial question of collecting racial data. At Potomac, the collection of such information was seen as an essential tool in measuring progress in civil rights. Fleming wrote in a memorandum for the Leadership Conference:

> Unglamorous as it may sound, this activity is indispensable to both governmental and private monitoring of the civil rights performance of private employers, the federal civil service, state and local governments, banks and other lending institutions, public school systems, state colleges and universities, hospitals and health services, housing authorities, and a host of other federally assisted or regulated services. Advocacy groups rely on this information to identify communities and institutions that persist in discrimination; the news media use it to report progress, or the lack of it, to the public; and the government itself cannot conduct meaningful compliance programs without such data.

Yet he also well understood those who were uncomfortable about identifying people by race.

> The collection of racial and ethnic data rankles administrators and defenders of the meritocratic viewpoint. Many university officials and teachers see it as an intrusion on sacrosanct processes of professional selection and advancement, as well as on personnel records that are regarded as inviolate in academe. Many employers see it as a burdensome (and often embarrassing) imposition on management. Government officials themselves tend to be reluctant to the point of recalcitrance about inflicting the chore of data-gathering on their subordinates, grantees, and contractors.
>
> The reasons for these negative attitudes toward data collection are several. One is the conviction that such censuses are inextricably related to the violation of merit standards and the imposition of quotas, overt or covert. Another is understandable resentment of time-consuming red tape that diverts energy and attention from the primary mission of the enterprise. Yet another is the surviving fear of civil rights adherents, white and black, that racial data will, in the end, inevitably be used to perpetuate rather than end discrimination.

Each of these objections is justified to some degree. Yet, when the alternative consequences are considered, it is difficult to sustain the argument against the collection and analysis of racial data, at least at this stage of history. If we are serious about finding and using the methods that will create equality in practice, we must have the means to measure the relative effectiveness or ineffectiveness of our efforts. That is what racial data collection is, or should be, all about.

Eventually, federal data collection requirements were maintained, but not without a continuing struggle through the Reagan years. By now, thanks to this persistent work, racial data collection is widely accepted and used.

By the end of Nixon's first term, his administration's hostility toward equal opportunity programs was underscored by two new initiatives: the impoundment of appropriated funds and the practice of revenue sharing. Revenue sharing was central to the grandly named concept of "new federalism," which included transferring control of assistance programs to the states. In an argument that resonates for the current debate about devolution of powers to the states, Fleming warned:

Generally speaking, [the New Federalism] is characterized by a predilection for . . . curtailment of domestic spending, distaste for federal intervention (particularly for social purposes), and the setting of public priorities by states and localities rather than the federal government.

As a general philosophy of government, decentralization has many attractive features. Washington politicians and bureaucrats are, in fact, often fatuous, ill-informed, wasteful, and arbitrary. To diminish their authority in favor of local decision-making processes is an appealing notion. In practical application, however, decentralization raises some unsettling social questions.

Local government processes, devoid as they frequently are of any national perspective, can be more bigoted, autocratic, and heedless of the general welfare than any decisions emanating from Washington. More specifically, in the area of equal treatment, national goals and standards achieved after decades of arduous effort are suddenly in danger of extinction.

Since the days of the New Deal, the Federal Government has been seen as the protector of the rights of the disadvantaged minorities and the poor in general. The recent emphasis on governmental decentralization, revenue sharing and block grants is, therefore, viewed by civil rights advocates as regressive. How much public money is being diverted from social needs to tax relief, physical facilities, hardware, and so on? How much citizen participation is there in the local decision-making that the New Federalism celebrates?

During Nixon's second term, CNPR took on a project to monitor the civil rights aspects of revenue sharing, and was able to document how the new distribution of federal largess shortchanged minorities and the poor. In many discussions with federal officials, the Leadership Conference task force set out to defuse the adverse effects of revenue sharing by advocating explicit equal opportunity guidelines, stronger enforcement guarantees, and special remedies in regions where minorities had been undercounted.

These efforts were fruitless. The Office of Revenue Sharing (ORS), ignoring OMB efforts to strengthen enforcement, was unwilling to hold back funds from jurisdictions that failed to comply with civil rights regulations, nor would it change the distribution formulas. Regulations issued by the Treasury in 1975, which reduced the department's capacity to act speedily and effectively against noncompliers, signaled a further retreat.

Attempts to encourage the Department of Justice to enforce Title VI of the Civil Rights Act were equally frustrating. It appeared that Justice had unilaterally abdicated the enforcement job vested in the Attorney General. By late 1975, the department was taking an interest only in Title VI matters that were subject to lawsuits by private parties.

When Nixon resigned and Ford took over, nothing changed. "A retrospective look at the public scene in 1974 arouses little nostalgia," Fleming wrote to his board:

> Some comfort might be derived from the fact that "Watergate" and associated scandals raised the issue of public morality to the top of the national agenda. But if morality is defined to include equality of

opportunity, the year ended no better than it began. In fact, in terms of unemployment, inflation, and publicly-supported programs, minorities ended the year in worse shape than they started it.

Some insights may be gained from the results of a poll conducted by the Gallup organization for our namesake Potomac Associates in mid-1974. The poll found "the problems of black Americans" at the very bottom of the list of Americans' concerns, and "improving the situation of black Americans" received the next to lowest rating as an object of government spending for domestic purposes.

One should not conclude from this that racial hostility and bias were on the upswing. Two other sets of responses indicated something different. Questions designed to measure discriminatory attitudes elicited more favorable responses than in earlier years. And yet another question indicated that the majority of respondents felt that blacks had recently made a great deal of progress, although blacks themselves did not see it that way.

These findings indicated that many Americans were taking their cues from influential national leaders, who generally tended to ignore minority problems or to imply blandly that they were steadily diminishing. Thus, public racial attitudes seemed to reflect less antagonism than indifference, based on complacency about minority progress. Such complacency appeared clearly unfounded. The latest census data showed a decline in minority status, both absolute and relative, with respect to income, employment housing concentration, and so on. One might suppose that national economic woes contributed to feelings of indifference toward minorities: widespread adversity does not encourage a spirit of generosity toward the less fortunate.

CHAPTER 20 ▪ *Beyond Federal Programs*

THE STRUGGLE TO MAINTAIN federal enforcement of civil rights mandates was not the only arena of Potomac activity. Widespread institutional segregation woven into the fabric of American society also demanded attention. Although basic constitutional questions had been settled and formal barriers to equal treatment in public life were removed, Fleming frequently spoke of how much more was necessary.

> Taking down the "white only" signs doesn't in itself create equal opportunity—though many Americans seem to think so.
>
> Over the years, segregation and discrimination have been thoroughly built into all of the major institutions of our society, north as well as south. These *de facto* discriminations reinforce each other and are perpetuated not only by prejudice, but by a host of impersonal influences—inertia, custom, habit, and the cumulative effects of deprivation among Negroes that discrimination has produced.
>
> A legal or policy change thus produces little practical result; it is only the prelude to a complicated and painful regearing of the given "system"—including public and private institutions—to overcome the effects of past discrimination and generate really meaningful opportunities for Negroes. This is a job for which few people have any relish, skill, or experience. But it must be done if the token and symbolic progress of the past twenty years is to become broader and more practically significant.

By the late 1960s, as the predominant mood of the country became less hospitable to far-reaching programs of social reform, Potomac undertook a series of private initiatives aimed at systematic institutional change and expanded opportunities for blacks. Working with combinations of political, professional, and interest groups, Potomac fostered projects ranging from minority business development to the revitalization of central cities. Much of this activity was spearheaded by James Gibson, who had joined Potomac's small staff in 1966. Gibson had years of experience with civil rights organizations in Atlanta, and brought to the staff his special interest in community and neighborhood development projects to support minority opportunity.

Among his first projects, for example, was the launching of the Mississippi Beef Project, which spoke to two Potomac interests: the need for rural economic development and the need to work with and support a new generation of black officials who were taking office in both North and South.

A newly elected black Mississippi state senator, Robert Clark, came to Fleming and Gibson to talk about the economic hardships of his rural constituents. Gibson drew on contacts he had established while working with Potomac board member Vivian Henderson, president of Clark College, on the National Advisory Commission on Rural Poverty. He convened a strategy group, including an Illinois cattle-grower whom he knew from the commission and a consultant from the Office of Economic Opportunity, to work out the details of a beef-raising cooperative. Within a few months, a beef cooperative was established with funding from OEO and the Ford Foundation, and $2.5 million in mortgage money for pasturage and cattle from the Farmers Home Administration.

Opening Up the Free Enterprise System

In the late 1960s, Potomac staff reached out through local groups associated with the Urban Coalition to expand corporate equal opportunity programs. Fleming, for example, worked for several months to help officials of the Kodak Corporation launch a broad set of new policies and procedures in its corporate headquarters in Rochester, New York.

But he sought at the same time a more far-reaching project to support minority business development. The result was the Council on Equal Business Opportunity (CEBO). Its origin is another example of how Potomac created a reassuring environment to bring together experts, consultants, and foundation executives to generate new ideas.

The plan was to provide business counseling, management skills training, and technical assistance to black entrepreneurs who were launching their own businesses. Beginning as a demonstration project in Baltimore, CEBO grew into an independent national organization.

The idea arose when board member Philip Hammer introduced Fleming to Benjamin Goldstein, who had left his post as president of Franklin Simon, the New York retail store chain, to head the minority loan program at the Small Business Administration (SBA). But now Goldstein wanted to work in a privately sponsored program. His interest fit with ideas Fleming had been discussing with John Coleman of the Ford Foundation, who wanted to make grants in the minority business area for projects that had a good chance of succeeding. A two-year Ford grant of $246,000 to Potomac began in early 1967.

Goldstein insisted on moving beyond traditional "ghetto" or marginal enterprises and toward mainstream market opportunities in retail, service, manufacturing, and building construction fields. In a few months the organization was in place, with Fleming and Hammer serving as CEBO board members. Goldstein and a staff of two other professionals, including Baltimore businessman Sam Daniels, were soon working with thirty minority business clients. CEBO also persuaded major corporations in the area to develop subcontractor capabilities among its clients by providing them with technical and training assistance.

CEBO had ambitious goals in its efforts to develop relatively large and stable businesses. It set high standards of financial accountability, required rigorous accounting, and was committed to intensive long-range consulting services for its clients. Progress was often rocky. Goldstein, a self-confident white outsider with foundation funds at his disposal, was tough and outspoken. A chronic shortage of clients with relevant previous experience led to continual debate about acceptable levels of risk.

As time went on, however, the most pressing problem was finding risk capital, which the conservative banking community was reluctant to make available for minority ventures. Goldstein proceeded to raise funds and put together support for the Baltimore Community Investment Company (BCIC), a unique new lending institution with sixteen blacks and six whites on its board. It took months of groundwork to overcome predictable but daunting conflicts over the sharing of management control and the definition of tolerable risk levels. The company's initial capitalization was financed by a sale of $600,000 in stock, matched by a $1.8 million loan from the SBA. CEBO worked with the new company to screen and train potential borrowers.

At the press conference announcing BCIC, Kenneth Wilson, vice president of the Afro-American Newspapers, set the tone: "We do not regard this financial involvement simply as a means of getting a few Negroes a break in the business world. More than that, we look at it as the beginning of a process to open up the free enterprise system to Negroes."

The results of the two-year Baltimore demonstration project were encouraging enough to warrant a broader application. Fleming obtained another three-year grant from the Ford Foundation to expand the idea to other cities, to fund a training program for business development specialists, and to give a challenge grant to Baltimore CEBO to enable it to become fully self-supporting.

Goldstein and his deputy, Cliff Henry, set up the National CEBO (N/CEBO), a new organization that worked with several cities to replicate the Baltimore results. Its first offshoot was the independent non-profit Washington Metropolitan Area Business Service.

One of N/CEBO's major interests was in promoting black-owned supermarkets. Using a network of investment bankers, wholesale grocers, supermarket chains, and universities located in black communities, the staff brought technical assistance and economies of scale to dozens of new enterprises. They also experimented with a "joint venture" process by which new black firms could become partners with experienced white businesses in shared undertakings.

Over time, N/CEBO moved beyond an exclusive concentration on entrepreneurial capitalism to focus on broad community development projects. It sponsored the National Urban Services Development Corporation, which helped set up and manage neighborhood commercial projects all over the country. Encouraged by the Ford Foundation to extend its reach by sharing its business skills with nonprofit and community organizations as well as commercial businesses, N/CEBO went on to work with groups such as the Delta Foundation in Mississippi, TWO in Chicago, and Geno Baroni's National Center for Urban Ethnic Affairs, in their efforts to generate and nurture viable economic enterprises.

Meanwhile, Baltimore CEBO met its matching requirement and became fully independent. By 1970 N/CEBO was also a thriving independent organization complete with its own leadership and constituency, as well as its own funding through grants and contracts for services it provided. As a national repository of important experience and skill, N/CEBO was even in a position to advise foundations on expanding similar programs. Within a few years of its creation, the CEBO project had established community mechanisms to generate minority business development in half a dozen major metropolitan areas; it produced more than a million dollars in project funding, and a much larger sum in SBA, foundation and commercial investment in the business enterprises themselves.

This project influenced two other ventures that turned out to have long-term value in the economic development field. One was the launching of the "program-related investing" (PRI) movement in the U.S. PRI involves the use of foundation investing (through debt, equity, and guarantees), rather than grants, to carry out philanthropic goals. This was a concept tried out in the eighteenth century by Benjamin Franklin but then almost wholly unused and untested for almost two centuries. Taconic Foundation president John Simon, a Potomac board member, had been exploring the legality and utility of this idea. When Potomac began the search for foundation capital to buy shares in Baltimore CEBO, this initiative was one of the triggers that led Simon to convene a group of foundations to discuss the PRI concept and the possibility of a multi-foundation PRI pool. Such a pool was established in 1968 under the name of the Cooperative Assistance Fund; for twenty-five years it has been investing in enterprise development projects in low-income communities. At the same time the Ford Foundation began a major PRI program (Louis Winnick at Ford had been thinking along the same lines for some time). These activities, in turn, encouraged other foundations to try out the PRI process; with Congressional and IRS approval, more than three hundred foundations have made such investments.

A more direct and exceedingly important by-product of the N/CEBO experience, however, was the exposure of young minority staff members and trainees to this particular brand of practical economic development skills, as a result of an internship and training program begun with a

$100,000 grant from the Economic Development Administration of the Commerce Department. N/CEBO also launched a training program for government employees who evaluated minority enterprise programs. In the words of Cliff Henry, former staff and trainees "are all over the country working successfully in economic development, financial management, housing development and government."

And Potomac, in "spinning off" the initial project into independence, had kept faith with its own style of putting together small, flexible operations which in turn generated new ideas and new leadership.

Technical Assistance to Central Cities

Jim Gibson played an important synthesizing role in Potomac's efforts to develop a new cadre of urban specialists who were prepared to tackle the problems of America's inner cities.

The cities, "which had risen from the ashes of the 1960s riots," Fleming wrote, "soon found themselves the repositories of the country's accumulated social ills. For the first time since the Great Depression, cities teetered on the brink of bankruptcy. Racial polarization, ghettoization and urban decay were all byproducts of this continuing national neglect."

At the same time, an enormous increase in the number of blacks registering and voting, coupled with the concentration of blacks in central cities, led to the election of black mayors and other local government officials in both the North and the South. The new leaders soon realized they had to deal with overwhelming problems on all fronts, from fiscal crises to the general deterioration of services and infrastructure—not to mention racial discrimination.

In 1968, soon after Richard Hatcher was elected the first black mayor of Gary, Indiana, he asked Potomac how it could help his new administration assess its problems and devise solutions. General government assistance was not in Potomac's portfolio, but after considerable discussion, Jim Gibson was loaned temporarily to Mayor Hatcher's administration. His role was to help assemble a team of specialists who would do brief surveys on the scene, recommend approaches, recruit useful personnel, and round up fiscal resources.

Gibson quickly discovered how difficult it was to attract high-level personnel to Gary. Salaries were low, and training and career-ladder opportunities limited. Potomac soon became seriously engaged in the problem of developing a new cadre of urban specialists.

During about eight months as special adviser to Hatcher, Gibson worked along with other concerned organizations, including the U.S. Conference of Mayors, National Urban Coalition, Urban America, Metropolitan Applied Research Corporation, and several foundations. As a result, Hatcher was able to develop and begin to secure funding for major local programs directed at reducing poverty, meeting health and welfare needs, fostering economic development, and increasing citizen participation in every aspect of political and cultural life. Once the major senior positions were filled in Gary, Gibson's and Potomac's involvement officially ended, but their ongoing policy consultation continued over the next few years.

By the end of the decade, more than two thousand black elected officials were in place. A new Institute of Black Elected Officials was established in Washington to conduct research and offer technical assistance to this important new group of leaders. Under the direction of Eddie Williams, a former faculty member at the University of Chicago, it took the lead in developing a body of experience and techniques to help local officials respond to the inherited problems that racked their predominantly black jurisdictions. The institute later evolved into the Joint Center for Political and Economic Studies, an influential source of research and policy leadership.

What was required in America's troubled cities by the end of the 1960s was nothing less than fundamental institutional change in corporate and municipal structures. But private capital investment was drawn to the suburbs, and the federal government offered little help. Race relations seemed more politically explosive than ever. The rise of white ethnic initiatives helped spur racial polarization, and minorities continued to be underrepresented on private and public governing bodies.

To help inner-city administrators deal with these problems, Potomac established a project called Central Cities Technical Assistance (CCTA). In the early 1970s, six jurisdictions—Gary, Newark, Los Angeles, Washington, D.C., Prichard, Alabama, and Greene County, Alabama—were chosen as laboratories for a collaborative venture with the National Center for Urban Ethnic Affairs, recently founded by the charismatic Washington priest Geno Baroni.

Gibson, calling on his far-flung network of friends and colleagues in civil rights and community organization circles for help, coordinated this broad effort to generate black participation in political life, private foundation work, economic development, and culture and the arts. The initial goal of the project was twofold: first, to give administrators in predominantly black jurisdictions access to mainstream skills and resources, and second, to bring about significant change in the old ways of doing business that had excluded minorities.

The project's method was to consult with black administrators to identify fundamental needs and then to draw out public and private sources of help. Project staff produced expert specialists, meetings with government agencies, or periodic assessments of each jurisdiction's progress in key goals. The knowledge gained from each experience was synthesized for the benefit of other jurisdictions.

In Gary, the CCTA focus was on a comprehensive regional economic development plan to lessen local dependence on the steel industry. The Greater Los Angeles Community Action Agency was the project's point of contact in that city; work centered on improving social service delivery. Planning and implementing neighborhood improvement projects was a high priority in Newark, as well as in Los Angeles and Greene County. Helping to resolve interracial conflicts over allocation of resources to specific neighborhoods also required attention in Newark and Los Angeles. CCTA worked with Mayor Maynard Jackson in Atlanta, helping him analyze the implications of changes in the city charter.

In Washington, D.C., achieving greater home rule authority and making municipal government more accountable to the city's citizens was in the forefront of CCTA's work, which included encouraging a citywide transportation program for the elderly and handicapped, child development centers, neighborhood cultural and performing arts centers, and shopping centers in underserved parts of the city.

Gradually, CCTA expanded its network of useful contacts and technical assistance resources to include organizations such as the Metropolitan Applied Research Center in New York, the National Center for Equal Business Opportunity, the National Urban Coalition, Public Technology, Inc., and a number of universities. The project itself remained small, and was often overwhelmed by the scale of requests for assistance. It used a small, flexible operation to illuminate a cluster of problems and come up with useful strategies to engage larger institutions. By 1974, CCTA activities had spun off in several directions:

- The U.S. Department of Housing and Urban Development funded a demonstration program in several cities known as the Gary Plan; it was modeled on the policy and program planning process developed in Gary with Potomac assistance.
- The Joint Center for Political Studies and the National Center for Urban Ethnic Affairs won companion grants of more than $1 million from the federal Intergovernmental Personnel Program to train minority city officials. Senior CCTA staff members were seconded to each organization to carry out the work.
- The Washington, D.C., Bicentennial Commission, which Jim Gibson chaired, received a contract from the Bicentennial Administration to make sure people of color played a role in the 1976 national birthday celebration.
- The new College of Public and Community Service founded by the University of Massachusetts in 1973 was based on the CCTA model. CCTA project staff also worked with the University of Southern California in establishing a Public Affairs Center in Washington, D.C., to train local government managers.

Although minority elected officials are by now far more numerous and experienced, they are still working with greatly diminished resources to realize the dream of living communities and economic opportunity for their poor and minority constituents.

Work in the District of Columbia

Even after the CCTA project had ended, Gibson continued to use the District of Columbia, where he was deeply involved in a variety of projects aimed at minority empowerment and economic development, as an urban laboratory. He was pivotal in the creation of the Cultural Alliance, an unusual approach to alleviating metropolitan racial and economic tensions. With financial aid from the National Endowment for the Arts and local foundations and corporations, the Cultural Alliance fostered arts investments in the inner city as a path both to greater diversity in the arts and to economic revitalization.

Another approach to economic development involved Harambee House, a new minority-owned and -operated hotel. It was one of the few businesses in the country to be spawned by a community development corporation. Traditional sources of capital would not risk investing in a project of this scale in an inner-city neighborhood, so Gibson negotiated with the federal Economic Development Administration (EDA) for public funds to leverage private investment. The project created hundreds of construction jobs and more than 250 permanent jobs, and a long-blighted commercial and residential area began to recuperate.

It thus came as no surprise that Gibson resigned from Potomac in 1979 to accept the call of newly elected D.C. Mayor Marion Barry to serve as assistant city administrator for planning and development. Potomac's experience was in fact brought to bear on a number of D.C. government problems. One was minority participation in construction contracting and the provision of goods and services to the government. Building on an earlier project in New York City assisting its mayor in redesigning enforcement of equal opportunity in public contracting programs, Potomac regularly consulted with District officials as they implemented new regulations to improve minority employment and business opportunity. Herbert Franklin co-chaired the new administration's transition task force on housing. Board member Philip Hammer, who had earlier helped establish a local corporation to assure genuine community participation in the redevelopment of the riot-damaged 14th Street corridor, co-chaired a task force on planning and economic development.

Immersing itself in demanding economic and urban issues impelled Potomac to move well beyond its early focus on federal programs. But grappling with historic institutional racism involved even more than working with corporations and city governments. Reform in mainstream private and professional organizations was to be another important target during the 1970s.

POTOMAC'S APPROACH TO conscious or unconscious institutional discrimination within professional groups and private organizations was to spot specific opportunities, often depending on personal suasion and discourse, that could be leveraged into lasting reform.

One avenue opened in 1970 through the American Institute of Architects (AIA), when Potomac board member William Slayton became executive director. Fleming was soon named the first public member of the AIA board, where he challenged professional architects to take the lead in more socially responsible urban and residential development. Over several years, he was instrumental in encouraging AIA to set up scholarships to architectural school for disadvantaged students, help black schools of architecture to obtain accreditation, and expand on-the-job minority training programs. He was a frequent speaker to AIA state and national audiences, and continued to serve on the editorial board of *City* magazine when it moved from Urban America to the AIA along with its creative editor, Donald Canty.

Meanwhile the American Institute of Planners began a series of institutional reforms. Philip Hammer, who served as president of the American Society of Planning Officials (ASPO) in 1968–69, brought Potomac staff into discussions with the major organizations of city planners and development officials about engaging members of these organizations more directly in urban social and minority issues. ASPO elected three black planners to its formerly all-white board, as well as a black vice president. It established a $500,000 scholarship fund and an ongoing Aid for Minority Planning Students program.

Arthur Levin continued his work with the International City Managers Association programs in race relations and urban growth, prompting strong policy statements and spreading their message through regional conferences and training sessions.

To correct the imbalance of minorities in the media, Potomac sponsored one of the earliest training programs for minority journalists, funded by the Ford Foundation. It was directed by Robert Spivak, head of the Reporters News Syndicate. His sudden death unfortunately ended the effort after only one group of trainees had been placed with newspapers and television networks, but other such training programs flourished in later years.

The universe of private charitable foundations was a natural milieu for Fleming. He served on the boards of the Taconic Foundation, the New World Foundation, and the Southern Education Foundation, and was an influential figure at the national Council on Foundations, where he served for several years as chairman of its Advisory Committee on Social Justice. There was in the 1970s little racial or ethnic diversity on foundation boards and staffs. Many deplored that situation, but without agreement on mandatory or voluntary actions to bring about change. Some foundations were also beginning to look beyond their internal operations to consider strategies for fostering equal opportunity practices among their grantees. Progress eventually came through peer pressures, minority access to foundation forums, and the continuing exposure of data about the race and gender composition of foundation staff and board members.

In addition to its major projects, Potomac had always sought to play a catalytic and advisory role with as many public and private groups and individuals as its limited staff capacity would permit. Potomac was "conceived in anti-Parkinsonianism and has maintained it pretty well over the years," Fleming noted to his board at the end of the 1960s. Its staff remained small, and its central operating budget did little more than keep pace with inflation. "The assumption, which dates back to the origin of Potomac, is that a knowledgeable staff can have as much impact on social change through its contribution to program conception and activity by others as through its own institutional projects."

As its reputation for reliable counsel expanded nationwide, a host of national religious, business, and civic organizations came seeking advice, information, and collaboration.

In 1981, President Reagan forced the distinguished former Cabinet member Arthur Flemming out of his post as chairman of the Civil Rights Commission because of his forthright opposition to the administration's efforts to gut civil rights enforcement. Potomac worked with Arthur Flemming as he put together his influential bipartisan group of former Cabinet members to form a "shadow" Citizens Commission on Civil Rights to maintain an informed critique of government policy.

Board memberships, speeches, and articles expanded the number of useful platforms for stimulating understanding and action. From the National Chamber of Commerce Foundation to the Harrison Institute for Public Law, from the Center for a Voluntary Society to the Washington Journalism Center, from the Conservation Foundation to the Episcopal Church, and from the American Jewish Committee to the Anti-Defamation League, Potomac staff actively participated in shaping major equal rights programs.

Fleming also kept up international links that went back to a 1966 visit to England by Stephen Currier, during which he set up contacts with individuals and organizations in that country engaged in private civil rights efforts similar to his own. Anthony Lester, a London barrister working with the Commonwealth Committee on Immigration and Race Relations, had at the time sought help with a conference on fair employment legislation for British industrialists, public officials, and labor leaders. Potomac commissioned a paper covering two decades of American and Canadian fair employment experience, and briefed Americans scheduled to attend. In later years, the British Embassy in Washington frequently called on Potomac to organize briefings on American experiences and problems for visiting British officials, and Fleming consulted occasionally with agencies in England.

A 1969 invitation from the United States–South Africa Leader Exchange Program (USSALEP) prompted Fleming to visit that country to examine its racial problems in the light of his own experiences in the American South and in Washington. He served on the USSALEP board for the next twenty years, as it promoted corporate responsibility among American firms doing business in South Africa, managed a special Neiman Fellowship program for South African journalists, and sponsored a variety of useful exchanges among labor, business, and professional leaders.

Over the years, "a host of visitors passed through the Potomac portals," Fleming wrote. They included "seekers after employment advice; federal, state, local, and private human relations agency personnel; 'Greeks' (of every organizational affiliation) bearing proposals; and . . . a new breed of cat seeking counsel on computer applications to the social sciences and urban problems."

The issues involved were as diverse as the visitors—housing, planning, southern cooperatives, immigration reform, voter registration, tax reform, Black-Jewish dialogue, community control, campus revolt, income maintenance, police-community relations, even federal disaster relief. The library was always available to writers, researchers, and students, as were the meeting rooms to like-minded groups. The staff continually provided information and analysis to a variety of journalists, broadcasters, congressional staff, and policy makers.

In all of these encounters and experiences, Potomac kept its sights on the long range goals. Although earlier optimism about social change had given way to a more cynical pessimism in the 1970s, Fleming believed that the pendulum would swing back.

> In addition to the black movement, the multiplicity of "revolutions"—youth, women, environment, peace—are contributing in their different ways to a new awareness of injustices and the need for fundamental change in our institutions.
>
> We know from past experience that it is folly to confine our efforts to what may be deemed at the moment "realistic," "politically feasible," and "publicly acceptable." Potomac sees the present period as calling for continued pressure on behalf of good faith implementation of existing policies, anticipation and definition of issues that have not yet emerged as major national challenges, sustained conception and advocacy of institutional change, and the cultivation of collaborative relationships among imaginative individuals and organizations. These are the activities that will assure a sound agenda when there is a resurgence of the national commitment to justice for all.

The election of Jimmy Carter in 1986 seemed to offer hope of that resurgence. The first president from the Deep South in more than one hundred years owed his slim victory to black voters, many of them newly enfranchised. American politics had been changed irrevocably by the Voting Rights Act and private efforts, such as the Voter Education Project, to register black citizens. For the first time, more than 70 percent of the black population of the country voted, and more than nine out of ten voted for Carter.

But the Carter administration fell short of expectations. "With inflation and energy the top concerns of 1977 and 1978," Fleming reported to his board, "social and civil rights programs were relegated to the back burner, if, indeed they even remained on the stove. The political legerdemain of budget balancing has obsessed not only Washington, but many states and localities, at the expense of the poor and near-poor. The past year was characterized by a new negativism in the American electorate which threatened to further erode hard-won minority gains." Nevertheless, in its customary role as broker of talent, ideas, and resources, Potomac would find ample opportunities for useful intervention even in the inhospitable climate of the 1970s and 1980s. Beyond riding herd on federal civil rights enforcement, and beyond its active work to expand opportunity and bring down barriers in mainstream private institutions, Potomac concentrated major resources on reforms in three critical areas covered in the next three chapters: equal education opportunity, metropolitan housing policies, and equal employment opportunity.

CHAPTER 22 ■ *Suffer the Little Children*

DESPITE THE 1954 *Brown v. Board of Education* decision that overturned legal school desegregation in 1954, equal or even improved education for minority children remained an elusive goal as the decades
passed.

Differing approaches to solving that problem had outspoken partisans. Some advocated more compensatory education for underachieving
poor and minority children wherever they are, and had a corollary interest in more neighborhood control of schools. Others were impressed by a
1968 report of the U.S. Civil Rights Commission, which documented the
connection between racial isolation and low achievement for minority
children; integration was not only a constitutional right, but probably
necessary to support a more positive sense of control and higher expectations. Still a third approach promoted court action to correct the widely
unequal investments in public schools resulting from different property
tax wealth in school districts.

Over the years Potomac explored and contributed to all of these
avenues toward educational equity. Their work convinced them that
remedies had to be adapted and combined according to the character-
istics of each school district.

The institute first determined for itself through a study by a professional consultant that many compensatory education programs were
strong on claims but deficient in documented results. Soon a number of
larger studies were published that confirmed and extended this view and
suggested to Potomac staff a useful collaboration with Dr. Robert Coles,
a distinguished child psychiatrist at the Harvard University Health Services, who had for a decade been working with and writing about poor
children in segregated and desegregated schools.

In September 1967, the institute asked Coles to examine in inner-city schools in thirteen cities what teachers and principals assumed about their students and what they expected them to achieve. He would look in turn at how students responded to these expectations. Coles's skills at eliciting the thoughts and feelings of children and teachers, as well as his use of children's drawings, resulted in a compelling picture of how children and teachers perceive and interact with each other. The study described and analyzed the successes and failures of education as measured by what really happens to children. It was addressed to all who share the conviction that public schools do need improvement, and who believe that every child has an equal claim upon a full measure of educational opportunity.

The chief lesson from the Coles report was that the leadership and commitment of the school principal determined the tenor and attitude of the teachers and pupils. A sensitive and dedicated principal created the best teaching and learning environment. The study was published by Potomac and widely used by public and teacher training schools as well as teachers' groups. Dr. Coles later incorporated the findings into his ground-breaking work, *Children of Crisis*.

Title VI of the 1964 Civil Rights Act, requiring the cut-off of all federal funds to noncompliant school districts, had given the federal government a powerful new mechanism for enforcing desegregation. During the Johnson years, Potomac had been much engaged in helping to design the administrative details of that machinery. Action was at first principally aimed at compliance in the South, with the ironic result that by 1974 the eleven states of the old Confederacy had in statistical terms the highest degree of school desegregation in the nation: fewer than 10 percent of black southern pupils continued to attend all black schools. Meanwhile, de facto segregation continued to grow in the North and West, where government intervention was minimal.

With the advent of the Nixon administration, federal enforcement of school desegregation came to a halt. Attorney General John Mitchell refused to enforce Office of Education guidelines, prompting the resignation of Leon Panetta, director of Civil Rights at the Department of

Health, Education and Welfare, and then of Dr. James E. Allen, the Education Commissioner.

Seeking a way to force the federal government to comply with Title VI, Arthur Levin had several years earlier initiated the idea of a generic lawsuit to speed up the slow pace of desegregation on a district-by-district basis. Months of consultation and research with the law firm of Joseph Rauh, John Silard, and Elliot Lichtman, with Jack Greenberg and Jean Fairfax of the NAACP Legal Defense Fund (LDF), and with a variety of other experts, now came to fruition.

Their novel legal theory, first put forward in a Potomac publication about housing desegregation in 1966, asserted the right of private citizens to sue the federal government for proper enforcement of Title VI. Winning such a suit with respect to education would mean that the courts would supervise the Office of Education's administration of school desegregation, thus overriding executive branch control.

Rauh and Greenberg forewarned the new secretary of HEW Elliot Richardson and his new civil rights director Stanley Pottinger about the impending suit. Absent any assurance by HEW of more vigorous Title VI enforcement, LDF went to court in October of 1970.

The plaintiffs in the suit, which became known as *Adams v. Richardson,* included black and white students attending segregated public schools and colleges, and citizens whose federal taxes were being used to support them. They sought to compel HEW to correct a host of sins of omission and commission in the enforcement of school desegregation: lack of compliance with court desegregation orders, no action on public college desegregation, no compliance by state departments of education, school district default on existing desegregation plans without penalty, no suspension of federal fund payments during administrative proceedings, and failure to revise desegregation plans to conform with ongoing Supreme Court clarifications of law.

Judge John H. Pratt soon handed down a crucial initial decision. He agreed that administrative enforcement of Title VI was subject to judicial review, thus affirming the principle that government officials can be held accountable by the courts for their administrative actions. On the basis of this preliminary ruling, Potomac immediately published *Administrative Repeal of Civil Rights Law: A Case Study.* The pamphlet explained the unique principal at stake in this case: it was now possible to seek judicial review of administrative abuse of legislated mandates.

After two years of motions, countermotions and testimony, Judge Pratt, generally considered a judicial conservative, surprised many (including perhaps the Justice Department) by finding in favor of the plaintiffs. He granted relief on all six of the plaintiffs' grievances, stating that "defendants now have no discretion to negate the purpose and intent of the statute by a policy described in another context as 'benign neglect,' but on the contrary, have the duty, on a case-by-case basis, to employ the means set forth in (the law) to achieve compliance."

A few months later his broad and uncompromising order for remedy received front-page newspaper coverage around the country. HEW would have to give the court a continuing detailed account of its progress in carrying out the earlier ruling. In due course a U.S. Court of Appeals unanimously upheld the Pratt ruling.

A rash of similar suits followed to compel federal enforcement of other laws. Levin's persistence in pursuing the idea that citizens can hold government agencies accountable for obeying the law had major implications not merely for education but for all federally assisted public services. The principle is now so taken for granted that it may be difficult to remember how novel it appeared at the time.

The favorable decision on Title VI in HEW not only accelerated elementary and secondary school desegregation but also made possible a new attack on discriminatory state higher education systems in southern states. The last bastions of legal segregation in state-supported higher education in the South had been breached by the admission of individual black students to formerly all-white state universities in the early 1960s, albeit with the usual bitter implications for federal-state relations. But almost nothing had been done to change the fact that two entirely separate state systems of publicly funded universities, colleges and junior colleges, one historically white and one historically black, continued to exist side by side.

The ruling in *Adams v. Richardson* required HEW to make sure that each state provided a nonracial system of higher education. But designing remedies for such discrimination presented especially knotty problems. Many black educators feared that state-supported black colleges would be abolished or submerged, as had happened to so many black elementary and secondary schools in the name of desegregation; that black administrators and faculties would be downgraded or discarded; and that black students would be given less, rather than more, opportunity for postsecondary education. There was, in fact, ample reason to believe that state commissions of higher education in the ten affected southern states, left to their own predilections, might adopt policies that could destroy many existing black public colleges.

Fleming and Levin consulted closely with Jean Fairfax of the NAACP Legal Defense Fund (LDF) to define acceptable criteria and standards for supporting state systems. Fairfax, supported in part by the Southern Education Foundation, took the lead in organizing a series of consultations with educators and civil rights leaders across the South to devise ways to create state systems in which black institutions could be upgraded, and opportunities expanded for black students. Out of this work came the document *Criteria for a State Plan,* submitted by the attorneys to HEW as a guide for future desegregation plans.

Potomac continued to work with LDF in monitoring the implementation of higher education desegregation for many years after Judge Pratt ordered the reluctant southern states to develop and implement statewide unitary plans. The process was slow, and the results often failed to meet the desired standards. Many states managed to keep negotiations going for ten years or more. The plans eventually approved under Reagan were far weaker than originally intended, and some state systems were still under court supervision years later.

Meanwhile, school desegregation efforts were often little more than meaningless gestures in large metropolitan areas with many different school districts, each predominantly white or black, with a vastly disproportionate concentration of blacks in the central city districts. Beginning in 1970, therefore, Potomac joined forces with other groups and experts to explore metropolitan solutions that required integration across the boundaries of school districts.

Plaintiffs in a number of suits argued that de facto public school segregation was in fact the result of public actions that officially sanctioned residential segregation. The logical extension of that argument was a requirement of official affirmative action to correct the situation. A few federal judges handed down decisions mandating unitary systems and ordering busing of pupils as one of several means to achieve a measure of racial balance even in metropolitan situations where residential segregation was a fact of life.

The controversy over court-ordered busing to achieve desegregation soon grew deeply emotional. "Forced busing" became a rallying cry against desegregation. Resistance fueled the primary campaigns of Governor George Wallace in Alabama, and Boston erupted in lengthy protest over court-imposed plans. (Little notice was taken of evidence published by the U.S. Commission on Civil Rights in 1976 that most school desegregation had in fact been accomplished without serious disruption, and with the support of both black and white parents—and that there had been a dramatic positive change in the attitudes of white parents once desegregation had taken place.)

Of course, school busing was scarcely a new practice, and one that traditionally had nothing to do with racial considerations. In 1971 an estimated 42 percent of school children were already bused, and only 3 percent for purposes of racial desegregation. Still, anti-busing pressures prompted Congress to enact in 1972 an amendment to the Higher Education Act that prevented any court-ordered busing plan from going into effect until all appeals were exhausted.

The overall question of racial concentration versus dispersion was in fact a terrain full of land mines. Apart from white resistance, many blacks strongly resented the intended or unintended consequences of desegregation that often occurred at the expense of black teachers and principals and often threatened a loss of cultural cohesion. Some argued instead for large-scale investments in the schools where black children were concentrated, and for more community control of those schools. School integration could follow later on, after integration of housing. Others, including members of the Civil Rights Commission, believed that if integration were postponed until the day when integrated housing patterns could be achieved, at least one more generation of children would be consigned to racially isolated and inferior schools. Fleming pointed out that the polarization of the public debate was born of frustration:

Since neither desegregation nor large scale compensatory programs is being pursued as a matter of vigorous national policy, the proponents find it easy to expend their pent-up feelings in an interminable argument over who has possession of the truth. Once large scale action becomes possible, one might hope that the public discussion will become more pragmatic. Any rational strategy must take into account the differing size, population, and racial make-up of American cities. . . . The relative emphasis will be different depending upon the degree of residential concentration, the percentage of Negro pupils involved, and geographic and logistical factors. Desegregation should remain the ultimate goal. . . . But Washington is not Peoria, and the antagonists should not be allowed to obscure that fact.

Rational strategy did not seem to be on the agenda, however. By 1974 judges were backing off the metropolitan remedies they had embraced only a few years earlier. When the Supreme Court overturned a Detroit plan to bus pupils across district lines to achieve metropolitan desegregation, Justice Thurgood Marshall, in his dissent, called the decision a "giant step backward." Both the courts and the Congress were serving notice that busing could not be relied on as a major remedy for the geographical and jurisdictional divisions that foster economic and racial isolation in the public schools.

Throughout these years there was another kind of inequity in schooling to which Potomac turned its attention: discrimination based on geographical distribution of public funds within states.

Although the traditional way of funding schools and the inequities that result from it are somewhat complicated and technical, the issue affects every public school child, parent, and property owner in the United States. Because public education spending in America is largely dependent on the local property tax, a public school district rich in taxable property can count on substantially more money per child for its schools—often at a lower tax rate—than the property-poor districts. The very great disparities in expenditures per child within the same state usually work to the advantage of children in the wealthier districts, and to the disadvantage of children in poor districts whose needs are even greater.

Law suits had been filed in the 1960s in several cities, including Detroit and Chicago, challenging these school financing patterns under the Equal Protection Clause of the Fourteenth Amendment and asking that state allocation formulas for school aid be revised to redress the grossly disparate results.

In November 1968, Potomac convened the first national conference of law professors, educators, taxation and finance specialists, litigating lawyers, and foundation representatives to consider the many educational, sociological, and constitutional ramifications of this issue. The agenda covered state school allocation formulas, details of pending legal cases, legal theories for constitutional change, and alternatives to litigation.

At the request of the conferees, Potomac and the Lawyers' Committee for Civil Rights Under Law undertook a clearinghouse and coordinating function on the subject, supported by the New World Foundation. Potomac staff also supervised a project sponsored by the Southern Education Foundation, whose Washington office was now housed at Potomac, to research data from six southern states.

After two years, with legal cases and research proliferating, the institute spun off to the Lawyer's Committee for Civil Rights Under Law the role of tracking and assisting individual litigants; to the Urban Coalition and to several university centers responsibility for the research agenda; and to the Urban Institute the consideration of legislative alternatives.

The national reform effort reached its zenith in 1971 with a landmark decision of the California Supreme Court. *Serrano v. Priest* held that it was unconstitutional for the amount spent on a child's education to be based on the taxable wealth of the district where the child happens to reside. In March 1973, however, reformers suffered a setback when the U.S. Supreme Court, in a similar Texas case known as *Rodriguez,* declined to adopt any equalization requirement under the federal Constitution. But only a few days later the New Jersey Supreme Court did issue an equalization mandate under the state constitution's public education clause. Reform efforts thereafter were forced to turn to state legal and legislative initiatives, rather than national ones.

Potomac remained especially active in pursuing the question of the educational and constitutional sufficiency of various potential remedies.

Contrary to the general early assumption that inner cities naturally would benefit from equalization legislation, there were now strong doubts on that score: inner cities might be worse off after equalization. Not only do cities have higher concentrations of children who require extra services such as compensatory and special education, but also they have higher costs for buildings, maintenance, security, food, vandalism repair, and salaries. In addition, the urban tax base must support the higher costs of other services, from garbage collection to street repair. Thus equalization of school tax efforts within a state, while constitutionally an advance, would not sufficiently address the severe inequality of costs between cities and suburbs.

Potomac therefore undertook a study of the urban implications of the *Serrano* decision. *Equity for Cities in School Finance Reform,* published in early 1973, convincingly demonstrated that the "equal protection" clause of the Fourteenth Amendment requires states to use a distribution formula for school aid that directly relates expenditures to educational costs and resources, and that such an "equal educational offering" standard is amenable to objective definition and measurement. Only such a standard, supplemented by a continuing but enlarged federal program of funding for compensatory education, could do justice to the exceptional service and cost requirements of inner-city districts, which came to be known as "municipal overburden." The booklet became an important resource for litigators and legal scholars, educators, professional organizations, federal officials, and civic and political leaders.

As a further impetus to urban school finance reform, Potomac joined in early 1974 with the National Urban Coalition and the Lawyers' Committee for Civil Rights Under Law to convene experts on urban school financing, education cost differentials, municipal overburden, alternatives for remedy, and possibilities for "second generation" litigation beyond the confines of *Serrano.* From the papers and debate emerged directly or indirectly a number of new reform strategies and state cases.

One of the most important came to trial in 1976 in New York State, brought by the school district of Levittown on behalf of property-poor school districts. It challenged the state's failure to provide the district with resources comparable to those of wealthier school districts. Soon the case was joined by the boards of education of Buffalo, New York City, Syracuse, and Rochester, asserting a separate constitutional claim: that the state school aid law failed in many respects to recognize the genuine burdens and needs of the city school districts, and was therefore discriminatory. Extensive testimony illuminated the vast burdens and problems of urban school systems in meeting the educational needs of the poor populations they serve, and quantified the costs of a variety of remedies.

Potomac made that information available to a much wider audience by publishing a summary of the testimony, *Central-City Schooling: Money Can Make a Difference.* Because the school conditions and learning needs in these urban areas of New York State were not significantly different from other city schools throughout the nation, the pamphlet offered another nationally useful resource.

In its continuing search for new approaches to old problems, Potomac welcomed a request in 1977 to sponsor a project to explore a new national service program that would attack two major national ailments. One was the alarming unemployment and disaffection of America's young people. The other was a host of untended social needs. Potomac was particularly interested in the implications of national service for minority youth, and in its promise of expanding the engagement of private organizations in social goals.

The project grew out of discussions with the Ford Foundation held by Harris Wofford, then president of Bryn Mawr College, and Jacqueline Wexler, then president of Hunter College, who became co-chairs. Dr. Roger Landrum, former director of The Teacher's Inc. and a former Peace Corps volunteer, directed the study. A broad-based Committee for the Study of National Service was put together, including Secretary of Labor Willard Wirtz, Rev. Theodore Hesburgh, Dr. Bernard Anderson, and Eddie Williams, among others. It met many times over sixteen months to wrestle with the broad issues inherent in this subject.

The idea of national service was not new. It had surfaced periodically, and significant local models already existed. The committee weighed all the arguments against a national service: the cost, the potential for new layers of bureaucracy, the infringement on individual liberty represented by compulsory service. It grappled with perennial issues: the merits of mandatory universal service versus a voluntary system with incentives and sanctions; methods for connecting volunteers with meaningful work without replacing job opportunities for minimum wage workers; and means of attracting noncollege-bound youth.

Finally the group reached consensus on a broad set of principles, based on a voluntary National Service with the capacity to provide a million or more youth with opportunities for service. A public corporation, chartered and funded by the Congress, would develop and regulate National Service, but implementation would be decentralized through private and public agencies.

After the committee's report, *Youth and the Needs of the Nation*, was released at a press conference in early 1979, an avalanche of requests for information deluged the project staff and committee members. Newspaper columns, TV and radio appearances, and congressional testimony soon followed. Eight governors set up study groups in their states and nine mayors in their cities. Thirty-five House members and five Senators furnished the printed report to all high schools in their respective districts or states. A total of twenty thousand copies was distributed to government and private opinion leaders all over the country.

In the wake of this widespread reaction, Landrum raised funds from corporations and foundations to hold a national conference of more than three hundred persons in Washington, chiefly for the young people most affected by the proposals. The report of that conference faithfully recorded the sense of ferment and controversy, along with the conviction that voluntary service could be a critical investment in building a sense of shared values to sustain a democratic society.

Publication of the second report marked the end of the work of the committee for the Study of National Service, and of Potomac's direct involvement in the debate. Landrum remained temporarily at Potomac, sponsored by the German Marshall Fund to undertake a six-week reconnaissance of national youth service programs in Germany and France to evaluate their experiences in relation to American needs. He went on to co-found Youth Service America, a national nonprofit organization that has become an important force in generating both local programs of national service and national policy, and a key influence on President Clinton's AmeriCorps. Rarely does an intellectual debate become translated so swiftly into policy and programmatic reality at the national level.

In 1979, the discouraging fact remained that twenty-five years after the *Brown* decision, half of the nation's children were still in segregated schools and minority children were still achieving far below the level of majority children. The Reagan administration addressed itself to those problems by appointing a presidential commission on the status of education. Fleming commented at the time that:

> In response to its recommendations, the President reaffirmed his commitment to four basic reforms—an end to busing for purposes of integration, a return to school prayer, sterner discipline, and tuition tax credits for patrons of private schools. (Government expenditures for public education, he maintained, have resulted only in declining test scores.)
>
> President Reagan's priorities are a recipe for disaster for the public schools and the children who are most dependent on them. A compelling case can be made for order and discipline in the classroom; but if this means only arbitrary expulsion of pupils who bring with them to school the liabilities of disturbed and inadequate family situations—and one can find no other definition in the Reagan lexicon—the public schools offer little promise for underclass children. Tuition tax credits can only encourage a retreat to private schools by middle-class families and the relegation of public schools to the status of warehouses for society's rejects, who can presumably find succour in school-sponsored prayers.

Clearly there would be little national leadership to further educational opportunity, and Potomac continued its search for other promising approaches. Fleming himself became increasingly concerned with the connection between disadvantage and discrimination. He worked with editor and historian Harry S. Ashmore of the Center for the Study of Democratic Institutions to extend the idea of national service to projects in which high school and college age young people would serve as tutors and mentors of young disadvantaged children.

Although funds were not available for the large national project they envisioned, Potomac was able to assist a model for such a program that in time had a significant impact. It had been developed by a student at the University of Miami, Norman Manasa, who organized official course credit to his fellow college students for tutoring services, to considerable local acclaim. When he moved to Washington, D.C., in 1980, he undertook to broaden the program nationally. With support from Potomac and others, and a remarkable degree of persistence, he created through his Washington Education Project a network of over twenty colleges and universities in five states sponsoring such tutoring credits. Thousands of young people growing up in desperate circumstances have been helped by this early support, and hundreds of college students have had a first-hand opportunity to understand and make a difference in urban America.

Behind all these strategies to make educational equity a reality, however, lay the inescapable fact that residential patterns based on race and economic status still to a large extent determined the educational opportunities of American children. In 1973, 75 percent of black Americans lived in metropolitan areas, more than three out of four of them in central cities. In contrast, approximately 66 percent of white Americans lived in metropolitan areas, but only two out of five lived in central cities. The process of white suburbanization was proceeding so rapidly, Fleming noted, that "even if cross-district busing and the redrawing of district lines had enthusiastic political and judicial blessing, it would be difficult, in some cases impossible, to overcome the effects of such unbalanced population distribution. . . . Without a radical shift away from residential segregation, the winning of scattered local battles will not prevent the loss of the war."

As a practical matter, the passage and enforcement of legislation to promote low-income housing and housing desegregation was a remote prospect. But Fleming always kept his eye on the long-range goal: "The tangled web of housing and school desegregation cannot be unsnarled on a case-by-case basis; the complex system of policy and practice that governs housing supply and location must be overhauled from the federal level down if apartheid is not to become the settled way of life in the United States."

And so Potomac devoted an increasingly large share of its research and resources to the question of housing patterns and urban growth.

CHAPTER 23 ∎ *Power to the People Who*
Got There First

THE GOAL OF RACIALLY inclusive housing had long had high priority among civil rights activists. But because most housing development and management was firmly controlled by the private sector, it appeared to lie beyond the reach of federal civil rights regulation.

For all of its active existence, Potomac was deeply involved with the entire range of housing opportunity issues. So, too, were multitudes of local governments, banks, other lenders, federal and state agencies, builders, land owners, developers, and, of course, renters, owners, and would-be owners. How Potomac sought to move this mountainous pile of interests toward its goal of good housing, fairly accessible to all, is the subject of this chapter.

The institute used by now familiar techniques: shaping new legal theories, publicizing "best practices" in private integrated housing, and collaborating with larger groups. In the 1970s they moved on to establish the long-running Metropolitan Housing Project, which successfully connected urban growth and zoning policy to civil rights requirements.

But it may be fair to say that these efforts illustrate chiefly the difficulty of large-scale purposeful reform in America. When Potomac took up the question, adequate and accessible housing was one of the sorest problems of American society. At the end of Potomac's exertions it still was.

In the 1960s, Arthur Levin worked intensively with attorney John Silard to develop a new legal tool to combat housing discrimination. They were convinced that Title VI of the 1964 Civil Rights Act, which prohibits discrimination in any activity supported by federal financial assistance, could be used for this purpose. Their 1966 pamphlet, entitled *Metropolitan Housing Desegregation,* argued that the many federal programs of direct benefit to private home owners and builders, such as sewer and water improvements, road construction, electrification assistance, and a wide range of supporting community services—not to mention the new federally funded rent supplements—created a clear federal obligation to assure compliance with housing desegregation standards even in private housing development.

They proposed an enforcement mechanism based on the federal requirement for comprehensive regional planning. At risk would be federal programs that displaced thousands of families each year: highway construction, public housing, slum clearance, urban renewal, and public works. An appendix to the pamphlet also set forth the legal basis for citizens to seek judicial relief from housing discrimination under the Title VI statute.

These far-reaching recommendations were much discussed and reprinted. Press coverage particularly noted the finding that the federal government already had in Title VI a weapon against discrimination in the sale and rental of housing which was stronger than the proposed fair housing law then languishing in Congress.

Although the model was not immediately applied to or legally tested in the field of housing, the principles it advocated were judicially adopted in the landmark *Adams v. Richardson* suit ordering the Department of Health, Education and Welfare to strengthen Title VI enforcement of school desegregation, and in a number of related legal actions based on Title VI.

Another useful publication soon followed. The success of the institute's recently completed study of practical methods to integrate employment in private business led them to plan a similar review of methods to integrate private housing, using the skills of the same consultant, George Schermer.

He and Potomac's research librarian, Margaret Price, surveyed over 150 real estate developments and neighborhoods that had achieved racial integration. The forty sites selected for closer examination and field work represented stabilized neighborhoods, profit-motivated suburban tracts, and large and small urban renewal projects. Schermer and Levin then wrote a set of guidelines for workable solutions. The manual was in great demand by both advocates and practitioners in the field after it was published in 1968 as *A Housing Guide to Equal Opportunity*. Its principal finding was that "stable patterns of racial integration in housing developments and neighborhoods do not just happen. They are the result of commitment, clearly established policy, imaginative and thorough planning, and competent management—all elements which go far beyond the requirements of the law."

In 1968, the Supreme Court gave a significant boost to fair housing in a decision (*Jones v. Mayer*) that established the principle that discrimination in housing is illegal in all private as well as public housing transactions. However, it took the wrenching national tragedy of the assassination of Martin Luther King Jr. to push Congress at last to enact a fair housing law in 1968. While the new law's coverage was not universal, in combination with the new judicial ruling it at least laid a basis for more effective antidiscrimination actions.

The Department of Housing and Urban Development (HUD) now had a much larger enforcement responsibility and asked Potomac for advice on implementing the act.

The problems HUD faced in establishing a complaint process recalled earlier discussions between the institute and the infant Equal Employment Opportunity Commission: How could they avoid getting bogged down in a high volume of slow-moving individual complaints and find a way to foster more generic and systemic changes? There was also the danger of delegating too many enforcement functions to HUD subagencies, whose self-policing might be less vigorous than a strong equal opportunity office at the secretary's level. Potomac staff made a host of suggestions for affirmative initiatives, including voluntary agreements with realtors, public education campaigns and, perhaps most important, financial aid and technical assistance to fair housing groups that could be counted on to tailor their pressures to local conditions. The Johnson administration scarcely had time to consider those initiatives in its waning days, although a few were adopted much later under President Carter.

With the advent of the Nixon administration, major civil rights and urban organizations decided that the time was ripe to coordinate their strategies on housing whenever possible. The National Committee

Against Discrimination in Housing (NCDH), whose members included fair housing groups all across the country, could play such a coordinating and convening role, but it first needed reorganization and a new funding commitment. At the request of NCDH's directors and its major funder, the Ford Foundation, Fleming joined fellow NCDH board member Robert Carter, the former general counsel of NAACP, on a two-man committee in the early 1970s to accomplish those goals.

The working alliance between Potomac and NCDH continued for many years. After Fleming was named chairman of the NCDH board in 1972, he worked closely with its president Robert Weaver, former secretary of HUD, and successive directors Ed Holmgren and Martin Sloan until the organization closed its doors in 1987.

There were many calls for Potomac's brand of help in the complex field of housing equity. Developers, real estate boards, private and governmental employer groups, and a host of church and voluntary organizations asked for advice and counsel.

In their own backyard in Washington, Potomac had a hand in launching the Fort Lincoln "new town in town" and Regency House, the first public housing in the affluent residential neighborhoods west of Rock Creek Park. Phil Hammer and Jim Gibson served by presidential appointment as chairman and member of the National Capital Planning Commission. They were thus able to give practical application to some of the concepts growing out of the institute's urban policy strategy discussions. Levin brought similar insights to bear in his work as president of the Montgomery County (Maryland) Fair Housing Association, and as a board member of the Metropolitan Washington Planning and Housing Association, of which Gibson also served a term as president.

But Fleming was seeking a broader way to influence national urban growth policy. It was a melancholy fact that in the 1970s the country was far more segregated, racially and economically, than ever before in its history. Zoning and lending practices that reinforced segregated housing were usually justified on economic and environmental grounds, rather than racial ones, but the effect was the same. Poor people and minorities were concentrated in the increasingly destitute central cities; whites took flight to the unplanned sprawl of the suburbs; and job growth was often in places not easily accessible to minorities.

The problem of massive and growing racial concentration was the result of a combination of both economic and racial exclusivity, Fleming wrote. "As long as so large a proportion of blacks is poor or near-poor, the two issues cannot meaningfully be treated separately."

But how was it possible to break down the barriers to genuine choice that would give minorities and poor people even a semblance of equal housing opportunity? Fleming was a great believer in self-interest as a key to successful social change.

> One of the roots of opposition to progressive social change is the widespread conviction that the minority poor can advance only at the expense, socially as well as economically, of others in the society. Our public policies have not been notably successful in dispelling this apprehension by fusing ethical and self-interested motives.
>
> Direct subsidies to low-income families, unlike grudging welfare payments and monolithic public housing, can enlist the energies of the market place in the service of upward mobility of the poor. Our studies of fair housing indicate that whites or non-whites who are indifferent or even somewhat hostile to integration in principle will readily accept desegregated living if it offers unusual advantages of price or convenience. A rational policy of urban growth will have much to offer to all of us, not only as homeowners but as business-men and industrialists, blue-collar and white-collar workers, build-ers and developers, and public officials at all levels of government. The carrot, then, rather than the less effective stick can and should become the main inducement for the creation of democratic pat-terns of living.

The problems were of course vast, the social and economic climate unpropitious, and the scale of Potomac's resources and operations ex-ceedingly modest. But Fleming believed in anticipating the next cycle of opportunity, and in working to perfect the best possible agenda of poli-cies and programs until such a day arrived. Nowhere was this more true than in the issues of housing and urban development.

By 1972 a number of national and local organizations were promoting low-income housing production and working on fair access to existing housing. Few, however, were looking systematically at ways to change federal, state, and local growth and zoning policies that created barriers to affordable housing outside the central cities. What was the potential for using such policies instead to reduce racial and economic polarization? Suburban jurisdictions increasingly leaned on arguments of private property, individual liberty, fiscal soundness, and protection of natural resources to justify turning their backs on their neighboring cities. As attorney Herbert Franklin wryly suggested, they had in effect adopted their own special slogan in the political arena: "power to the people who got there first."

Into this gap stepped the Potomac Institute, establishing its Metropolitan Housing Project (MHP) with support from the Ford Foundation.

A couple of years earlier, Potomac had convened a series of conferences specifically focussed on strategy for launching legal attacks on exclusionary zoning practices. These meetings of lawyers, scholars, and planners from all parts of the country were initially sponsored by the Taconic Foundation under the leadership of John Simon. When the clearinghouse function outgrew Potomac's resources, it was transferred to the National Urban Coalition, where Herbert Franklin, executive associate for Housing and Urban Development, took over the responsibility. Although he had since left the coalition to join a private law firm, Franklin was invited to direct the new Potomac project and he did so for the next twelve years as a consultant.

At the heart of the program was the clearinghouse function, with periodic meetings of planners, lawyers, and public interest professionals to debate current issues and marshal support for timely strategies. Franklin produced a monthly newsletter featuring prompt analysis of important judicial, legislative, and administrative developments around the country. These "Metropolitan Housing Memoranda" soon became known as an indispensable source of information to a readership of several hundred key policy makers. He also brought expert technical resources to the aid of citizens' groups, legal scholars, and activists. On key issues, the Potomac project produced its own publications.

The Metropolitan Housing Project pursued two main lines of argument over the years. The first was that government forces are never neutral but have far-reaching effects, intended or unintended, on residential patterns. What people think of as life choices are increasingly influenced by public policy, and most particularly by federal action or inaction. As Fleming observed:

> The reality is that most middle-class Americans did not achieve their present housing circumstances through their own unaided efforts. The stigma of "handouts" does not attach to Veterans Administration or F.H.A. guarantees, to tax deductibility of mortgage interest and property taxes, or to the roads and other elements of government financed infrastructure that make suburban housing possible. These are seen as well-deserved entitlements, in contrast to the grudging charity associated with public housing.

The second line of argument was that no part of a metropolitan area can really be insulated from the economic and social realities of its neighbors. "We must be very clear that the goal of a new national policy is not to do something special for minorities. The motive is to assure the health of the cities and the entire society. The goal is to reverse a pathological pattern that has resulted from the whole society's failure to deal with some of its most pressing human problems."

The first major publication of the Metropolitan Housing Project addressed the impact of policies to control urban growth on the supply of affordable housing. The rapid population increase in metropolitan areas over the previous decade had produced what many considered alarming results. Many large housing developments sprang up unsupported by community facilities such as schools and by infrastructures such as sewer and water treatment. Increases in real property taxes provoked citizen dismay. A number of cities therefore adopted a combination of land use, ecological, and urban planning policies often described as "no growth" or "controlled growth" or "timed development" policies. Little attention had been paid, however, to the effect of such growth control policies on low- and moderate-income housing.

Franklin took as an example a typical "development timing" ordinance, in this case adopted by the town of Ramapo in New York State and upheld by the influential New York Court of Appeals. His booklet, *Controlling Urban Growth—But For Whom?*, documented the ways in which a potentially useful planning and regulatory device in fact greatly limited the housing opportunities of lower-income households. He spelled out the preferable social, fiscal, and ecological ingredients of a controlled growth policy, pointing out that unless a balanced growth goal is set when a policy is initially designed, negative social consequences are inevitable.

Potomac board member Vernon Jordan, then executive director of the National Urban League, warned that some no-growth laws have motivations other than ecological ones. He made the point succinctly at a later Smithsonian Institution task force on land use and urban growth: "A concern for the environment and for proper land use can never be accepted as a cover for efforts to exclude people on racial or class grounds from living in a community of their choice."

Hundreds of local communities had by the early 1970s passed measures to plan or control growth within their jurisdictions. Legal challenges to these actions produced a welter of confusing and often conflicting lower court decisions. The Metropolitan Housing Project stepped in to publish a document summarizing criteria that a court might use to determine the acceptability of such measures. It was based on an earlier MHP study commissioned by officials in Hartford, Connecticut, to help them determine whether a planned "new town" development would pass muster if challenged in court. Franklin and fellow attorney David Falk wrote *Local Growth Management Policy: A Legal Primer* for the benefit of hundreds of local officials, planners, and equal housing advocates.

At this point national housing policy took a surprising turn. The Nixon administration had at first seemed inimical to fair housing regulation and to federally subsidized low- and moderate-income housing programs. They impounded budgeted funds and proposed to eliminate the only mechanisms through which dispersed housing opportunities for most minority group members could realistically be achieved. Potomac joined with many other organizations in a successful legal challenge to this abuse of executive discretion, based on the same Title VI enforcement strategy that had been used in the *Adams v. Richardson* suit. A federal district judge ordered HUD secretary James Lynn to resume the programs.

Shortly, however, federal policy made a dramatic shift. President Nixon and Congress compromised their differences and enacted the

Housing and Community Development Act of 1974. For the first time national housing policy was directed to the problem of economic as well as racial segregation. The act recognized the host of problems arising from metropolitan growth and the concentration of poor people in the central cities. Its primary objective was to provide "decent housing and a suitable environment and expanding economic opportunities, principally for persons of low and moderate income." The act consolidated, expanded, and simplified community development aid. It vested control over these block grants firmly in local communities.

By linking a locality's eligibility for federal housing and community development aid to its provision for low-income housing, the act made it possible to challenge the exclusionary practices of suburban jurisdictions. It was a logical next step for Potomac to monitor HUD's first-year implementation.

The findings were not encouraging: HUD was approving local Housing Assistance Plans uncritically and routinely without reference to whether they proposed the objective of producing and dispersing lower-income housing. Potomac's report, which produced an avalanche of attention, concluded that HUD was frustrating the intent of Congress. Secretary Carla Hills eventually undertook a more serious review of the plans, and in time disapproved at least one on the basis of a history of racial discrimination. But the pace of federal housing subsidies slowed to a trickle; in the first year of the new act only three hundred families were actually placed in housing in the entire country.

This new federal requirement that all jurisdictions must frame their land use controls in terms of social equity opened new opportunities for more progressive zoning practices. The history of land use control, however, did not inspire confidence that local jurisdictions were well equipped to meet this challenge. Potomac therefore obtained funds from the National Science Foundation to analyze and distill workable "inclusionary" ordinances. Its 1974 publication *In-Zoning: A Guide for Policy-Makers on Inclusionary Land Use Programs* was a primer for policy makers on land use controls that would foster a greater socio-economic mix in urban growth areas by assuring a supply of new housing for lower-income households.

This comprehensive guide found a ready audience in government, planning, and academic circles. It covered the reasons why a locality with vacant land might find public and regional benefits in adopting an avowedly inclusionary land use program, not to mention protecting itself against judicial intervention. The ingredients of an inclusionary program followed, such as planned unit development, special regulatory treatment of subsidized housing, regional housing allocation plans, and land banking.

Potomac's work on metropolitan land use issues received solid judicial support in early 1975. A notable decision of the New Jersey Supreme Court in the *Mount Laurel* case for the first time imposed on a local government an affirmative inclusionary zoning obligation, based on regional housing needs. Reversing a whole line of previous New Jersey lower court decisions upholding exclusionary practices, the high court set up a new principle of judicial review in determining whether a local zoning ordinance promotes the general welfare. Because of the historic importance of this decision, and its applicability to other states, Potomac reproduced the decision as *Zoning "For the Living Welfare of People."*

Potomac and the MHP later took considerable comfort when one of the most important anti-exclusionary rulings of the decade was handed down by the New Jersey Supreme Court. Popularly known as *Mount Laurel II,* this remarkable 1983 opinion upheld the previous decision, but it also found the previous ruling vague and without practical effect. It therefore laid down detailed statewide guidelines for access to housing by lower-income residents (heavily minority) in communities hitherto closed to them. Potomac published excerpts, together with a thoughtful analysis by Herbert Franklin, so that court systems and public officials in other states could have ready access to this ground-breaking model.

Another key housing case, on which Franklin served as a consultant, was the famous *Gautreaux* case in Chicago, which came before the Supreme Court in 1976. Even more important than the finding—that public housing had been consistently and unlawfully sited in racially concentrated areas—was the issue of remedy. The Supreme Court ruled that although the violation of federal law occurred within city boundaries, relief beyond the city was permissible because both HUD and the Chicago Housing Authority had authority to operate outside city limits. The remedy fashioned in this case is still working and forms the basis for what may prove to have been a significant HUD initiative in the Clinton administration.

Constantly seeking broader audiences for equitable land use policies, the Potomac Institute collaborated with the Center for the Study of Democratic Institutions in California, whose president was former University of Chicago president Robert Hutchins. They jointly sponsored two important conferences on land use decisions in 1975 and 1977 in Santa Barbara. Fleming, Franklin, and Levin contributed papers that were published in two issues of the *Center Magazine*.

On another front in the fair housing battle, Potomac tackled the issue of discriminatory mortgage lending by financial institutions. Consultant Zina Greene and Arthur Levin wrote a *Lender's Guide to Fair Mortgage Policies*. Based on the requirements of the Home Mortgage Disclosure Act of 1976, the booklet was a useful tool not only for local groups attacking discriminatory practices but also for banking institutions trying genuinely to carry out the legislated mandate.

When Jimmy Carter was elected president in 1976, Potomac was ready to share its experience and recommendations with a new administration that seemed to have a strong commitment to civil rights. An early contribution was a detailed and specific set of recommendations: *Equal Housing Opportunity: The Unfinished Federal Agenda*. Although the Carter White House did turn to the Metropolitan Housing Project on occasion for policy advice, the president's and HUD secretary Patricia Harris's strong statements in support of fair housing enforcement and opening up housing in the suburbs to minorities were not matched by departmental action.

Some advances took place, particularly when Sterling Tucker was named assistant secretary for fair housing late in the administration: new programs of grants to state antidiscrimination agencies and nonprofit housing advocacy agencies, spotchecking realtor practices, and lifting a ten-year freeze on issuing guidelines to implement Title VIII of the 1968 Act. But in the end, almost none of Potomac's recommendations for systematically reducing discrimination in housing, lending, and zoning were enacted by the Carter administration. The Civil Rights Commission charged in 1979 that although court decisions had helped to remedy discriminatory practices, federal efforts had in recent years done nothing to strengthen Title VIII or its enforcement.

After President Reagan took office, Fleming reported to his board:

> The fifty year old federal housing program did not escape the rapacious attention of the Reagan Administration. Soon after taking office, the Chief Executive appointed a President's Commission on Housing. Its report found no national shortage of rental housing, except in some few areas, and hence no need for a federal program of housing construction. It held that the problem of the poor was in affording, not finding, housing and thus federal housing policy should be demand-oriented rather than supply-oriented.

The new commission recommended consumer housing assistance grants or vouchers rather than any effort to subsidize housing units. OMB director David Stockman went further, proposing to dismantle all HUD programs in the name of reducing inflation and interest rates.

The Reagan administration displayed the same aversion to fair housing regulation as it showed to other forms of equal opportunity enforcement. Civil rights groups persuaded Congress to introduce a tougher new fair housing bill, only to be overtaken by a Reagan bill that preserved the weak and cumbersome enforcement provisions of the past. During its first thirty months, the Reagan Justice Department filed only six housing discrimination suits, as compared to forty-six under Carter. Moreover, the administration jettisoned a Carter-instituted policy of selecting cases that would set significant nationwide precedents, and instead picked cases at random.

For all civil rights groups, including Potomac, the work of the 1980s in housing was a continuing effort to preserve existing housing programs from attack and erosion. There could be little thought of breaking new ground.

The Metropolitan Housing Project closed down in 1984. The Ford Foundation concluded its grants after twelve years of support, ending the long series of publications, policy explorations, and Metropolitan Housing Memoranda, to the regret of a large group of activists and scholars who had come to depend on their timeliness and accuracy.

Throughout its history, the Potomac Institute was deeply engaged in the complex policy and legal issues of housing integration. Its consistent goal was never simply salt-and-pepper integration, but the achievement of rational and responsible public actions to reduce massive and involuntary racial concentrations. To the argument that dispersion of the black population would have an adverse effect on black political power, Fleming always replied: "Black political 'control' of impoverished and deteriorating cities is an unenviable form of black power; it should at least be supplemented by black participation in more affluent and influential jurisdictions, so that more elected officials, white as well as black, will be responsive to minority and low-income constituents."

He also took on those who claimed that prevailing majority attitudes would always prevent residential integration, reminding them that the history of the preceding years was proof that such attitudes at any given time should not determine the goals to be set for ourselves and for society. "If we are convinced that large-scale and increasing isolation of racial and low-income groups threatens the well-being of society, and that such isolation will not be remedied by purely voluntary methods, then we will not so easily despair of achieving public policy remedies."

CHAPTER 24 ▪ *Can Justice Be Color Blind?*

IN 1896 JUSTICE JOHN MARSHALL HARLAN wrote his famous dissent from the Supreme Court decision that enshrined the "separate but equal" doctrine as the law of the land: "In the view of the Constitution, in the eye of the law, there is in this country no superior, dominant ruling class of citizens. There is no caste system here. Our Constitution is color-blind, and neither knows nor tolerates classes among its citizens." Eighty years later Harold Fleming noted:

> Harlan's was a courageous and farsighted stand—so farsighted, in fact, that it remained a minority one until 1954, when the Supreme Court finally held that segregation violated the 14th Amendment to the Constitution. At the time of that decision, it was commonly assumed that the ethical principle undergirding equal treatment was legally established once and for all. What remained, it seemed, was the arduous but morally uncomplicated job of putting the principle into practice throughout the society. In retrospect, however, this view seems innocent indeed.

From its inception, Potomac played a central role in what turned out to be the extremely complicated work of putting that principle into practice. In the 1960s, the institute designed, installed, and provided models for compliance mechanisms that, with later refinements, are still in effect today. In later years, as these programs came under attack for violating Justice Harlan's "color blind" precept, Potomac's public education efforts and publications played a key part in untangling the "moral complications" Fleming had in mind, and in defending and preserving effective compliance practices against distortion and attack.

In its early days, Potomac had helped the Defense Department establish and implement standards of equal employment among the many large corporations with which it did business. It moved on to advise Franklin Roosevelt Jr. in establishing the federal Equal Employment Opportunity Commission, which would bring those standards to bear on private industry and labor unions all across the country.

By the end of the 1960s it had, at the request of Mayor John Lindsay of New York, developed a model system of equal employment compliance among contractors doing business with that city, a system second only to the federal government in the dollar volume of its contracts. A number of other cities requested copies of the report to help them implement their own practices, and the model was frequently used.

In 1966, Potomac decided to look at the actual results of newly legislated national and state fair employment mandates, in order to review what was and was not working in real corporate experience.

George Schermer, a human relations consultant with extensive experience in Philadelphia and Detroit, was commissioned to survey firms known to have above-average minority employment records and to analyze what practices led to their relative success. The resulting publication, *Employer's Guide to Equal Opportunity,* concluded that while antidiscrimination laws are an essential first step, "color-blind" neutrality did not by itself produce significant gains in nonwhite employment. The study demonstrated that equal employment worked best when top management adopted an explicit, firm, and fair employment policy and made sure it was effectively communicated down the line. Large firms must set specific goals and follow through procedures to overcome bureaucratic inertia. The survey also revealed that, contrary to common assumptions, organized labor unions and established labor rights rarely jeopardized such programs. Another noteworthy finding was that the greatest progress was made by firms in cities where fair employment was backed by publicity and public programs involving all segments of the community.

This how-to-do-it manual laid out specific steps that management could take beyond the minimum requirements of state and federal laws: judicious use of psychological tests along with race-sensitive training, promotion practices, and labor relations. It also warned that "unless employers themselves can find ways of employing and upgrading . . .

minority personnel at a considerably accelerated pace . . . new forms of direct pressure and intensified regulation can be anticipated."

Press coverage of the report was good, and demand was strong among state agencies, human rights commissions, business associations, church groups, and universities. The roster of companies requesting copies of the *Guide* represented virtually all federal contractors, and federal agencies themselves were among the largest bulk purchasers. A sign of the changing times was that among the groups placing large orders were Road Builders' Associations in Alabama, Mississippi, and Georgia.

Before long, however, many of the newly implemented equal employment regulations were under fire. By the time Nixon took office, the phrase "affirmative action" had begun to be clouded by controversy. In speeches and articles in the early 1970s, Fleming analyzed the problem:

> Affirmative action as a governmental concept is scarcely more than a decade old. It dates back to President Kennedy's Executive Order of 1961 requiring government contractors to practice equal employment opportunity. The thought that blacks or similarly disadvantaged minorities might be seen as favored at the expense of whites would have been laughable then. The very fact that such issues can be argued today is testimony to the volatility of our society.
>
> The subject of the debate is color-blindness vs. color-consciousness. Those who are most articulate on the negative side of this debate are not the traditional defenders of segregation and the racial status quo. On the contrary, they include . . . the kind of individuals customarily identified with egalitarian values. This suggests, quite correctly, that there are issues here that should not be lightly brushed aside as the progeny of racism.
>
> The case of the latter-day advocates of color-blindness is essentially a meritocratic one: solely individual ability and achievement, not group identity, must determine who receives what rewards in society. They decry discrimination . . . [and] recognize that past discriminations have resulted in inequities that should be rectified. They maintain, however, that past injustices must not be remedied at the expense of individuals who happen to belong to favored (or less unfavored) groups. Hence it is acceptable, even obligatory, to

provide extra education and training for one who has been denied such opportunities in the past because of group identity. But it is improper and unjust to give preference at the point of selection to such an individual over a better qualified person from a more advantaged background.

Taking the dimensions of the problem is a difficult matter. As in the case of school busing, one hears a great deal about injustice and hardship inflected on innocent individuals, but solid evidence in support of the complaint is exceedingly scarce. How many whites in what situations have in fact suffered from "discrimination in reverse"? Conversely, how many blacks have benefitted from preferential treatment? How many institutions of higher learning have had their federal funds cut off because they refused to give statistical evidence of affirmative action? How many government contractors have been terminated or debarred for failure to give favored treatment to minority workers?

The likely answer to all of these questions is, Very few. Yet there have been enough instances of alleged discrimination in reverse, at least proposed if not actually carried out, to convince some commentators that the basic principle of equal treatment is in jeopardy.

Early in the Nixon administration, a curious dichotomy occurred. Business executives, disliking the welter of diverse rules about contracting with the government, encouraged the administration to pronounce a single new government-wide affirmative action standard. It is often forgotten today that it was President Nixon who in 1971 promulgated Executive Order No. 4, which established the policy of "goals and timetables" directed toward all minorities, not just blacks and women. This mandatory affirmative action policy spread throughout government and government-related industries, frequently by court order. In the next several years, blacks made significant progress in all occupational categories in private employment.

On the other hand, Nixon and his Cabinet freely indulged in inflammatory rhetoric against "reverse discrimination," "racial quotas," and bureaucratic excesses, playing to his electoral strategy to capture right-wing sentiment.

Because it had been a pioneer in the field, the Potomac Institute felt a special obligation to provide a reasoned defense of affirmative action. Fleming wrote a number of articles, beginning with one in *City* magazine in 1972 that was reprinted by the HEW Office of Civil Rights for distribution to all its employees, by the Equal Employment Opportunity Commission, by the National Civil Service League, and by other public and private groups.

Arthur Levin undertook the special mission of debating the subject with the boards and special committees of several national and local Jewish agencies, which carried on a vigorous battle against quotas of any kind. Their concern stemmed from their own well-remembered and painful battles against exclusionary quotas; the challenge from blacks provoked strong group feelings.

Many of those opposed to affirmative action had a distorted view of what the process actually involved. Thus one of the first steps of its defenders was to define it accurately. The affirmative action program recommended by Potomac and initially implemented was very straightforward. Federal agencies and private companies holding contracts with the government must maintain statistics on the number of minority and women employees in their various job classifications. Agencies and companies must supply these data to the compliance offices. If there is significant underrepresentation of women or minorities, agencies and companies must set reasonable goals and timetables to correct the situation based on the availability of qualified employees in the workforce of their respective areas.

"The difference between non-discrimination and affirmative action should be clearly understood," Fleming wrote. "Non-discrimination is firmly rooted in American law and protects every individual. Affirmative action is group-directed and can have differing policy goals: the historical reparations goal of remedying the effects of past discrimination, or the forward-looking goal of bringing 'out-groups' into the mainstream."

He thought that insistence on pure meritocracy overlooked some important realities. For generations, blacks were excluded from employment and higher education not only by outright discrimination but also by such indirect methods as word-of-mouth recruitment, announcements directed to a mainly white public, job qualifications not related to job performance, "culturally biased" testing, and a variety of signals intended to discourage black applicants or would-be applicants. Such a pattern can be changed only by a conscious effort to reverse the methods and their inequitable results until such time as the historical imbalance is redressed.

Meritocracy also assumes, he pointed out, that there are precise methods of measuring and comparing the qualifications of applicants.

> As every experienced employer or admissions officer knows, this is not the case. In practice, the employer who is free to do so takes into account not only "objective" test results, but many intangible factors as well—his perception of the applicant's character, personality, motivation, family circumstances, ability to work harmoniously with others, and so on. In general, these factors have worked to the disadvantage of nonwhites, since the white selectors have tended to prefer the applicants who most resembled themselves in appearance, dress, speech, family, and community background. We have also come to realize that employment tests are not the impartial instruments they once were thought to be. Most of them still put an unwarranted emphasis on verbal facility, at the expense of other aptitudes and skills that under-educated nonwhites are more likely to have.
>
> Under these circumstances, it is simplistic to argue that the applicants can be put into some indisputable rank order of qualification. In most cases there is room for legitimate flexibility of judgment in choosing among a group of applicants, all of whom may justifiably be regarded as "qualified." If an employer or admissions officer uses that flexibility to remedy racial imbalance resulting from past exclusion, he is not necessarily guilty of discrimination in reverse. On the contrary, it can be strongly argued that he is fulfilling an ethical obligation to reexamine and modify selection criteria that are racist in effect, if not in intent.

Another flaw in the strictly meritocratic position is that it neglects the question of social benefit. Fleming believed that a society such as ours aspires to be is in grave danger if rigid adherence to traditional standards of credentialing and formal testing deny social and economic mobility to the have-nots.

Many years ago, the most prestigious Eastern universities recognized that the regional differentials in secondary education were such that few Southerners or other "provincials" could be expected to make it through their admissions screen. Consequently, they waived college-board examinations for the non-Easterners, substituting instead the criterion of the applicant's high school performance—a straight-forward example of "preferential treatment" that no one was heard to complain of.

At that time, when the beneficiaries were overwhelmingly white, such affirmative efforts to achieve a pluralistic result were consid-ered laudably democratic. The important point is that these uni-versities recognized the value to themselves as institutions and to their students of pluralistic rather than elitist student bodies. And since education at one of the prestigious universities has a decidedly favorable influence on later career advancement, these institutions may be said to have had a "democratizing" effect on business and professional leadership and thus to have benefitted the society as a whole. The importance of including racial minorities in this process would seem to justify a similarly affirmative approach.

Fleming particularly enjoyed using the analogy of this university en-trance program, because as he often recounted he himself had been one of the graduates of a designated "provincial" high school who thereby gained a place at an Ivy League university.

The issue of setting numerical goals remained a persistent stumbling block in the discussion. The history of affirmative action unfortunately includes many regulatory excesses on the part of government agencies, which have provided ammunition over the years to opponents seeking to discredit the entire concept. Fleming acknowledged that the line between a numerical goal and a rigid quota may on occasion be crossed, and may in practice lead to abuse. But he insisted that this was not a reason to abandon goal-setting in the first place.

The central question is not whether the goal-setting requirement is sometimes misapplied, but whether the requirement itself is nec-essary and defensible. Even a cursory review of the history of equal opportunity programs demonstrates that it is. Experience with nondiscrimination laws, state and federal, has invariably shown that little or nothing happens so long as the employer or institution is not held accountable for measurable results. The federal contract compliance program, for example, yielded more protestations of good faith than black employees until goals and timetables were introduced. Similarly, school desegregation in the South was mainly an exercise in tokenism until target figures were established for black pupils and faculty members. The old plaint, "We've tried but we just can't find any who are qualified," tends to prevail unless some specific standard of achievement is applied.

Measuring results, of course, required collection of racial and ethnic data, always a controversial subject. Requiring individual racial identification during the process of application and selection, as opposed to ongoing organizational "outcome" statistics, was even more complicated. Apart from philosophical objections with respect to merit standards and the fears of civil rights advocates about the misuse of racial data, the paperwork burdens were formidable. Nevertheless, the need for a means to determine whether equality in practice has been achieved was indisputable, just as a business examines its balance sheet and a school examines its pupils' achievement scores.

Opposition to affirmative action in employment and higher education deepened during the Nixon and Ford administrations. A recession in the mid-1970s, followed by double-digit inflation, halted economic progress for nearly everybody, and blacks more than most. The rise in unemployment was also steeper among blacks and reached catastrophic rates for black youth.

As the debate over affirmative action became ever more charged and overheated, the institute's research librarian, Margaret Price, began a factual assessment of a decade of equal employment efforts in three arenas: the federal government, private contractors doing government business, and institutions of higher education. Consultant Virginia Willis gathered this material into a manuscript that was published in 1973 as *Affirmative Action: The Unrealized Goal.*

The report came as a surprise to those who assumed that affirmative action rules had made sweeping changes in minority employment opportunity. The analysis made it disquietingly clear that more than a decade of affirmative action policy had yielded little progress. Token programs of recruitment and upgrading were geared more to public relations than results. The study showed clearly that minorities continued to be heavily overrepresented in the lower-paid and less skilled jobs traditionally reserved for them, although there had been a frantic scramble on the part of industry and higher education to attract a small number of the most highly qualified minority individuals for executive positions.

During the relatively prosperous 1960s, blacks, particularly black women, increasingly penetrated the workforce, albeit in entry-level grades and lower skilled jobs. Although the black-white income gap closed somewhat, and fewer black families were living below the poverty line, the basic pattern of black disadvantage had not changed. Affirmative action did not accomplish the hoped-for results because of the ill-defined, voluntary nature of the effort.

College programs of "open" and "preferential" admissions certainly had begun to increase minority enrollment, but progress was slowed by cutbacks in federal educational opportunity grants to colleges. The statistics also demonstrated that new policies benefitted the children of white, blue-collar workers as much or more than blacks.

Nonetheless, the study pointed out some progress. The courts in particular were forcing recalcitrant government and private employers and unions to hire minorities and women on a more equitable basis as well as awarding large sums in back pay and damages. Herbert Hill, an indefatigable NAACP lawyer, made the relevant point in remarks quoted in the study: emerging judicial interpretations of Title VII, which allowed proof on the basis of statistical data and could reach an employer's entire enterprise and result in substantial monetary judgments, were a great impetus to a meaningful change in employment practices.

The booklet stressed that if the results of past discrimination were to be undone and equal opportunity programs made productive, they needed a framework of monitored goals and timetables. It was also essential to include some method of measuring results. Once again the difference between "goals" and "quotas" was defined and discussed.

The publication proved to be a valuable continuing resource to hundreds of training programs and seminars. It was widely used to bolster the practices of those organizations and agencies, public and private, which were more concerned with reality than rhetoric. Harvard University reprinted the higher education portion of the booklet for distribution in academic circles.

Prospects for affirmative action during the deep recession of 1974 and 1975 were not bright, however, although the lines at the unemployment compensation windows were well integrated. The eventual fate of affirmative action still depended on seminal cases working their way up through the court system.

Among them were suits affecting the divisive debate about admissions to colleges and universities. For several years the U.S. Department of Health, Education and Welfare, in addition to conducting a very public war of words with the academic community, had been publishing and enforcing its higher education guidelines. These rules carefully defined the need for affirmative action plans with goals and timetables, emphasizing more effective recruitment practices. In no way did the guidelines contemplate any reduction in academic standards, and numerical quotas were explicitly prohibited.

As agreements between universities and HEW were gradually (and reluctantly) adopted, some new programs were challenged by white applicants for admission who believed that "reverse racism" was unjust and unconstitutional. One case, that of Allan Bakke, symbolized the entire debate. A white applicant, he had been rejected by the University of California Medical School at Davis, which had reserved sixteen places for minorities, many of whom had significantly lower test scores than Bakke did.

The case attracted volumes of informed and uninformed comment and over fifty amicus curiae briefs by the time it reached the Supreme Court in 1977. Deep divisions persisted within civil rights constituencies, and the court showed signs of a split between those who would abolish affirmative action altogether and those who would strongly uphold it.

Fleming saw, more clearly than most, that the *Bakke* case was not a "morally uncomplicated" one: He wrote about it with characteristic courage and candor, observing that it was an example of misplaced solidarity:

It was a wholly inadequate vehicle for these issues. The ruling assumption seems to be that to yield anything to the critics is to yield everything. But it is self-defeating to maintain that there are no unnecessary or needlessly onerous civil rights regulations, that all parents who object to busing are racists, or that human services programs are not in need of stricter "targeting" on individuals and areas of real disadvantage. Privately, few civil rights advocates would deny that the Davis Medical School admissions plan, which Mr. Bakke challenged, was in fact a quota system. Such quotas have long been held justified by the courts when institutions have been found guilty of persistent past discrimination. But the Davis school had no history of discrimination and was not under court order. Nevertheless, most of the civil rights groups joining in the litigation heeded the call for a united front, swallowed their misgivings, and rallied to the defense of the Davis plan.

Not surprisingly, a majority of the sharply divided Supreme Court found the admissions program impermissible. Luckily a differently composed majority voted to preserve the essential principle: that race can legitimately be taken into account, along with other factors, in a unified admissions program.

In this climate, Potomac staff seized every opportunity to spread factual information about why affirmative action programs were necessary to bring about social justice, how they actually worked, and what results they had achieved. In many articles and speeches, Fleming sought to keep the discussion focused clearly on the well-being of society, rather than on the advancement of a particular group. When the potential of large numbers of minority youths is blighted, when a permanent underclass is created, society as a whole is diminished. He distinguished between the legal issue—the extent to which the suspect classification of race can be considered in publicly condoned actions—and the larger issue of fairness. He wondered why some were squeamish about taking race into account where it can be constitutionally done, given the fact that Americans readily give preferential treatment to many groups, such as veterans, when the national interest appears to be at stake.

He helped the Center for the Study of Democratic Institutions to plan another "dialogue" in 1978, this time about the *Bakke* case, in two issues of the *Center* magazine. Using his own contribution to point out again how rarely meritocracy has been practiced in all areas of admissions to higher education or to business and professional opportunities, he said, "We should look very carefully at the extent to which we apply a double standard of purity when we deal with these knotty questions of race."

The years immediately following the highly publicized *Bakke* case were critical ones for maintaining government affirmative action programs. At first there were some positive signs. Even the Burger Court upheld most rulings against corporations that failed to employ minorities at all levels. In a key but narrow test of affirmative action plans, the 1978 *Weber* case, the Supreme Court held that voluntary plans by businesses and unions, even including quotas, were constitutional. Two years later the Court also upheld the right of Congress to legislate the allocation of percentages of federal program funds to minority-owned businesses.

Progress on the administrative front was in part due to the strengthening of the Office of Federal Contract Compliance Programs during the Carter administration. In an important move, EEOC Chair Eleanor Holmes Norton was finally able to introduce a new program concentrating on major lawsuits to end patterns and practices of discrimination in key industries, rather than relying on individual complaints, which were inevitably backlogged and often had no general effect once resolved—a recommendation made by Potomac as long ago as 1965 in its consultations with the EEOC's first chairman, Franklin D. Roosevelt Jr.

The election of President Reagan, however, signaled open opposition to affirmative action, and indeed to civil rights enforcement in general. Reiterating his belief that yesterday's battles are never definitively won, Fleming reported to his board at the end of 1983:

> The administration seems determined to destroy a half century's gains in social equity, care for the poor, provisions for the old, education for the young, preservation of the environment, safety for the worker, and honesty for the consumer.
>
> The President and his appointees are systematically dismantling or nullifying programs that were put in place with great effort

during the past twenty-five years. Moreover, they are challenging longstanding principles of fairness and equal treatment that the federal courts and Congress have embodied in law. It is a deadly serious campaign, waged with great persistence and, thus far, considerable success.

The battle goes forward in two areas—the first that of public opinion, the second that of bureaucracy, congressional relations, and the courts. Thanks largely to the predilections of the media, public attention has centered most heavily on the rhetoric of the President and his lieutenants, especially the occasional graceless utterances to which they are prone: Edwin Meese's declaration that there is no evidence of "rampant" hunger in America; Linda Chavez's announcement on behalf of the Reagan-dominated Civil Rights Commission that underemployment of women and minorities in high-tech industries results only from their ineptitude in math and science; the President's own casual suggestions that Martin Luther King Jr. may eventually be shown to have been a communist sympathizer and that street people are "homeless by choice."

These and like pronouncements have angered the civil rights constituency and encouraged civil rights opponents—although they have aroused no widespread or lasting public indignation. The lack of adverse popular reaction must be attributed largely to Reagan's remarkable personal style. No president of recent memory could successfully have combined such unfeeling rhetoric with an image of geniality and benevolence.

Deplorable as callous statements by high public officials may be, they are of far less consequence than the administration's determined effort to redefine the federal civil rights role as one of neutrality and, arguably, not-so-benign neglect.

Specifically, the new administration set about dismantling or vitiating federal enforcement efforts, the Equal Employment Opportunity Commission, the Civil Rights Commission, school desegregation enforcement, and voting rights enforcement. Its tools were budget cuts in relevant staff and programs, appointment of weak and unskilled officials to key jobs, and relaxation of regulations in fair housing and education.

Secretary of Education Terrel Bell made it clear that he would not uphold any desegregation laws on the books with which he was not in tune. Assistant Attorney General William Bradford Reynolds declared that the government should not compel children who didn't want an integrated education to have one.

Many of the policies and programs under attack were those that Potomac had helped bring into being, Fleming noted. "While little can be done to induce a recalcitrant administration to maintain vigorous implementation, it is possible to combat efforts to abolish civil rights and equal opportunity programs outright."

The organizations allied in the Leadership Conference focused their energy on strengthening legislation. One highlight, indeed one of the few bright spots of the Reagan years, was the extension of the Voting Rights Act of 1965 after a hard-fought battle. Civil rights groups mobilized their constituents to a pitch of intensity not seen since the sixties. With the help of a small group of committed senators and congressmen (including Republicans who broke ranks with the White House), what was arguably the most powerful civil rights law since the Fourteenth Amendment was reauthorized in 1982.

Potomac's long-standing relationships with many private foundations allowed it to play a special supporting role in this effort. While direct lobbying was not permitted for tax-exempt organizations like the institute, public education was. A number of foundations contributed to a coordinated campaign to foster broad public understanding of the need to continue voting rights protection. Some groups put together case material documenting the varieties of discrimination that still existed, from crude disfranchisement efforts to subtle forms of discouragement. Others, including the Voter Education Project in the South and its Hispanic counterpart in the Southwest, kept up their registration work in places where resistance was still endemic.

In 1981, a group of foundations asked Potomac to sponsor an exchange of information among foundations and grantee organizations working in the field. The institute periodically issued comprehensive bulletins reporting activities underway and calling attention to work still to be done. The bulletin was disseminated until the new voting rights measure was signed into law a year later.

Victories were few, however. Affirmative action barely survived a sustained attack. Reagan appointees proposed regulatory changes that would have exempted 75 percent of the businesses then subject to goals and timetables, removed class action remedies for noncompliance, and otherwise set the tone for a reversal, if not elimination, of affirmative action. The attorney general himself refused to supply statistical information on his own agency's employees by race and sex, thereby failing to comply with an EEOC requirement that had applied to all federal agencies for many years. The Justice Department repeatedly sought to join legal attacks on municipal affirmative action plans in police and fire departments, even voluntary ones, although it was largely rebuffed by the federal courts. The administration even prevented publication of its own Labor Department's study of the effectiveness of federal contract compliance programs.

Potomac and its colleagues set out to refute such misrepresentations and regressive actions by marshalling the facts. It seemed an opportune moment to bring the institute's 1973 survey of affirmative action results up to date.

The result was a comprehensive statistical examination by labor economist Herbert Hammerman and Arthur Levin of the progress made by minorities and women in those institutions, public and private, that were subject to affirmative action requirements. Like the suppressed Labor Department study, the Potomac report offered much encouraging news. Since 1973, when Potomac's previous study of employment was published, women and minorities had made notable gains, especially in higher skilled and better paid job categories. The gains were uneven, and in most areas parity was still remote, but the trend was unmistakably in the direction of equal opportunity, particularly in the higher positions that had for so long been closed to the traditional victims of discrimination.

The report, *A Decade of New Opportunity: Affirmative Action in the 1980s,* was published in late 1984. Its wealth of statistical information was lightened by a lucid summary of the significance of the data. The introduction reviewed once again the value of setting numerical goals and gathering employment data. It again laid to rest the myths that had grown up around affirmative action practices and delineated what should and should not be included in affirmative action policy and practice.

Overnight the report became an indispensable document. It received favorable editorial treatment in the *New York Times* and in *Business Week,* and led to numerous interviews and talk show appearances by Fleming and Hammerman. Fleming reported to his board with some satisfaction on the fortuitous timing of the report.

> As you know if you've been following the news during the Dog Days (August 1985), Messrs. Meese and Reynolds of the "Justice" Department are proposing to kill the Affirmative Action program as now defined. They want the President to amend the existing Executive Order so as to forbid all use of numerical measures in determining compliance of government contractors with equal employment requirements. This would take us back to the Eisenhower days when there was no accountability, but instead reliance on good will and voluntary action by employers. In fact, even the voluntary use of goals and timetables by employers apparently would not be sanctioned. Such action would be the most drastic step yet taken in the Administration's campaign to dismantle civil rights enforcement.
>
> Fortunately, the Meese initiative, which he had hoped to slip by during the unguarded days of summer, has encountered significant opposition. Labor Secretary Brock, who administers the program, is waging a cautious counter-strategy. The National Association of Manufacturers and some other business leaders are publicly opposed to the proposal. Many Senators and Congressmen, some in the President's own party, are upset. The civil rights coalition is working hard to rally public and political opposition. As a concession to this vocal opposition, Meese has agreed to submit the proposal for discussion by the Cabinet, probably in the next week or two. There is a better than even chance that a majority of Cabinet members will oppose the change. The danger is that Meese will persuade the President to ignore the Cabinet majority and simply issue the new order anyway. It wouldn't be the first time.
>
> I'm glad to say that our work on Affirmative Action is playing a critical part in these developments. Our report and its findings are

being used by the media and representatives of business, labor, and the civil rights groups as the currently definitive evidence that Affirmative Action is working effectively and should be continued. While we can't claim that the timing of our report was the result of shrewd calculation, luckily it couldn't have been better.

In the end, Meese's attempt was defeated. Affirmative action, in the sense of setting numerical goals and tracking progress, seemed to have become a permanent feature of corporate management and was widely supported by the business community. Continuing public education and vigilance, however, would be required to keep it from vanishing from the federal agenda.

Meanwhile, a number of relevant cases wound their way through the courts. Three of them, involving teachers, firefighters, and sheet-metal workers, were decided by the Supreme Court in 1986. Fleming thought the results warranted wider discussion and commissioned Herbert Franklin to analyze the rulings. His paper, *Reading the Supreme Court Tea Leaves on Affirmative Action: Affirmative Hiring Goals Reinforced,* was distributed in 1986.

After sorting out the welter of opinions in the three cases, Franklin was able to show that the Reagan administration's claim that the Supreme Court had vindicated its opposition to "racial quotas" was simply not justified. "Any fairminded analysis of these opinions will indicate that the Court has in many respects reinforced the use of voluntary affirmative goals and timetables in appropriate situations where identifiable non-minority workers are not adversely affected and has established a new standard for the federal courts in ordering involuntary affirmative action," said Franklin. He extracted from the opinions the key elements of an effective plan which would pass the Court test, as a guide for employers and public officials.

Franklin concluded that the extensive efforts of the Reagan years to reverse public policies of the previous five administrations, both Democratic and Republican, had virtually no effect on Supreme Court jurisprudence.

Nevertheless, the overall legacy of the Reagan-Bush years was the loss of a carefully constructed machinery of law enforcement. Such lasting damage would take both time and energy to repair.

For more than two decades, Potomac had defined the essential principles of affirmative action, designed mechanisms that made affirmative
action work, and defended government mandates from persistent attack.
In all of their work, the board and staff of Potomac held to a consistent
view on the fundamental issue. It was expressed in a guest editorial by
Fleming in the summer 1980 edition of the *Civil Rights Quarterly:*

> Historically, discrimination has been inflicted, not on particular
> individuals, but on identifiable members of entire groups. It was
> not selected blacks, for example, who were denied equal access to
> schools, jobs, and housing, but blacks as a race. Discrimination is a
> wholesale process, and it was intricately woven into the social and
> economic fabric of our society. To undo it requires an equally sys-
> tematic process.
>
> Eighty-four years ago, in a famous dissenting opinion, Supreme
> Court Justice John Harlan declared that "our Constitution is color-
> blind." We can only guess at what he might say today. Perhaps it
> would be something like this: "Our Constitution is color-blind.
> But until our society translates that ideal into everyday practice, the
> decision-maker who is color blind is blind to injustice."

CHAPTER 25 ▪ *To Everything There Is a Season*

AS FLEMING NEARED RETIREMENT age in the mid-1980s, Potomac activities began to draw to a close.

James Gibson had left in 1979 to join the District of Columbia government, and later to become a leader in private foundations concerned with social justice. In 1982, Arthur Levin retired after twenty-one years of invaluable service. Fleming had since then relied on consultants and project personnel to carry on Potomac's undertakings, as always with the indispensable administrative support of Eleanor Ambrose.

The decision to close the institute rather than to seek new leadership and new funding sources was not an easy one. All those associated with it felt a deep satisfaction at the role it had played over more than twenty-five years. But Fleming's dispassionate view of organizational realities was set out in a 1986 memorandum to board members, who regretfully concurred.

> As we all know, the social climate is unpropitious for most public interest organizations, perhaps especially so for those concerned with civil rights.... The current regressiveness cannot, of course, be attributed to Reaganism alone. It is also attributable to a popular belief that further governmental action and institutional reform are unnecessary as well as prohibitively expensive in this era of Gramm-Rudman.
>
> Undergirding this opinion is the widespread perception that the economic problems and social pathology that afflict the minority "underclass" can be addressed effectively only by minority leadership and self-help.

The prevalence of these views has had a sharply negative effect on the funding and effectiveness of most organizations committed to the advancement of equal opportunity. Many foundations—particularly those that came to the arena late and reluctantly—have dropped out. Others have shifted their priorities in this field away from national policy development and advocacy to service delivery and community-based programs. As a result, many organizations in Potomac's orbit are struggling for survival.

The problem is not just the capriciousness of funding sources. It also has to do with effectiveness. Organizations like Potomac must depend heavily on pressures for positive change generated by large social and political forces. It is these that create opportunities for the shaping of new policies and programs. In their absence, organizational energy is largely absorbed by defensive battles—and even those need troops in the field. For these reasons, the national civil rights oriented groups that are best positioned today are those with sizable constituencies, broadly based financial support, and strong minority leadership.

It is no disparagement of Potomac's record of achievement to recognize that, at least as it is now conceived, its period of greatest usefulness is over. We anticipated this eventuality at the beginning, when we deliberately ruled out the assumptions and trappings of permanence.

Thus in 1987 the Potomac Institute closed down its formal operations in the brick townhouse near Dupont Circle in Washington that had been the scene of so many useful gatherings.

Throughout its existence, the Potomac Institute had remained entirely faithful to the initial vision that Fleming suggested to Stephen Currier in 1961: a small, independent, unpretentious, and flexible center in Washington for the cultivation of ideas and associations that would advance public policy and private practices affecting race relations.

This chronicle has detailed much of the large terrain covered by Potomac projects over the years, beginning with the initial decision of the Curriers and Fleming to focus on legislative and administrative change at the federal level. The rationale for that was described in a board memorandum of 1962:

No other institution compares with the Federal Government in the variety and extent of its influence on minority rights and opportunities. . . . Federal benefits and programs affect the lives of virtually all citizens—government contracts; housing loan guarantees and subsidies; military installations, reserve units, national guard, and ROTC; education grants and loans; national parks and forests; veterans' services; regulation of business, commerce, labor, and transportation, etc.

With few exceptions, these vast benefits and services are not conditioned on effective guarantees of non-discrimination. Where explicit policies of non-discrimination apply . . . there is seldom effective administrative machinery and follow up. For example, though departmental regulations have forbidden racial discrimination in Federally-aided vocational education since 1948, the policy has never been enforced. By presidential orders, discrimination in employment by government contractors has been forbidden since World War II. Yet no firm has ever lost or been denied a contract because of discrimination, and only recently (through machinery developed by the Potomac Institute) has affirmative administration of the non-discrimination clause begun to be provided for. . . .

So habitual and ingrained are administrative practices foreclosing equal opportunity to Negroes that they go on automatically unless a considerable and sophisticated effort is made to redirect them.

This perception led to a stream of activities: technical assistance in enforcing contractor compliance with Kennedy's 1961 Executive Order, assuring that the Justice Department had ample opportunity to understand the real situation in the South with respect to repressive state and local actions, activating the "compliance underground" to lay the groundwork for the new Civil Rights Act, bringing many federal agency programs in line with it after it was passed, and helping to design two new federal agencies—the Community Relations Service and the Equal Employment Opportunity Commission. The experience and credibility arising from these activities made Fleming and his colleagues respected counselors to both the Kennedy and Johnson administrations.

After 1967, as federal initiatives on social programs and equal opportunity began to decline, Potomac shifted gears and direction. It kept its focus through the years on three of the largest areas of equal opportunity: housing, education, and employment. Among the most important of its contributions was the identification of a powerful new tool by which private citizens can hold the government accountable, under judicial supervision, for enforcement of civil rights legislation. This strategy, first victorious in the *Adams v. Richardson* case requiring implementation of school desegregation law, spawned many similar actions in other fields from environmental protection to women's rights. The institute also played a central role in shaping legal strategy in school finance equity and in zoning and urban growth policy.

Throughout the years of diminished federal leadership, Potomac maintained close ties with other civil rights agencies—chiefly the Leadership Conference on Civil Rights—in defensive action to protect legislative and administrative gains already won. Among the most important were the victorious struggles to keep alive affirmative action guidelines and data collection requirements.

The institute never put its sole reliance on government enforcement of civil rights, however. An equally important role was to facilitate action by private forces through "social interventions." Notable among those interventions were creation of the National Urban Coalition, the Council for Equal Business Opportunity, the Central Cities Technical Assistance project, and hundreds of collaborations and consultations with and publications addressed to professional, religious, charitable, and civil groups across the country.

Potomac's fundamental objective was always to diminish racial discrimination in public and private arenas, but experience taught that it often could not be tackled head on. The challenge was to develop approaches that built on perceived self-interest (of employers, housing developers, restaurant owners, and others) and also on what Fleming believed to be the residual decency of most human beings—what Lincoln referred to as "the better angels of our nature."

"Potomac's style of working is not easy to describe briefly," Fleming once wrote, "for much of it involves working with, through, and on other people and groups. The tired old word catalyst comes to mind, but, aside from being trite, it really is not very appropriate. In our more frivolous moments, we have come up with such concoctions as *Poto-synthesis*." Whatever it might be called, the method consisted of spotting an important emerging issue and bringing fruitful new combinations of talent, resources, and self-interest together around it. When an opportunity seemed to have enough payoff to warrant a place on the short list of active priorities, the role of Potomac in putting together the pieces was worked out. Board member Herbert Franklin thought the apt description was an aphorism attributed to Louis Pasteur: "Fortune favors the prepared mind."

An essential part of the formula was the long and steady support for the institute's modest core operating budget by the Taconic Foundation, based on an annual review of performance. Potomac also earned the respect and trust of a number of other private foundations that confidently funded special projects, in many years expanding the institute's funding by two or three times the base grant.

The institute's status as a tax-exempt charitable organization of course precluded legislative lobbying and involvement in electoral campaigns. But it found ample opportunity to contribute documentation, interpretation, and strategy advice that directly influenced public policy and action.

Because it was not burdened with the fund raising and constituency building demands of a general membership organization, it did not need to take self-serving public postures; it had no axe to grind but that of effective program. Its positions were tested for intellectual integrity and factual accuracy and not for their ability to please any group of special pleaders.

Potomac's method of reconnaissance and probing for opportunities for action entailed continually opening new lines of communication to new audiences, often explaining complex issues in a way that all could understand. Fleming's forte was pointed analysis, explanation, and examination of alternatives, rather than judgment or confrontation.

Another important ingredient of the Potomac style was strong relationships with the best and most influential of the Washington press corps, cultivating a reputation as a reliable source of information and analysis in the field of civil rights. The emphasis was always on substance and content rather than on Potomac as the source.

The audience for the institute's public information was in general the government, or the majority community, helping them come to terms with minority demands for equality. Many activities brought government and private representatives together who would not otherwise have occasion to meet and exchange views in a relaxed atmosphere. Conferences were typically small, informal, off-the-record, and sharply focused.

The publications of Potomac remain today a mine of useful, and usefully explained, information. Their success was in large part due to the skills of Arthur Levin, a relentless foe of muddy prose and unchecked facts. They frequently gave practical intellectual content and coherence to ideas that may have rocketed off on the first-stage fuel of moral truths but needed the sustaining power of technical workability and legal persuasiveness. Potomac's publications armed practitioners and policy makers with ideas that could be used in courts of law and councils of government.

Throughout the institute's existence Fleming resisted the temptation to expand, and thus did not compete with related organizations for operating funds. Fleming liked to say that Potomac "was conceived in anti-Parkinsonism and has maintained it pretty well over the years." That self-imposed exemption from the need for self-justifying claims that go along with larger scale fund raising suited his style.

As organizations go, Potomac was tiny: Fleming, Levin, Eleanor Ambrose, Margaret Price, after a while Gibson, and modest research and clerical support. But the appearance was deceptive. They made up in skill and versatility for whatever they may have lacked in numbers. It is hard to imagine a staff more frequently recruited by other organizations for boards, task forces, commissions, and advice. Fleming's diversity of leadership roles and board memberships outside Potomac itself sometimes made him seem an "institute" by himself. And if the Potomac staff seemed infinitely exploitable by others, such availability for service was simply the evolved realization of a hope Currier and Fleming had had from the start.

The institute's knowledgeable board members and skillfully chosen consultants were in and out of its work continually, as were strategically placed friends inside and outside government. Floating coalitions with other like-minded organizations provided extra leverage. Together, these resources always enabled Potomac to assemble a show of force that made it seem bigger and more powerful than its actual size. In time, Potomac became unintentionally a model for small activist "think tanks" that were to burgeon later in the 1970s and 1980s.

The Potomac way of operating—seeding new ground and moving on, forging alliances around many different projects, and foregoing public credit—made it at once superbly effective and hard to define. That flexibility at times lent a slight air of mystery to the institute. Fleming himself was always amused at the occasional assumption that the institute must be a "cover" for some well-funded enterprise of more nefarious purpose. His habit of calling all his southern friends "Cousin Harry" or "Cousin John" also led to some confusion—including at least one often-recounted inquiry by the FBI about one of his "relatives."

But for the far-flung circle of those who knew and relied on it, Potomac remained throughout its time a calm island of clarity and good sense, of reliable information, of hope and direction, in a sea of social change.

At Potomac they never threw their weight around and rarely claimed ownership of an idea or project. They cooperated, shared resources, and encouraged collaboration. Fleming acted as a wise counselor, whose roles ranged over that of teacher, adviser, encourager, convener, intermediary, negotiator—even poet and philosopher. His ability with the English language, his southern charm and good humor, his selflessness, all enabled him uniquely to play these roles. Those who worked with him know the profound effect he had on others whose names appeared far more frequently in the media.

Many of the important collegial relationships were fostered by the genial atmosphere in Potomac's comfortable brick townhouse on a quiet Washington street, which was formerly the parish house of St. Thomas Episcopal Church, whose rector and landlord, Henry Breul, occasionally frequented the precincts contributing his own well-informed perspective on issues of the day. Fleming understood, with his southern instincts, that good humor and fellowship can encourage consensus.

A revealing measure of Potomac's influence might have been gauged at five o'clock on many weekday afternoons. The social custom that came to be called "Fiveses" began early in Potomac's history: while Fleming and his colleagues finished up the day's business a visitor or two or more would drop in. The refreshment was never more elaborate than mixed nuts, lubricated by a little bourbon or gin. What happened then was an hour or two in which government people and private agency people and journalists came to know one another better, more personally. They exchanged information and ideas, argued fine points in a friendly manner, and grew to a deeper understanding of the common problems.

Harold Fleming would be the first to say that Potomac's achievements and victories, and those of its many colleagues and allies in the field of civil rights and urban policy, would never be final. They remain to be defended, refined, and rewon in a constant search for racial understanding and equity in each generation. But his remarkable sense of history, of human nature, and of humor enabled him to stay steadily, creatively, and dispassionately in the arena of social justice for nearly fifty years.

An expression of that humor was his bent toward topical verses or songs accompanied on his ukelele, the satirical wit that released his anger at injustice and animated the Potomac Institute for many years. Some of the particular names and references may have faded from memory, but it seems fitting to exit laughing with excerpts from Harold Fleming's New Year's observations in 1965 and 1966.

ODE ON A BROKEN CROCK
CIVIL RIGHTS 1965

January (two-faced Janus)
Started this momentous annus
With Johnson's bid for unity—
The Council on Opportunity.
Everybody raised a cheer . . .
    (But where are the snows of yesteryear?)

The problem was there for all to see—
The fractured Negro family.
And just the man to coin a plan
Was Daniel Patrick Moynihan.
His data made the pundits swoon . . .
    (But where are the snows of yesternoon?)

To LBJ 'twas clear the polity
Demanded we have real equality.

At Howard he said, "Let us gather
All the experts; let them blather.
Bring on the Irish and the Jews and all the militants you choose.
Give me your ideas, foreign or native,
Just so they're fresh and innovative."
Everybody said, "How keen!" ...
     (But where are the snows of yestere'en?)

"Tis better, they say, to light a spark
Than sit around and curse the dark.
And so they did in Watts, L.A.,
And lit a fire as bright as day.
(Baby, baby, burning bright
In the ghetto late at night,
Say, what studies, what commissions
Will ever really change conditions?)
Everybody studied Watts
And said, "We must improve their lots;
Then they will neither burn nor thieve."
     (But where are the snows of yestereve?)

Came November and sweet sessions
Of silent thought and loud professions.
Scarcely a man is now alive
Who planned those sessions in 'sixty-five.
For who is loved by LBJ
In December as in May?
Where went our blood, our sweat, our tears? ...
     (Gone, with the snow of yesteryears.)

Off with the old, on with the new!
Face the future with derring-do!
Sometimes the dice must come up sevens,
Notwithstanding Novak and Evans.
And for the old snows, shed no tear ...
     (For there'll be snowjobs all next year.)

BALLAD OF RECEDING GOAL
CIVIL RIGHTS 1966

Lyndon Johnson took an axe
To make inflation bygone.
He gave the budget forty whacks
And sent the chips to Saigon.
While war and space go on apace,
Both funded in entirety,
The needs of poverty and race
Are of the chopped variety.
            For each man kills the thing he loves;
            Farewell, oh Great Society.

Although the New Year may appall,
Pray, let us not prejudge it.
The Congress may surprise us all
And pass the Freedom Budget.
And maybe we will come to see
We're on a burning deck,
That drifting in the galaxy
The earth's a tiny speck,
            And that peace will save what each man loves—
            To wit, his bloody neck.

APPENDIX A ▪ *Potomac Institute Board of Directors, Staff, and Fellows*

BOARD MEMBERS

Stephen R. Currier	President 1961–67
Harold C. Fleming	Executive Vice President 1961–67
	President 1967–87
	President Emeritus 1987–92
Herbert M. Franklin	1983–93
Lloyd K. Garrison	1961–91
	Treasurer 1962–76
Philip G. Hammer	1961–93
	Vice President 1968–87
	President 1987–93
Vivian Henderson	1966–76
Vernon E. Jordan Jr.	1968–93
Burke Marshall	1965–68
Melvin A. Mister	1976–93
Andrew E. Norman	1962–93
Lois Rice	1978–93
	Vice President 1987–93
John G. Simon	1961–93
	Secretary 1962–93
William L. Slayton	1966–93
	Treasurer 1977–93

STAFF

Harold C. Fleming	Executive Vice President 1961–67
	President 1967–87
	President Emeritus 1987–92
Arthur J. Levin	Staff Director 1961–67
	Executive Vice President 1967–82
James O. Gibson	Staff Associate 1966–71
	Executive Associate 1971–79

Eleanor Ambrose	Administrative Assistant 1961–93
Carole A. Baker	Assistant to James Gibson 1969–74
Analoyce E. Clapp	Program Assistant 1964–66
Rosa M. Grillo	Secretary to Arthur Levin 1972–76
	Archivist 1985–87
	Research Associate 1992–93
Catherine B. Hare	Research Associate 1971–72
Benigna Marciukaitis	Research Librarian 1978–85
Surekha Desai Patel	Research Clerk 1965–68
Amelia Perazich	Research Associate 1972–78, 1985–87
Margaret Price	Research Associate 1961–70
Marian Ambrose Smith	Research Librarian 1986–87
Cecilia Dade	Secretary to Arthur Levin 1965–68
Larene Flack	Secretary to James Gibson 1973–78
Helen J. Hester	Secretary to Arthur Levin 1962–64
Mildred Flowers Johnson	Secretary to Harold Fleming 1961–62

FELLOWS

Benjamin Muse	1965–67 To assist in his documentation of the civil rights movement, published in 1968 as *The American Negro Revolution: From Nonviolence to Black Power, 1963–67*
Marion A. Wright	1977 To assist in the publication of the history of his civil rights work published in 1978 as *Human Rights Odyssey*

APPENDIX B ■ *Potomac Institute Publications and Projects (in chronological order)*

PUBLICATIONS

J. Kenneth Morland. "School Desegregation—Help Needed?" (1962).

John Silard and Arthur J. Levin. Based on research by Harold Galloway. *State Executive Authority to Promote Civil Rights* (1963).

Arthur J. Levin and John Silard. *The Federal Role in Equal Housing Opportunity* (1964).

Margaret Price and Arthur J. Levin. *Service for All Citizens* (1964).

———. *Opening Public Accommodations to All* (1964).

———. *The Civil Rights Act of 1964: A Summary* (1964).

———. *Americans Are Law-Abiding Citizens* (1964).

———. *The Federal Dollar and Nondiscrimination* (1965).

Arthur J. Levin and Margaret Price. *Fair Employment Is Good Business* (1965).

Arthur J. Levin and John Silard. *Metropolitan Housing Desegregation* (1966).

George Schermer. *Employer's Guide to Equal Opportunity* (1966).

George Schermer and Arthur J. Levin, with editorial assistance by Margaret Price. *Housing Guide to Equal Opportunity* (1968).

Robert C. Coles, M.D. Advised by Dr. Kenneth Haskins, former principal of Morgan Community School; Dr. Thomas Pettigrew and Dr. Robert Rosenthal, Department of Social Psychology, Harvard University; and Dr. David K. Cohen, Harvard School of Education. Preface by Arthur J. Levin. *Teachers and the Children of Poverty* (1970).

Arthur J. Levin. *Administrative Repeal of Civil Rights Law: A Case Study (Adams v. Richardson)* (1972).

John Silard, Norman Drachler, and Arthur J. Levin. *Equity for Cities in School Finance Reform* (1973).

Virginia Willis, with research by Margaret Price and Amelia Perazich and a chapter by Harold C. Fleming. *Affirmative Action: The Unrealized Goal* (1973).

Herbert M. Franklin, with Arthur J. Levin (ed.). *Controlling Urban Growth—But for Whom?* (1973).

Herbert M. Franklin, David Falk, and Arthur J. Levin. *In-Zoning: A Guide for Policy Makers on Inclusionary Land Use Programs* (1974).

David Falk and Herbert M. Franklin. Edited by Arthur J. Levin. *Local Growth Management Policy: A Legal Primer* (1975).

Herbert M. Franklin. *Zoning "For the Living Welfare of People"* (1975).

David Falk and Herbert M. Franklin. "Equal Housing Opportunity: The Unfinished Federal Agenda" (1976).

Zina Greene. Edited by Arthur J. Levin. *Lender's Guide to Fair Mortgage Policies* (1976).

John Silard, Elliot Lichtman, Mary Levy, and Arthur J. Levin. *Central-City Schooling: Money Can Make a Difference* (1977).

Roger Landrum, Jacqueline Greenan Wexler, and Harris Wofford. Foreword by Harold C. Fleming. *Youth and the Needs of the Nation: Report of the Committee for the Study of National Service* (1979).

Roger Landrum, ed. *National Youth Service: What's at Stake?* (1980).

Herbert M. Franklin. *Fundamental Fairness in Zoning: Mount Laurel Reaffirmed* (1983).

Herbert Hammerman. Edited by Arthur J. Levin. *A Decade of New Opportunity: Affirmative Action in the 70s* (1984).

PROJECTS

Charles H. Slayman Jr. "Racial Identification of Federal Employees." Unpublished report to Potomac Institute (June 1961).

John Hope II, Arthur J. Levin, Ronald Haughton, and John Feild. "Contract Compliance Recommendations," "Recommendations for Manning of Air Force Equal Opportunity Program," "Recommendations on Training for the Air Force Equal Opportunity Program," "Affirmative Actions in the Air Force Equal Employment Opportunity Program," "Air Force Equal Opportunity Program: A Manual of Procedures." Reports to the U.S. Air Force under EEO Contract (1961).

Arthur J. Levin, John Hope II, Ronald Ziegler, and John Feild. "Training for U.S. Army Equal Employment Opportunity Program," "U.S. Army Equal Employment Program: A Manual of Procedures," "Recommendations for U.S. Navy Equal Employment Opportunity Program," "Recommendations for Training: U.S. Navy Equal Employment Opportunity Program," "U.S. Navy Equal Employment Opportunity Program: A Manual of Procedures," "Recommendations for Defense Supply Agency Equal Employment Opportunity Program," "Defense Supply Agency Equal Employment Opportunity Program: A Manual of Procedures." Reports to U.S. Army/Navy/DSA under EEO Contract (1961–62).

John Silard. "Federal Authority with Regard to Racial Discrimination in Public Services and Accommodations." Report to U.S. Commission on Civil Rights (1962).

Conference on Legal Representation for Negroes in the South (December 1962).

Arthur J. Levin, Furman L. Templeton, and Ronald Ziegler. "Equal Employment Opportunity for Civilians in the Armed Forces." Report to U.S. Department of Defense under EEO Contract (1963).

Arthur J. Levin. *The City Government and Minority Groups.* Joint publication of International City Managers Association, Southern Regional Council, and Potomac Institute (1963).

Margaret Price and Arthur J. Levin. "The Economic Impact of Racial Unrest." Report distributed to press and selected policy makers (1963).

Arthur J. Levin. "NASA Equal Employment Survey of Wallops Island Station." Report to National Aeronautics and Space Administration (1963).

Harold C. Fleming, H. Ben Sissel, and Will D. Campbell. "Report to the Agenda Committee of the United Presbyterian Commission on Religion and Race" (1963).

Seminars with U.S. Urban Renewal Administration staff (1963–65).

"Operation Compliance." A project in coordination with U.S. Department of Justice and Southern Regional Council. (See publications by Price and Levin above.) (1964–65).

Arthur J. Levin. "Directory of Municipal Human Rights Agencies." Compiled for International City Managers Association (1964).

"The Police and the Civil Rights Act." Report of the Conference of Police Executives at the University of Oklahoma, co-sponsored by the International Association of Chiefs of Police, the Southwest Center for Human Relations Studies and the Southwest Center for Law Enforcement Education of the University of Oklahoma, the Anti-Defamation League of B'nai B'rith, and the Potomac Institute (1964).

David Apter. "Civil Rights Information Center." Report to the Potomac Institute (1964).

W. G. Foster. "Guidelines for Implementation of Title VI in Schools." *Saturday Review of Literature* (March 20, 1965). Distributed by Potomac Institute.

Daniel Schreiber. "Improving Academic Achievement of the Negro Child." Report to Potomac Institute (1965).

Consultation on organization and operating plan of new Equal Employment Opportunity Commission (1965).

J. Kenneth Morland. "Educational Problems Occasioned by Desegregation; Views of Southern School Personnel." Report to Potomac Institute (May 1965).

Arthur J. Levin and James O. Gibson. "Recommendations to Improve Community Relations at Job Corps Conservation Centers." Report to the Office of Economic Opportunity (1965).

Harold C. Fleming, Special Consultant to the White House Conference "To Fulfill These Rights." Planning Session (November 1965) and Conference (June 1966).

Arthur J. Levin and James O. Gibson. "Civil Rights Functions in the Office of Economic Opportunity." Report to the Office of Economic Opportunity (1966).

Arthur J. Levin, James O. Gibson, Kenneth C. Jones. Recommendations to the Department of Health, Education and Welfare: "Equal Educational Opportunities Program." Office of Education; "Equal Opportunity Program." Social Security Administration; "Special Assistant for Civil Rights." Office of the Secretary; "Office of Equal Health Opportunity." Public Health Service (1966).

Arthur J. Levin and James O. Gibson. "Human Resources in Economic Development: The Application of Title VI to Programs of Economic Development." Report to the Economic Development Administration, U.S. Department of Commerce (1966).

"Minority Group Considerations in the Selective Service and Other Proposed Systems of National Service." Report to the Chairman, National Advisory Commission on Selective Service (1966).

Arthur J. Levin. Based on research by Harry Fleischman, Race Relations Coordinator of the American Jewish Committee. "A Fair Employment Contract Compliance Program for New York City Agencies." Report to the Office of the Mayor, New York City (1967).

Beryl Radin. "Fair Employment in the United States." Report to the National Committee for Commonwealth Immigrants for the London Conference on Racial Equality in Employment (1967).

Council on Equal Business Opportunity (CEBO). A project on management services to minority entrepreneurs. Benjamin Goldstein, Director; Cliff Henry, Deputy Director. (1967–71).

School District Inequities Conference (September 1968).

Harold C. Fleming, Potomac staff and Board members, Melvin Bergheim, and Robert Hearn. Urban Strategy Project (1968–69).

Consultation to the Department of Housing and Urban Development on implementation of the 1968 Fair Housing Act (1968–69).

Robert Spivack. Reporters' News Syndicate Journalism Training Project (1969).

Carl F. Stover. "The Relationship of the Private Sector to the Realization of Domestic Public Goals." Report to National Institute on Public Affairs (1970).

Monthly conferences on fair housing of National Urban League, NAACP, National Urban Coalition, Urban America, Lawyers' Committee for Civil Rights Under Law, Leadership Conference on Civil Rights, American Friends Service Committee, and U.S. Commission on Civil Rights. Jointly sponsored with National Committee Against Discrimination in Housing (1970–72).

Ben Goldstein and Clifford Henry. *Business Packaging*, handbook prepared for the U.S. Department of Housing and Urban Development by National Council on Equal Business Opportunity, Inc. (1971).

Central Cities Technical Assistance Project (CCTA), 1971–74. James O. Gibson, Director; Arthur J. Naparstek, Co-Director; Jesse E. Bell Jr., Co-Director; Carroll B. Harvey, Senior Associate; Carole A. Baker, Information Clearinghouse Officer; Jose Gutierrez, Policy Development Associate; Bette Treadwell, Administrative Resource Intern.

Jean Fairfax. "Criteria for a State Plan for Higher Education Desegregation." Report to the U.S. Office of Education (1971).

Herbert M. Franklin et al. "Accommodating Environmental and Social Objectives in Land Use Decision-Making." Background paper for the Woodstock Conference on Accommodating Environmental and Social Objectives in Land-Use Decision Making, in cooperation with the Sylvia and Aaron Sheinfeld Foundation (May 1974).

Urban School Finance Conference, co-sponsored with National Urban Coalition and Lawyer's Committee for Civil Rights Under Law (February 1974).

Herbert M. Franklin and Arthur J. Levin. "The Housing Assistance Plan: A Non-Working Program for Community Improvement?" A review of compliance in Atlanta, Boston, Chicago, Cleveland, Detroit, and San Francisco (1975).

Consultation to Robert Patricelli, Administrator, Urban Mass Transportation Administration, Department of Transportation, on use of transportation policy to shape desirable land-use patterns (1975).

Sidney Howe. "Environment and Equity." Report funded by the New World and Rockefeller Fundations (1976).

Herbert M. Franklin and William L. Slayton. Members, Special Commission of American Bar Association, which published "Housing for All Under Law" supporting judicial actions to overcome exclusionary zoning (1976).

Harold C. Fleming. "The Social Constraints." Herbert M. Franklin. "Houser of Last Resort." *Center* magazine, Center for the Study of Democratic Institutions, Santa Barbara (January/February 1976).

Arthur J. Levin. "Government as Partner in Residential Segregation." James O. Gibson, "Majoritarian Standards and Self-Interest." *Center* magazine, Center for the Study of Democratic Institutions, Santa Barbara (March/April 1976).

Herbert M. Franklin. "A New Metro Approach." *Center* magazine, Center for the Study of Democratic Institutions, Santa Barbara (September/October 1976).

Michael McManus. American Town Meeting Project, funded by the Ford Foundation (1977).

Joel Brenner and Herbert M. Franklin. "Rent Control in North America and Four European Countries." Funded by the German Marshall Fund (1977).

National Planning Conference on Human Rights and Racism, convened for the National Institute of Mental Health (1978).

Consultation to Center for Minority Group Mental Health Programs, National Institute of Mental Health, on racism and mental health programs (1978).

Seminars on effectiveness of civil rights programs, convened for the U.S. Commission on Civil Rights (1978).

Immigration and Refugee Policy Project, for the Citizens' Committee for Immigration Reform, Rev. Theodore Hesberg, Chairman (1981).

Metropolitan Housing Conferences, co-sponsored with National Committee Against Discrimination in Housing (1981, 1983).

Voting Rights Information Exchange for Grantors and Grantees (1981).

Harry Ashmore, with Wilson Riles, Bettye Caldwell, and Shirley Hufstedtler, consultation on national service programs and underclass children, funded by the Drown Foundation (1982–84).

Edward Holmgren. "Fair Housing in a Post Civil Rights Era: Does Anyone Care?" Report to the Ford Foundation (1983).

Fred Jordan. Project to evaluate citizen involvement in community planning, funded by the Ford Foundation (1983).

John Feild. Project to strengthen the capacity of community-based nonprofit groups to sponsor low-income housing, in collaboration with the Local Initiative Support Corporation and the Neighborhood Reinvestment Corporation (1984).

Norman Manasa, Washington Education Project (1984).

Herbert M. Franklin. "Reading the Supreme Court Tea Leaves on Affirmative Action: Affirmative Hiring Goals Reinforced" (1986).

APPENDIX C ▪ *Selected Articles and Speeches by Harold C. Fleming, 1961–1986*

ARTICLES

"Equal Job Opportunity—Slogan or Reality?" *Personnel Administration* (March/April 1963).

"The Federal Executive and Civil Rights: 1961–1965." *Daedalus* (Fall 1965).

"On Black Power." Unpublished memorandum to John Stewart, Office of the Vice President (1967).

"Social Strategy and Urban Growth." Unpublished (January 19, 1969).

"Report on a Visit to South Africa." *U.S. South Africa Leader Exchange Program Reports,* October 2, 1969.

"The Multiple Revolution and the Seventies." *Issues* (1970).

"School Integration: The Evolution of National Policy." *The Teachers Handbook* (Glenview, Ill.: Scott, Foresman and Company (1971).

"Riding Herd on Government Programs." *Foundation News* (May/June 1972).

"Some Notes on the Next Four Years." Unpublished (1972).

"The 'Affirmative Action' Debate: Can Justice Be Color-Blind?" *City* (Summer 1972).

"Minority Affairs." *State of the Nation,* Watts and Free, eds. (Washington, D.C.: Potomac Associates 1973).

"A Decade of Affirmative Action," *Contact* (Summer 1974).

"The Social Constraints." *Center* (January/February 1976).

"The Old New South: A Recollection," *New South* (Fall 1973).

"Public Interest Is Monitoring Purpose." *Council on Foundations Regional Reporter* (June 1974).

"Brown and the Three R's: Race, Residence, and Resegregation." *Journal of Law and Education* (January 1975).

"Foundations and Affirmative Action." *Foundation News* (September/October 1976).

"Slouching toward a Divided Society," *Nation's Cities* (July 1977).

"Architecture and Consumerism." *AIA Journal* (May 1980).

"Consumerism and the Profession." *Texas Architect* (July/August 1980).

"Putting Down Affirmative Action." *Perspectives: The Civil Rights Quarterly* (Summer 1980).

"The Demands of a Changing Society," Report to the University of Texas School of Architecture (1984).

"An Outsider's Inside View of Architecture." *Architecture* (March 1984).

"Comments on 'The Civil Rights Act: Twenty Years Later.'" *Southern Changes* (March/April 1985).

SPEECHES

Untitled, New York University Conference (February 6, 1962).

Untitled, Annual Meeting of the Tampa Urban League (May 14, 1962).

Script for Voice of America program on Negro Voting Rights in the South (July 25, 1962).

Untitled, National Civil Liberties Clearing House Conference (March 19, 1964).

Untitled, National Association of Social Workers Human Rights Assembly (March 23, 1964).

"Building Tomorrow's Communities" (December 3, 1964).

"The End of the Beginning." National Association of Intergroup Relations Officials (November 15, 1966).

"The Sick Society and the Idea of SRC." Southern Regional Council (November 1967).

Untitled, American Council of Jewish Women (February 27, 1968).

Untitled, National Association of Intergroup Relations Officials (November 12, 1968).

"Renewing the Idea of Community." Allegheny Conference on Community Development, Pittsburgh, Pennsylvania (November 18, 1968).

Untitled, National Association of Housing Rehabilitation Officials (1969).

"Community Control—Its Meaning and Implications: A Growing Issue for the Nation." National Civil Liberties Clearing House Conference (March 1969).

"Community Control." Women's City Club Institute on Community Participation and Decision Making (April 19, 1969).

Untitled, Clemson University College of Architecture (October 14, 1983).

Untitled, Harvard Class of 1944 40th Reunion (June 7, 1984).

Untitled, National Committee Against Discrimination in Housing (September 24, 1986).

NOTES

1   Senator John F. Kennedy, response to question following campaign speech, Minneapolis, Minn., October 1, 1960 (Boston: Kennedy Library).

2   Harris Wofford, Speech to the National Civil Liberties Clearinghouse, spring 1961.

3   Memorandum from Harold Fleming to Berl Bernhard, Staff Director, U.S. Commission on Civil Rights (Washington, D.C.: Library of Congress, Potomac Institute Archives).

4   William Manchester, *The Glory and the Dream,* 3rd ed. (New York: Bantam, 1975), 936-7.

5   Burke Marshall, *Federalism and Civil Rights* (New York: Columbia University Press, 1964), 81.

6   U.S. Congress, House Subcommittee on Manpower Utilization of the Committee on Post Office and Civil Service, *Hearings on Use of Contractors: Equal Opportunities in the Military Services,* 88th Cong., 1st sess., November 5-6, 1963, 48-106.

7   Arthur M. Schlesinger, *Robert Kennedy and His Times* (Boston: Houghton Mifflin, 1978), 311.

8   Godfrey Hodgson, *America in Our Time* (Garden City, N.Y.: Doubleday, 1976), 214.

9   Mayor Ivan Allen Jr. Testimony before Congress on Title X of CRA. Potomac Institute, *Service to All Citizens* (Washington, D.C.: Potomac Institute, 1964), 1.

10 Gary Orfield, *The Reconstruction of Southern Education* (New York: Wiley-Interscience, 1969), 101.

11 Harry McPherson, *A Political Education* (Boston: Atlantic–Little, Brown, 1972), 348.

12 Ibid, 350.

13 *The Kerner Report: The 1968 Report of the National Advisory Commission on Civil Disorders,* 1st Pantheon ed. (New York: Pantheon, 1988), summary, 1-2.

INDEX